Florida Community Association Litigation

HOMEOWNERS' ASSOCIATIONS AND CONDOMINIUMS

2017

RON M. CAMPBELL

Daily Business Review
One S.E. 3rd Ave.
Suite 1750
Miami, FL 33131
800-756-8993
www.dailybusinessreview.com
www.alm.com
www.lawcatalog.com

This book is not intended to offer advice or counsel. Nor is it intended to serve as a substitute for professional representation. Since the information in this book may not be sufficient in dealing with a client's particular problem, and because this area of law constantly changes, lawyers and others using this publication should not rely on it as a substitute for independent research.

International Standard Book Number
978-1-62881-285-5 (Print)
978-1-62881-286-2 (eBook)

Printed in the United States of America

An eBook or online version of this publication is included as part of your purchase. To download, follow the instructions below. *Please note the eBook or online product cannot be returned once the file has been downloaded.*

Login or register at: www.lawjournalpress.com/activate
Please enter code 537266 to download your product.

SUPPORTED DEVICES: We recommend Apple® iPad® or iPhone®, SONY® Reader, or Adobe® digital Editions for PC or MAC users).

For help using this product, visit our FAQ page: www.lawjournalpress.com/help

For Returns:

In Care of: ALM Media
545 Wescott Road
Eagan, MN 55123
For QUESTIONS please contact Customer Service at 1-877-256-2472

Subscriptions to books are auto-renewed to avoid disruptions in service. Print editions must be returned within 30 days in resalable condition for refund. For downloadable eBook or Online products, a refund will be granted if the eBook or Online product has not been downloaded.

Acknowledgements

I owe my deepest gratitude to my wife, Lindsey, whose tireless support made this book possible. I gladly take this opportunity also to thank my family at Cole, Scott, and Kissane. The firm's dedication to hard work and excellence guided the development of my career. To Barry Postman, for his mentoring and guidance. To Michael Shiver, Julie Kornfield, Katie Merwin, Lindsay Lee, Patrick Boland, and Angela Hernandez for their friendship and encouragement.

About this Book

This book is about the legal issues that arise repeatedly in litigating homeowners' and condominium association lawsuits in Florida. Homeowners' and condominium associations are common forms of community living in Florida, and the law regulating their operation touches on the lives of each of the owners and residents who own property and live within their purview. The book covers a broad range of topics because practice in this area of the law is multifaceted. Attorneys that practice community association law regularly prosecute and defend against claims that sound in the law of contracts, real property, civil rights, and more. Each of these topics is discussed to provide the reader with a set of practical tools that may be used to approach community association disputes. Students of this area of the law will also benefit from detailed discussion of the Florida statutes regulating community associations and construing case law.

This book also discusses the motivations that underlie common community association disputes. Emotions run high when neighbors feud. By placing the dry legal issues in their context, the goal is to create a framework for understanding the root cause of the legal dispute. With some tact, the attorney may lead the client to adopt an objective perspective of the given circumstances and overcome his or her entrenched position. Of course, no amount of reason will resolve all differences. If litigation and trial is inevitable, then an understanding of the motivations underlying the dispute aids the attorney in effectively advocating in mediation and arbitration, and before the court.

This book draws heavily on the Condominium Act, Chapter 718, and the statutes governing homeowners' associations, found in Florida Statutes Chapter 720. There is a great deal of similarity between these two chapters. To the extent possible, the book attempts to avoid repetition by referencing both chapters simultaneously where their provisions mirror one another. Some repetition was necessary to avoid confusion.

Introductory information on the nature of the various forms of Florida community associations is in the first chapters of the book. The book focuses almost exclusively, however, on the most common forms: homeowners' associations and condominium associations. There is very little discussion of cooperatives, timeshares, and mobile home subdivisions, because there are simply not enough disputes involving these types of community associations to warrant lengthy discussion.

This is an ever changing area of the law. As such, this book should serve as a springboard for the reader's own research. It is true that some critical principals discussed herein have guided the courts for decades, but the Florida Legislature revisits the statutory regulation of Florida community associations on a regular basis. In addition, Florida courts continuously create new law regarding issues affecting the operation of community associations on which we previously had little or no guidance. Moreover, there is no "one size fits all" approach to all community association litigation. Most cases are highly fact specific, and the courts typically approach them on a case-by-case basis. This book only aspires to guide and equip those who wish to learn more about community association litigation, providing direction as to issues impacted by statutory regulation and published case law.

Ron Campbell
May 2017

About the Author

Ron M. Campbell is a trial attorney who has been litigating Florida community association cases since 2004. He is one of the managing partners of the Southwest Florida office of Cole, Scott, and Kissane, which is located in Bonita Springs, Florida. Cole, Scott, and Kissane is one of the largest insurance defense firms in Florida. He earned his Bachelor of Arts degree from the University of Florida, and his Juris Doctorate from Fordham University School of Law.

Summary of Contents

Chapter 1: Introduction to Florida Community Associations 1

Chapter 2: The Governing Documents....................................19

Chapter 3: Developer Obligations and Turnover 35

Chapter 4: Board of Directors..59

Chapter 5: Operation of the Community Association 81

Chapter 6: Member and Board Meetings.............................123

Chapter 7: Covenant Enforcement......................................135

Chapter 8: Alternative Dispute Resolution...........................163

Chapter 9: Collection Practices...177

Chapter 10: Fair Housing Litigation 199

Chapter 11: Attorney's Fees...231

Table of Cases...245

Index 253

Table of Contents

Chapter 1: Introduction to Florida Community Associations 1
1-1   INTRODUCTION..1
    1-1:1   Definition of Community Association Litigation 1
    1-1:2   Governing Documents...2
    1-1:3   Community Association Duties and Rights..................2
1-2   HOMEOWNERS' ASSOCIATIONS.....................................4
    1-2:1   The Homeowners' Association Act;
              Legislative Intent 4
    1-2:2   Protections Afforded to the Membership.....................5
    1-2:3   Scope of the Homeowners' Association Act 5
           1-2:3.1   Residential Communities 5
           1-2:3.2   Exclusion of Condominiums and
                     Cooperatives...6
           1-2:3.3   Homeowners' Associations
                     Are Comprised of Parcel Owners 6
    1-2:4   Common Areas and Individual Parcels.........................7
1-3   CONDOMINIUM ASSOCIATIONS.....................................8
    1-3:1   Governing Statutes 8
    1-3:2   Distinguishing Features of Condominiums 9
    1-3:3   Condominium Association Tests 10
1-4   COOPERATIVES..12
    1-4:1   Distinguishing Features of Cooperatives 12
    1-4:2   Statutory Definition of Cooperative 14
1-5   MOBILE HOME SUBDIVISION HOMEOWNERS'
    ASSOCIATIONS 14
1-6   TIMESHARE OWNERS' ASSOCIATION............................15
    1-6:1   Florida Vacation Plan and Timesharing Act..............15
    1-6:2   Statutory Definition of Timeshare Plan......................15

Chapter 2: The Governing Documents..19
2-1   INTRODUCTION..19
2-2   THE DECLARATION 20

	2-2:1	Basic Characteristics of the Declaration	20
	2-2:2	Restrictions in the Declaration	21
	2-2:3	Invalid Restrictions	22
	2-2:4	Required Declaration Provisions for Condominium Associations	23
2-3		ARTICLES OF INCORPORATION	24
2-4		BYLAWS	25
2-5		CONFLICTS BETWEEN GOVERNING DOCUMENTS	26
2-6		RULES AND REGULATIONS	26
2-7		PROHIBITED PROVISIONS	27
	2-7:1	Prohibited Provisions for Homeowners' Associations	27
	2-7:2	Prohibited Provisions for Condominium Associations	29
2-8		AMENDING THE GOVERNING DOCUMENTS	30
	2-8:1	Amending Homeowners' Association Governing Documents	31
	2-8:2	Amending Condominium Governing Documents	31

Chapter 3: Developer Obligations and Turnover **35**
3-1		INTRODUCTION	35
3-2		DEVELOPER OBLIGATIONS AND HOMEOWNERS' ASSOCIATIONS	35
	3-2:1	Developer-Made Contracts	37
	3-2:2	Disclosures Prior to Sale	38
3-3		DEVELOPER OBLIGATIONS AND CONDOMINIUM ASSOCIATIONS	40
	3-3:1	Recreation Facility Leases	41
	3-3:2	Sale Prior to Completion	43
	3-3:3	Developer Warranty	45
	3-3:4	Developer-Made Contracts	46
	3-3:5	Disclosures Prior to Sale	48
3-4		TURNOVER OF HOMEOWNERS' ASSOCIATIONS	51
	3-4:1	Conditions Triggering Turnover	51
	3-4:2	Developer Obligations Following Turnover	52
3-5		TURNOVER OF CONDOMINIUM ASSOCIATIONS	53
	3-5:1	Conditions Triggering Turnover	53
	3-5:2	Developer Obligations Following Turnover	56

Chapter 4: Board of Directors **59**
| 4-1 | | INTRODUCTION | 59 |
| 4-2 | | ELECTION OF THE BOARD | 59 |

4-2:1   Qualification for Board Membership 59
4-2:2   Election Procedures 60
4-2:3   Required Condominium Association
Election Procedures 60
4-2:4   Filling Vacancies on the Board 62
4-2:5   Election Disputes 64
4-3   DUTIES OF THE MEMBERS OF THE BOARD 67
4-3:1   Fiduciary Duty 68
4-3:2   Director Compensation Prohibited 70
4-3:3   Business Judgment Rule as Applied
to Board Members 71
4-3:4   Self-Dealing and Unjust Enrichment 73
4-3:5   Business Judgment Rule as Applied
to Community Associations 74
4-4   BOARD MEMBER DISCIPLINE AND REMOVAL 75
4-4:1   Civil Penalty for Condominium
Board Members 75
4-4:2   Recall of Board Members 77

Chapter 5: Operation of the Community Association 81
5-1   INTRODUCTION 81
5-2   HOMEOWNERS' ASSOCIATION FINANCES 82
5-2:1   Homeowners' Association Budgets 82
5-2:2   Homeowners' Association Reserves 83
5-2:3   Homeowners' Association Assessments 85
5-3   CONDOMINIUM ASSOCIATION FINANCES 86
5-3:1   Condominium Association Budgets 86
5-3:2   Condominium Association Reserves 87
5-3:3   Condominium Association Assessments 88
5-4   FINANCIAL REPORTING 89
5-5   COMMON PROPERTY MAINTENANCE,
REPLACEMENT, AND IMPROVEMENT 92
5-5:1   Homeowners' Association Common Areas 92
5-5:2   Condominium Association
Common Elements 93
5-5:3   Limited Common Elements 99
5-6   THE CONDOMINIUM ACT AND INSURANCE 100
5-6:1   Condominium Property Insurance Coverage 101
5-6:2   Failure to Maintain Condominium
Property Insurance 102
5-6:3   Other Types of Condominium
Association Insurance 102

	5-6:4	Condominium Owners' Residential Property Insurance	103
	5-6:5	Reconstruction Work After Property Loss	103
	5-6:6	Multicondominium Associations	105
5-7	OFFICIAL RECORDS		106
	5-7:1	Homeowners' Association Official Records	106
	5-7:2	Condominium Association Official Records	109
5-8	WRITTEN INQUIRIES		114
5-9	HIRING MANAGERS, CONTRACTORS, ATTORNEYS, AND ACCOUNTANTS		114
	5-9:1	Competitive Bids	117
5-10	CONDOMINIUM ASSOCIATION EMERGENCY POWERS		118
5-11	RIGHT TO SUE AND BE SUED		120
	5-11:1	Homeowners' Associations' Right to Sue and Be Sued	120
	5-11:2	Condominium Associations' Right to Sue and Be Sued	121
	5-11:3	Class Action Suits	121

Chapter 6: Member and Board Meetings **123**
6-1	INTRODUCTION		123
6-2	BOARD MEETINGS		123
	6-2:1	Homeowners' Associations	123
	6-2:2	Condominium Associations	125
6-3	MEMBER MEETINGS		128
	6-3:1	Homeowners' Associations	128
	6-3:2	Condominium Associations	129
6-4	VOTING PROCEDURES		131
	6-4:1	Homeowners' Associations	131
	6-4:2	Condominium Associations	132
	6-4:3	Electronic Voting	133

Chapter 7: Covenant Enforcement **135**
7-1	INTRODUCTION		135
7-2	USE RESTRICTIONS		136
	7-2:1	Homeowners' Association Use Restrictions	137
	7-2:2	Condominium Association Use Restrictions	137
7-3	ARCHITECTURAL CONTROL		139
	7-3:1	Homeowners' Association Architectural Controls	139
	7-3:2	Condominium Association Aesthetic Controls	142
7-4	MANDATORY MEMBERSHIPS		142
7-5	SCHEME OF DEVELOPMENT		144
7-6	TRANSFER RESTRICTIONS		147

7-6:1   Association Approval of Transfers 149
7-6:2   Rights of First Refusal 150
         7-6:2.1   Prohibition Against Forced Sales............. 150
         7-6:2.2   Right of First Refusal Does Not Violate
                    the Rule Against Perpetuities.................. 151
7-7   ENFORCEMENT METHODS... 152
       7-7:1   Fines and Suspensions 152
       7-7:2   Mandatory Mediation and Arbitration..................... 155
       7-7:3   Statute of Limitations.............................. 156
7-8   ESTOPPEL 156
       7-8:1   Selective Enforcement.............................. 159

Chapter 8: Alternative Dispute Resolution.. 163
8-1   INTRODUCTION TO ALTERNATIVE
       DISPUTE RESOLUTION...................................... 163
8-2   HOMEOWNERS' ASSOCIATION DISPUTES 163
8-3   CONDOMINIUM ASSOCIATION DISPUTES 166
       8-3:1   Arbitration Procedures 171

Chapter 9: Collection Practices... 177
9-1   INTRODUCTION... 177
9-2   ASSESSMENT LIABILITY..................................... 179
       9-2:1   Homeowners' Associations 179
       9-2:2   Condominium Associations...................... 179
9-3   STATUTORY PROTECTION AGAINST UNFAIR
       AND ABUSIVE ASSESSMENT COLLECTION
       PRACTICES 182
9-4   LIEN RIGHTS 186
       9-4:1   Homeowners' Associations 186
       9-4:2   Condominium Associations...................... 189
9-5   PENALTIES... 191
9-6   ASSESSMENT GUARANTEES................................. 193
       9-6:1   Homeowners' Associations 193
       9-6:2   Condominium Associations...................... 194
9-7   LIABILITY FOR ASSESSMENTS FOLLOWING
       FORECLOSURE SALE 195
9-8   SLANDER OF TITLE 197

Chapter 10: Fair Housing Litigation 199
10-1   INTRODUCTION... 199
10-2   ADMINISTRATIVE PROCESS 201
       10-2:1   Exhaustion of Administrative Remedies.................. 201

Table of Contents

10-2:2   The United States Department of Housing
          and Urban Development 201
10-2:3   The Florida Commission on Human Relations 202
10-2:4   Administrative Procedures.....................................203
          10-2:4.1   Admissibility of Determinations..............205
          10-2:4.2   Post-Determination Proceedings..............206
10-3   CLAIM ANALYSIS..208
        10-3:1   Standing to Bring a Claim 209
        10-3:2   Discrimination in Sale or Rental.............................210
                  10-3:2.1   Intentional Discrimination 210
                  10-3:2.2   Disparate Impact 211
        10-3:3   Reasonable Accommodation 212
                  10-3:3.1   Elements of a Reasonable
                              Accommodation Claim...........................212
                  10-3:3.2   Necessity and Reasonableness..................214
        10-3:4   Relief From Discriminatory Housing Practices 216
10-4   COMPANION ANIMALS 219
        10-4:1   Emotional Support Animals for Mental
                  and Emotional Disabilities.......................................220
        10-4:2   Service Animals vs. Emotional Support Animals......221
        10-4:3   Emotional Support Animals
                  and the Fair Housing Act 221
10-5   HOUSING FOR OLDER PERSONS 226
10-6   CONCLUSION..229

Chapter 11: Attorney's Fees..231
11-1   INTRODUCTION...231
11-2   THE "AMERICAN RULE" 232
11-3   PROPOSALS FOR SETTLEMENT 234
11-4   FEES AS SANCTIONS...235
11-5   AMOUNT OF FEES...236
        11-5:1   Contingency Risk Multiplier 238
11-6   LOSING ENTITLEMENT TO FEES...............................239
        11-6:1   Failure to Plead Entitlement 239
        11-6:2   Time Limit for Motion Service 240
        11-6:3   Losing Entitlement Before Suit Begins....................241
11-7   CONCLUSION..242

Table of Cases..245

Index 253

Chapter 1

Introduction to Florida Community Associations

1-1   INTRODUCTION

Community association litigation is a complex topic that does not lend itself to generalizations. Community associations are sued for many reasons and are frequently parties to litigation involving alleged statutory violations, tort law, property law, and contract disputes. A community association may also find itself embroiled in employment claims, fair housing litigation, and collection practices litigation. Indeed, some wrongful conduct on the part of an association may be subject to a combination of several different causes of action.

1-1:1   Definition of Community Association Litigation

Community association litigation is defined as any legal dispute regarding the rights and duties of the association and the property owners that make up its membership. Community associations, which include homeowners' associations, condominiums, and cooperatives are typically non-profit corporations that govern ownership and property uses within a community. Membership in the community association is usually mandatory for all property owners. In purchasing property in a community governed by a community association, an owner submits him or herself to the authority of that community association. Community association litigation tends to foment in the space where the legal rights and obligations of the association meet and potentially clash with those of the property owner.

1-1:2   Governing Documents

Community association litigation frequently arises from covenant enforcement disputes, which involve the set of documents that establish the association regime and set forth the rights and obligations of the owners and the association. Such governing documents are contracts between the association and the property owners and they have some of the attributes of covenants running with the land, "circumscribing the extent and limits of the enjoyment and use of real property."[1]

Homeowners' associations are typically governed by a declaration of covenants and restrictions, while condominium associations are established and governed by a declaration of condominium. The documents governing a cooperative include the lease providing the owner with exclusive use of the cooperative unit, the document evidencing the owner's interest in the cooperative association, and bylaws that may include use restrictions. If the community association is in a larger master planned community, it may also be subject to a master declaration of covenants and restrictions governing varying uses of property and different types of community associations.

The association's governing documents typically set forth prohibited uses of the property, architectural controls, the association's right to assess for common expenses, and procedural guidelines for community governance. The overall purpose of governing documents is to establish a set of rules to facilitate group living and to promote the common goals of health, safety, quality of life, and property values in a community. While the purpose and intention of community association living is positive, balancing the rights of the individual property owner with those of the community association itself is sometimes difficult.

1-1:3   Community Association Duties and Rights

The community association functions as a hybrid participatory/ representative democracy. The owners in the community make up the voting membership that elects a board of directors. On the one hand, there are many opportunities for each of the owners

---

[1] *Woodside Vill. Condo. Ass'n v. Jahren*, 806 So. 2d 452, 456 (Fla. 2002) (quoting *Pepe v. Whispering Sands Condo. Ass'n*, 351 So. 2d 755, 757 (Fla. 2d Dist. Ct. App. 1977)).

to participate directly in the operation of the community by contributing to discussion and decision making at board and membership meetings. On the other hand, the members of the board of directors, as elected officials, have the power to give effect to the wishes of the membership and use their own business judgment in the exercise of their authority.

Florida statutes and the governing documents dictate what unilateral actions the board may take on behalf of the community and what actions require the direct approval of the membership. This is an issue that is heavily litigated. The Florida statutes governing homeowners' associations, condominiums, cooperatives, and other types of community associations provide that the officers and directors of the association have a fiduciary relationship to the owners. Courts are continually asked to rule on the appropriateness of board actions and to determine whether they comport with Florida statutes and the authority granted by the association's governing documents.

The governing documents that guide and restrict use of the property, and provide procedural guidance for community governance, exist in a larger legal context defined by the property rights inherent to the ownership structure of the community association itself. Homeowners' associations, condominiums, and cooperatives are each unique forms of community living that distinguish themselves according to the property interests held by the owner in relation to the community association. Each of these forms of ownership has its own challenges and benefits. In recognition of this, the Florida Legislature codified separate acts regulating each form of Florida community association. As such, Florida community associations are truly creatures of statute. The statute in effect on the recording date of the community association's governing documents "control[s] as if engrafted onto" the purchase and sale contract itself.[2]

Community association litigation typically arises when the community or an owner asserts their rights or demands fulfillment of an obligation as set forth in the governing documents or the overarching statutory scheme. Florida statutes describe

---

[2] *Tranquil Harbour Dev. v. BBT*, 79 So. 3d 84, 86 (Fla. 1st Dist. Ct. App. 2011), *reh'g denied* (Feb. 13, 2012).

(1) community associations' obligation to maintain official records, budgets, and financial reporting; (2) the right of owners to assemble; (3) the obligations of members and their legal remedies; (4) the ability of the community to fine and suspend owners' rights to use common facilities; (5) the procedures to be used in meetings and elections; (6) prohibited provisions in governing documents; and (7) procedures for dispute resolution.

When the statutory scheme conflicts with the governing documents, this is a battle between a legislative declaration of public policy and the contract rights inherent in the mutual agreement between the community association and its property owners. How the court resolves this conflict may have far-reaching implications on the operation and management of the community itself.

1-2   HOMEOWNERS' ASSOCIATIONS

1-2:1   The Homeowners' Association Act; Legislative Intent

Florida Statutes Chapter 720 (the Homeowners' Association Act) gives statutory recognition to homeowners' associations and applies to not for profit corporations that operate residential communities in Florida.[3] While the Homeowners' Association Act sets forth comprehensive operating procedures for homeowners' associations and gives protection to association members, its stated goal is to avoid unduly "impairing the ability of such associations to perform their functions."[4]

The Homeowners' Association Act is not meant to control community management or circumscribe self-governance. The Florida Legislature recognizes that the contractual relationship established in the community's governing documents ultimately defines a homeowners' association's rights and obligations. Homeowners' associations are meant to operate with "minimal governmental oversight" and the regulations imposed by Florida Statutes "shall not constitute an unconstitutional impairment of contract."[5]

---

[3] Homeowners' associations may also be subject to Chapter 607, the Florida Business Corporation Act, or Chapter 617, the Florida Not For Profit Corporation Act, if incorporated under those chapters. *See* Fla. Stat. §§ 607.0101 et seq, 617.01011 et seq.

[4] Fla. Stat. § 720.302(1) (2016).

[5] Op. Att'y Gen. Fla. 2001-01 (2001).

1-2:2   Protections Afforded to the Membership

The Homeowners' Association Act protects association members in part by imposing a fiduciary relationship between the officers and directors of the association and the membership.[6] It also provides "legal redress against the association, members, directors, and officers for failure to comply with statutes, association documents, or community rules."[7] Certain types of disputes are subject to pre-suit mediation as a statutory prerequisite to filing suit. The stated purpose is to reduce court dockets and trials and offer "a more efficient, cost-effective option to litigation."[8]

1-2:3   Scope of the Homeowners' Association Act

1-2:3.1   Residential Communities

The Homeowners' Association Act applies to residential communities only.[9] Communities that are not designed as residential communities for either mobile homes, permanent or semi-permanent structures, or any structure designed, intended, or used as permanent living quarters are not "homeowners' associations" within the meaning of the statute. Chapter 720 also excludes the commercial or industrial parcels in mixed residential and commercial communities.[10] This is true regardless of whether a declaration of restrictive covenants is used as a tool to control property usage.[11] Thus, Chapter 720 does not apply to parks for transient recreational vehicles[12] and communities composed of property primarily intended for commercial, industrial, or other nonresidential use.

[6.] Fla. Stat. § 720.303(1) (2016).

[7.] *Baratta v. Valley Oak Homeowners' Ass'n at the Vineyards*, 891 So. 2d 1063, 1065 (Fla. 2d Dist. Ct. App. 2004).

[8.] Fla. Stat. § 720.311(1) (2016).

[9.] Fla. Stat. § 720.302(1) (2016).

[10.] Fla. Stat. § 720.302(3) (2016).

[11.] *Clark v. Bluewater Key RV Ownership Park,* 197 So. 3d 59 (Fla. Dist. Ct. App. 2012).

[12.] *Clark v. Bluewater Key RV Ownership Park,* 197 So. 3d 59 (Fla. Dist. Ct. App. 2012) (holding that a recreational vehicle (RV) park is not a "homeowners' association" within the meaning of Chapter 720, because it specifically prohibits mobile homes, permanent or semi-permanent structures, and any structure designed, intended or used as permanent living quarters and its primary purpose is the use and rental of RV lots without permanent residency; park's use of declaration of covenants to regulate property use has no bearing on the applicability of Chapter 720 and "does not necessitate a finding that Chapter 720 applies to this development").

1-2:3.2   Exclusion of Condominiums and Cooperatives

In addition, Chapter 720 does not apply to condominiums and cooperatives, which are governed by Chapters 718 and 719, respectively.[13] Questions arise when individual condominium associations are members of a master homeowners' association. In this scenario, condominium associations are not bound by Chapter 720, since this chapter does not apply to any association that is subject to regulation under Chapter 718.[14]

1-2:3.3   Homeowners' Associations Are Comprised of Parcel Owners

Homeowners' associations are corporations responsible for operating communities or mobile home subdivisions "in which the voting membership is made up of parcel owners ... and in which membership is a mandatory condition of parcel ownership.[15] Membership in the community consists of parcel owners or associations who represent parcel owners.[16] "Parcel" is defined as "a platted or unplatted lot, tract, unit, or other subdivision of real property within a community," which "is capable of separate conveyance" the owner of which is obligated to "be member of an association that serves the community; and [t]o pay to the homeowners' association assessments that, if not paid, may result in a lien."[17] Other types of corporations that manage and operate residential communities or mobile home subdivisions do not necessarily meet Chapter 720's definition of "homeowners' associations." For instance, property management companies do not meet Chapter 720's definition of "homeowners' association."[18]

---

[13] Fla. Stat. § 720.302(4) (2016).

[14] *Circle Villas Condo. Ass'n v. Circle Prop. Owners' Ass'n*, 957 So. 2d 1207, 1210 (Fla. 4th Dist. Ct. App. 2007) (in a community comprised of several individual condominium associations, one of the condominium associations brought suit against the master homeowners' association based on the homeowners' association's failure to live up to its maintenance responsibilities; the court held that the condominium association's refusal to comply with section 720.311(2)(a)'s condition precedent to filing this type of lawsuit, which requires pre-suit mediation, was immaterial since Chapter 720 does not apply to any association that is subject to regulation under Chapter 718).

[15] Fla. Stat. § 720.301(9) (2016).

[16] Fla. Stat. § 720.301(10) (2016).

[17] Fla. Stat. § 720.301(11) (2016).

[18] *Greenacre Props. v. Rao*, 933 So. 2d 19, 24 (Fla. 2d Dist. Ct. App. 2006) (parcel owner in a homeowners' association (1) sued the homeowners' association's property management company based on its failure to make the association's official records available for

1-2:4   Common Areas and Individual Parcels

Most homeowners' associations have common areas that are maintained and regulated by the association for use by homeowners. Common areas may include streets, entrance gates, landscaping, recreational facilities, and water maintenance systems. Common areas in homeowners' associations are defined as "real property within a community which is owned or leased by an association or dedicated for use or maintenance by the association or its members."[19] The rights and privileges associated with homeowners' association membership, which include use of the common areas, are an essential component of home ownership within the community.[20]

Homeowners' associations are distinguished by the respective property interests held by the members and the association. Members typically own their parcel and the association typically owns the common areas, unlike condominium associations, in which the members own an undivided share in the common elements.[21] This is the critical distinction between the property interests of owners in homeowners' associations and those in condominium associations. While the owners in homeowners' association typically only own their parcel, owners in condominium associations also have an undivided interest in the common elements that is not capable of conveyance separate and apart from the individual unit, as discussed below.

While homeowners' associations are exercises in group living, the owner is usually further removed from his neighbor than in the case of condominiums or cooperatives, both literally and figuratively. The owner is afforded some freedom to maintain and improve his or her property subject to the architectural and aesthetic constraints imposed by the governing documents. At the same time, the owner is afforded the beneficial use of certain common areas, the cost of maintenance of which is borne by the community as a whole.

---

inspection, as is required by statute, and (2) sought statutory damages for violations of section 720.305(b), which would entitle him to "minimum damages for ... willful failure to comply" with inspection requests ($50 per day for a maximum of 10 days); the court held that the parcel owner failed to state a cause of action against the management company because property management companies do not meet section 720.301's definition of "association" as "a Florida corporation responsible for the operation of a community ... in which the voting membership is made up of parcel owners").

[19] Fla. Stat. § 720.301(2) (2016).

[20] *Savanna Club Worship Serv., Inc. v. Savanna Club Homeowners' Ass'n*, 456 F. Supp. 2d 1223, 1229-30 (S.D. Fla. 2005).

[21] Fla. Stat. § 718.103(11) (2016).

1-3   CONDOMINIUM ASSOCIATIONS

1-3:1   Governing Statutes

Condominium associations are governed by Florida Statutes Chapter 718, which is known as the Condominium Act.[22] Every condominium in Florida is subject to this chapter.[23] Condominium associations are also governed by Chapters 607 and 617, the Florida Business Corporation Act and the Florida Not For Profit Corporation Act, respectively. Chapters 607 and 617 do not apply to the extent they conflict with Chapter 718.[24] In addition, the relationships between the condominium unit owners and the condominium association are governed by the declaration of condominium, which courts have referred to as the condominium's "constitution."[25]

Chapter 718 protects association members in part by imposing a fiduciary relationship between the officers and directors of the association and the membership.[26] It also provides a statutory cause of action for damages or injunctive relief against owners, tenants, and other invitees, and the association for violations of the Condominium Act, the declaration, the documents creating the association, and the association bylaws which are deemed expressly incorporated into any lease of a unit.[27]

Certain types of disputes are subject to pre-suit non-binding arbitration as a statutory prerequisite to filing suit. The stated purpose is to level the playing field between owners and the condominium association, which

> with its statutory assessment authority, is often
> more able to bear the costs and expenses of
> litigation than the unit owner who must rely on his

[22.] Fla. Stat. § 718.101 (2016).

[23.] Fla. Stat. § 718.102 (2016).

[24.] Fla. Stat. § 718.111(2) (2014); *Heron at Destin W. Beach & Bay Resort Condo. Ass'n. v. Osprey at Destin W. Beach*, 94 So. 3d 623, 631 (Fla. 1st Dist. Ct. App. 2012), *reh'g denied* (Aug. 21, 2012).

[25.] *Woodside Vill. Condo. Ass'n. v. Jahren*, 806 So. 2d 452, 456 (Fla. 2002) (quoting *Schmidt v. Sherrill*, 442 So. 2d 963, 965 (Fla. 4th Dist. Ct. App. 1983)).

[26.] Fla. Stat. § 718.111 (2016).

[27.] Fla. Stat. § 718.303 (2016).

or her own financial resources to satisfy the costs of litigation against the association.[28]

In addition, the Legislature recognizes that "alternative dispute resolution has been making progress in reducing court dockets and trials and in offering a more efficient, cost-effective option to court litigation."[29]

1-3:2   Distinguishing Features of Condominiums

Condominiums can be residential or commercial or both. What distinguishes the condominium form of ownership is the fact that owners own the common elements. Without shared ownership of the common elements, the community is not a condominium. Units themselves are subject to exclusive ownership;[30] but the unit is just one part of the condominium parcel, which includes both the unit and an undivided share in the common elements.[31] By definition, "condominium" is ownership of real property "comprised entirely of units ... and in which there is, appurtenant to each unit, an undivided share in common elements."[32] The common elements are "those portions of the condominium property not included in the units."[33] The common elements may include the land on which the condominium building is built, the structural elements of the condominium building, the lobby, the garage, elevators, and recreational facilities.

The "association," as defined by the Condominium Act, is the "entity responsible for the operation of common elements owned in undivided shares by unit owners."[34] In condominiums, the owners typically have no options for improving any of the condominium property outside the walls of their units. With that said, they are typically also free from the burden of having to maintain the external elements of the condominium building, landscaping, and other common elements.

---

[28]. Fla. Stat. § 718.1255(3)(a) (2016).
[29]. Fla. Stat. § 718.1255(3)(b) (2016).
[30]. Fla. Stat. § 718.103(27) (2016).
[31]. Fla. Stat. § 718.103(12) (2016).
[32]. Fla. Stat. § 718.103(11) (2016).
[33]. Fla. Stat. § 718.103(8) (2016).
[34]. Fla. Stat. § 718.103(2) (2016).

These benefits come at a price. Courts recognize that condominium living is unique and involves a greater degree of restrictions upon the rights of the individual owners.[35] The difficulties of living in close-proximity to one's neighbors and sharing common ownership of condominium property create the need for greater "limitation[s] upon the rights of the individual owner than might be tolerated given more traditional forms of property ownership."[36] "[I]nherent in the condominium concept" is that each owner must give up a certain degree of freedom of choice "to promote the health, happiness, and peace of mind of the majority of the unit owners."[37]

1-3:3   Condominium Association Tests

Only community associations that govern condominium property as defined by the Condominium Act are rightly referred to as condominium associations. To determine whether a community association is a condominium association or is subject to some other ownership regime, the courts apply a constituency and/or a function test. The constituency test asks whether the community association's membership is comprised of only condominium unit owners. The function test asks whether the community association exercises powers and performs actions comparable to those performed by condominium associations under Chapter 718.[38]

For instance, the Court applied the constituency test to a community association consisting of both single-family home owners and condominium owners and determined that

---

[35] *Woodside Vill. Condo. Ass'n v. Jahren*, 806 So. 2d 452, 456 (Fla. 2002).

[36] *Seagate Condo. Ass'n v. Duffy*, 330 So. 2d 484, 486 (Fla. 4th Dist. Ct. App. 1976). *See Sterling Vill. Condo. v. Breitenbach*, 251 So. 2d 685, 688 (Fla. 4th Dist. Ct. App. 1971) ("Every man may justly consider his home his castle and himself as the king thereof; nonetheless his sovereign fiat to use his property as he pleases must yield, at least in degree, where ownership is in common or cooperation with others. The benefits of condominium living and ownership demand no less. The individual ought not be permitted to disrupt the integrity of the common scheme through his desire for change, however, laudable that change might be.").

[37] *Hidden Harbour Estates v. Norman*, 309 So. 2d 180, 181-82 (Fla. 4th Dist. Ct. App. 1975) ("Condominium unit owners comprise a little democratic sub society of necessity more restrictive as it pertains to use of condominium property than may be existent outside the condominium organization.").

[38] *Downey v. Jungle Den Villas Recreation Ass'n*, 525 So. 2d 438 (Fla. 5th Dist. Ct. App. 1988).

the association did not meet the definition of "condominium association" set forth in the Condominium Act since the single-family home members were not subject to the condominium form of ownership.[39] The nature of the community was critical to the courts inquiry into whether each property owner would be entitled to the benefits and protections of the Condominium Act. Similarly, the Court held that a community association that controls common properties for the benefit of multiple condominiums, as well as for properties yet to be developed, is not a condominium association subject to Chapter 718.[40]

In contrast, the court applied the constituency and function tests and held that a recreation association that owned and managed facilities used by condominium unit owners, in which each owner was required to maintain non-transferable membership, should be treated as a condominium association subject to Chapter 718, and not as an independent not-for-profit corporation.[41] In deciding that condominium unit owner members were entitled to the protections and benefits of the Condominium Act in this case, the court considered the following factors under the constituency test:

[39.] *Raines v. Palm Beach Leisureville Cmty. Ass'n*, 413 So. 2d 30, 32 (Fla. 1982) (applying the constituency test to determine whether every property owner in a community association that consisted of 1803 improved lots with single-family homes and 502 condominium apartments was entitled to the Condominium Act's benefits and protections; each of the 21 apartment buildings had its own condominium association, with a master community association serving as a maintenance/management entity for the entire community; while each of the condominium associations and condominium owners was subject to their respective declaration of condominium and Chapter 718, the single-family lots were not protected under the Condominium Act).

[40.] *Department of Bus. Regulation, Div. of Land Sales v. Siegel*, 479 So. 2d 112, 114 (Fla. 1985) (four condominium buildings existed in a development and two parcels remained undeveloped, with each of the condominiums subject to its own declaration of condominium; if the overarching community association was deemed a "condominium association" under Chapter 718, then subsection 718.301(1) would entitle non-developer unit owners to control at least one-third of the association's board of directors; the Court held that the community association did not meet the Condominium Act's statutory definition of "association," since the community association could impose assessments upon non-condominium properties and the community "might eventually be partially comprised of non-condominium dwellers").

[41.] *Downey v. Jungle Den Villas Recreation Ass'n*, 525 So. 2d 438 (Fla. 5th Dist. Ct. App. 1988) (developer constructed recreation facilities then conveyed to a "recreation association" title to the recreation building and an adjacent vacant lot; a bare majority of recreation association members decided to assess each unit owner $450 to construct a swimming pool on the lot; opposing unit owners filed an action for declaratory and injunctive relief to determine whether the recreation association had the authority to acquire land, build a swimming pool, and assess the members without unanimous approval as required under Chapter 718); *see* Fla. Stat. § 718.110(4).

(1) the recreation association was entirely owned and controlled by the condominium unit owners; (2) the property owned by the association was expressly held for the use and benefit of the condominium unit owners; and (3) the association existed solely to serve the unit owners.[42] In applying the function test, the court held that the association's functions and actions were in substance those of a condominium association under Chapter 718.[43] The court noted that associations should not be allowed to circumvent legislative intent to protect the rights of condominium owners by simply "setting up an ostensibly independent corporation ... to perform some of the functions of a condominium association but without the unit owner protection" of Chapter 718.[44]

1-4 COOPERATIVES

1-4:1 Distinguishing Features of Cooperatives

Cooperatives are governed by Florida Statutes Chapter 719, which is known as the Cooperative Act.[45] The cooperative association can be for-profit or not for-profit corporation.[46] The cooperative association itself owns all of the cooperative property, including all lands, leaseholds, and personal property,[47] and retains full responsibility for its operation.[48] When an individual purchases a unit in a cooperative, he or she purchases a share in the cooperative association. The association then conveys a lease to the owner as part of the consideration for the purchase of the share.[49]

---

[42] *Downey v. Jungle Den Villas Recreation Ass'n*, 525 So. 2d 438, 440-441 (Fla. 5th Dist. Ct. App. 1988).

[43] *Downey v. Jungle Den Villas Recreation Ass'n*, 525 So. 2d 438, 441 (Fla. 5th Dist. Ct. App. 1988).

[44] *Downey v. Jungle Den Villas Recreation Ass'n*, 525 So. 2d 438, 441 (Fla. 5th Dist. Ct. App. 1988).

[45] Fla. Stat. § 719.101 (2016).

[46] Fla. Stat. § 719.103(2) (2016).

[47] Fla. Stat. § 719.103(15) (2016).

[48] Fla. Stat. § 719.103(2) (2016).

[49] *Southern Walls v. Stilwell Corp.*, 810 So. 2d 566, 572 (Fla. 5th Dist. Ct. App. 2002) ("Under the cooperative form of ownership, the owner receives shares in the cooperation and a long term lease as evidence of his or her title rather than a deed of conveyance.").

The unit owner holds both the share in the cooperative association and a lease entitling them to exclusive use and possession of the unit.[50] "Cooperative" ownership is therefore defined as

> ownership of real property wherein legal title is vested in a corporation or other entity and the beneficial use is evidenced by an ownership interest in the association and a lease ... granted by the association as the owner of all the cooperative property.[51]

The "cooperative parcel" is

> the shares or other evidence of ownership in a cooperative representing an undivided share in the assets of the association, together with the lease or other muniment of title or possession.[52]

The term "cooperative documents" shares this definition, and includes (a) the documents that create the cooperative, (b) the document evidencing a unit owner's membership or share in the association, and (c) the document recognizing a unit owner's title or right of possession to his or her unit.[53] A purchase and sale agreement also satisfies the definition of a "cooperative document" under section 719.103(13)(c) as a "document recognizing a unit owner's title or right of possession to his or her unit."[54]

Each unit owner is entitled to exclusive possession of his or her unit.[55] In addition, the cooperative parcel has a number of appurtenances, including evidence of membership, ownership of shares or other interest in the cooperative, voting rights, an undivided share in the association's assets, an exclusive right to use a portion of the common areas, an undivided share in the common surplus attributable to the unit, and any other appurtenances provided for in the cooperative documents.[56]

---

[50] Fla. Stat. § 719.103(26) (2016) ("unit owner[s]" hold "share[s] in the cooperative association and a lease or other muniment of title or possession of a unit that is granted by the association as the owner of the cooperative property").

[51] Fla. Stat. § 719.103(12) (2016).

[52] Fla. Stat. § 719.103(14) (2016).

[53] Fla. Stat. § 719.103(13) (2016).

[54] *McAllister v. Breakers Seville Ass'n*, 981 So. 2d 566 (Fla. 4th Dist. Ct. App. 2008).

[55] Fla. Stat. § 719.105(2) (2016).

[56] Fla. Stat. § 719.105(1) (2016).

1-4:2   Statutory Definition of Cooperative

Courts look to the form of ownership vested in the unit owners and the day-to-day means of operation of the property as set forth in the governing documents to determine whether a community meets the statutory definition of cooperative. For instance, the court determined that a "cooperative campground" was a cooperative and subject to all the procedural requirements for approval of site plans set forth in Chapter 719 based on the following factors: (1) owners purchased a leasehold interest in a unit that entitled them to a share in the corporation,[57] and (2) the co-op's bylaws provided that all Florida laws "regulating ... this Cooperative Campground shall be considered incorporated by reference herein and shall control in case of any conflict with these By-Laws."[58] The court rejected the association's argument that it could not be considered a cooperative because it failed to follow certain technical requirements in Chapter 719,[59] in part because equitable estoppel prevented the association "from improving its legal position based upon [its] own failure to comply with the law."[60]

1-5   MOBILE HOME SUBDIVISION HOMEOWNERS' ASSOCIATIONS

If the owners of lots in a mobile home subdivision do not create a homeowners' association pursuant to Chapter 720, they can create a mobile home subdivision homeowners' association governed by Chapter 723,[61] which is known as the Florida Mobile Home Act.[62] "Mobile home" is defined by Chapter 723 as a transportable "residential structure," 8 feet or more in width and over 35 feet in length, "designed to be used as a dwelling when connected to the required utilities, and not originally

---

[57.] *Key Largo Ocean Resort Co-Op v. Monroe Cty.*, 5 So. 3d 31, 34 (Fla. 3d Dist. Ct. App. 2009).

[58.] *Key Largo Ocean Resort Co-Op v. Monroe Cty.*, 5 So. 3d 31, 34 (Fla. 3d Dist. Ct. App. 2009).

[59.] Fla. Stat. § 719.1035 (2016) (requiring that the cooperative's documents be recorded in the county in which the cooperative is located).

[60.] *Key Largo Ocean Resort Co-Op v. Monroe Cty.*, 5 So. 3d 31, 34 (Fla. 3d Dist. Ct. App. 2009).

[61.] Fla. Stat. § 723.0751(1) (2016).

[62.] Fla. Stat. § 723.001 (2016).

sold as a recreational vehicle."[63] Chapter 723 applies to any residential tenancy in which a mobile home is placed upon a rented or leased lot in a mobile home park in which ten or more lots are offered for rent or lease.[64] Chapter 723 does not apply to any other tenancy, including those in which both a mobile home and a mobile home lot are leased or a tenancy in which a rental space is offered for occupancy by recreational vehicles that are primarily designed as temporary living quarters for camping or travel. When both the mobile home and lot are rented or when fewer than ten lots are available for rent or lease, the tenancy is governed by Chapter 83, Part II, the "Florida Residential Landlord and Tenant Act."[65]

1-6   TIMESHARE OWNERS' ASSOCIATION

1-6:1   Florida Vacation Plan and Timesharing Act

Florida Statutes Chapter 721, the Florida Vacation Plan and Timesharing Act,[66] gives statutory recognition to real and personal property timeshare plans in Florida.[67] Recognizing that timeshare plans are a significant part of the Florida tourism industry, the purpose of this chapter is to establish procedures for the creation, sale, exchange, promotion, and operation of timeshare plans. The Florida Legislature created Chapter 721 in part to "safeguard Florida's tourism industry and the state's economic well-being" and to protect consumers who purchase timeshare plans by requiring full and fair disclosure of terms, conditions, and services of timeshare plans.[68]

1-6:2   Statutory Definition of Timeshare Plan

A "timeshare plan" is any arrangement, "other than an exchange program," whereby a purchaser receives ownership rights in or a right to use accommodations and facilities for a period less than a full year during any given year, but not necessarily for

---

[63.] Fla. Stat. § 723.003(3) (2016).
[64.] Fla. Stat. § 723.002(1) (2016).
[65.] Fla. Stat. § 83.40 et seq.
[66.] Fla. Stat. § 721.01 (2016).
[67.] Fla. Stat. § 721.02 (2016).
[68.] Fla. Stat. § 721.02 (2016).

consecutive years.[69] This includes ownership rights or a right to use accommodations, such as apartments, condominiums or cooperative units, cabins, lodges, hotel rooms, campgrounds, cruise ship cabins, houseboats or other vessels, recreational or other motor vehicles, "or any private or commercial structure which is real or personal property and designed for overnight occupancy by one or more individuals."[70] "Timeshare unit" is "an accommodation of a timeshare plan which is divided into timeshare periods."[71] A "facility" is any permanent amenity, including furnishings, fixtures, equipment, real or personal property, other than an accommodation, which is made available to the purchasers of a timeshare plan.[72] Collectively, the owners of timeshare interests in a timeshare plan, including developers, make up the timeshare "owners' association."[73]

While the legislature intends Chapter 721 to be interpreted broadly in order to encompass all forms of timeshare plans,[74] a program must meet the basic statutory definitional elements to qualify as a timeshare under this chapter. For example, lifetime campgrounds licenses are not covered by Chapter 721 because they lack (1) timeshare plans containing timeshare periods, and (2) accommodations or facilities as defined by the Florida Vacation Plan and Timesharing Act.[75] Under a lifetime campgrounds license, purchasers do not buy a plan which gives them the "right to use accommodations, and facilities, if any, for a period of time less than a full year during any given year."[76] Nor does a campsite qualify

---

[69] Fla. Stat. § 721.05(39) (2016).

[70] Fla. Stat. § 721.05(1) (2016).

[71] Fla. Stat. § 721.05(41) (2016).

[72] Fla. Stat. § 721.05(17) (2016).

[73] Fla. Stat. § 721.05(27) (2016).

[74] Fla. Stat. § 721.02(6) (2016).

[75] *All Seasons Resorts v. Dep't of Bus. Regulation, Div. of Land Sales, Condos. & Mobile Homes*, 455 So. 2d 544, 547-548 (Fla. 1st Dist. Ct. App. 1984) (holding that Chapter 721 does not apply to licenses for nonexclusive use of plots for RVs, campers, or tents, improved by utility services and amenities such as a general store, recreation hall, swimming area, and tennis courts, under which members' stays are limited to 14 days at one time, with minimum seven day periods in between stays, because such licenses lack (1) timeshare plans containing timeshare periods, as well as (2) accommodations or facilities as defined by the Florida Vacation Plan and Timesharing Act).

[76] Fla. Stat. § 721.05(39) (2016). The statute's plain language suggests that the timeshare period is a single period of time less than a year, within a year. In the *All Seasons Resorts* program, purchasers did not buy a license for a single period of time within a year. They

as an "accommodation," which is defined by the general statutory language as a "structure."[77] As such, a lifetime campgrounds license does not qualify as a timeshare plan governed by Chapter 721.[78]

---

could use their membership to stay at campgrounds at any time of the year they chose for as many stays as could be accommodated, so long as they limited themselves to 14 days on and 7 days off. *All Seasons Resorts v. Dep't of Bus. Regulation, Div. of Land Sales, Condos. & Mobile Homes*, 455 So. 2d 544, 546 (Fla. 1st Dist. Ct. App. 1984).

[77.] *All Seasons Resorts v. Dep't of Bus. Regulation, Div. of Land Sales, Condos. & Mobile Homes*, 455 So. 2d 544, 547-548 (Fla. 1st Dist. Ct. App. 1984).

[78.] *All Seasons Resorts v. Dep't of Bus. Regulation, Div. of Land Sales, Condos. & Mobile Homes*, 455 So. 2d 544, 548 (Fla. 1st Dist. Ct. App. 1984).

Chapter 2

The Governing Documents

2-1 INTRODUCTION

The community association's governing documents establish the association regime by setting forth the rights and obligations of the owners and the association. A community association's governing documents include the recorded declaration of condominium or the recorded declaration of covenants; the articles of incorporation; bylaws; and any duly adopted and recorded amendments, supplements, and recorded exhibits thereto. A declaration of covenants and restrictions typically governs a homeowners' association, while a declaration of condominium governs condominium associations. The governing documents for cooperatives include the lease providing the owner with exclusive use of his or her unit, the document evidencing the owner's interest in the association, the bylaws, and any use restrictions.

The governing documents are treated as contracts between the association and the property owners and they have some of the attributes of covenants running with the land.[1] The governing documents typically restrict use of the property, and set forth architectural controls, the association's right to assess for common expenses, and procedures for community governance.

---

[1] *Pepe v. Whispering Sands Condo. Ass'n*, 351 So. 2d 755, 757 (Fla. 2d Dist. Ct. App. 1977).

2-2   THE DECLARATION

2-2:1   Basic Characteristics of the Declaration

The declaration serves as the community association's constitution.[2] The Condominium Act defines "declaration" as "the instrument or instruments by which a condominium is created, as they are from time to time amended."[3] The declaration of condominium may include covenants and restrictions concerning the use, occupancy, and transfer of the units.[4] Florida courts recognize that "restrictions concerning use, occupancy, and transfer of condominium units are necessary for the operation and protection of the owners in the condominium concept."[5]

Chapter 720, which governs homeowners' associations, defines "declaration of covenants" as

> a recorded written instrument or instruments in the nature of covenants running with the land which subject the land comprising the community to the jurisdiction and control of an association or associations in which the owners of the parcels, or their association representatives, must be members.[6]

While they have characteristics of covenants running with the land, restrictive covenants are considered contract rights and not interests in real estate.[7] When a developer subdivides a tract of land and imposes restrictions on the separate parcels sold to individual grantees, those restrictions may be enforced by any grantee against any other grantee, either on the theory that there is a "mutuality of covenant and consideration," or that the restrictions constitute "mutual negative equitable easements,"[8] which are enforceable as contractual rights.[9]

---

[2] *Heron at Destin W. Beach & Bay Resort Condo. Ass'n v. Osprey at Destin W. Beach*, 94 So. 3d 623, 628 (Fla. 1st Dist. Ct. App. 2012).

[3] Fla. Stat. § 718.103(15) (2016).

[4] Fla. Stat. § 718.104(5) (2016).

[5] *White Egret Condo. v. Franklin*, 379 So. 2d 346, 350 (Fla. 1979).

[6] Fla. Stat. § 720.301(4) (2016).

[7] *Cudjoe Gardens Prop. Owners Ass'n v. Payne*, 779 So. 2d 598, 599 (Fla. 3d Dist. Ct. App. 2001).

[8] *Hagan v. Sabal Palms*, 186 So. 2d 302, 307 (Fla. 2d Dist. Ct. App. 1966).

[9] *Dade Cty. v. Matheson*, 605 So. 2d 469, 474 (Fla. 3d Dist. Ct. App. 1992).

Restrictive covenants are not favored in law, and are strictly construed in favor of unrestricted use of real property.[10] They will be enforced, however, when "carried in all deeds with a view to preserve the symmetry, beauty, and general good of all interested in the scheme of development."[11] In construing restrictive covenants, the court will interpret the text to give effect to the parties' intentions, with any doubt as to the meaning of the words resolved against those seeking enforcement.[12]

The declaration spells out the rights and obligations of the owners, setting forth the use interest purchased by the owner of the property in the community association.[13] Both Chapters 718 and 720 provide a statutory cause of action against the association, any member of the association, any director or officer, or any tenant, guest, or invitee for failure or refusal to comply with the association's declaration or any governing document.[14]

2-2:2   Restrictions in the Declaration

Restrictions found in a declaration are given a strong presumption of validity. This is true because each owner purchases his unit with notice that his property is subject to the restrictions found in the declaration, which is recorded among the public records. The owner is considered to have knowledge of the restrictions and to have willingly accepted them.[15] Such restrictions have attributes of covenants running with the land and will only be invalidated if shown to be "wholly arbitrary in their application," in violation of public policy, or repugnant to a fundamental constitutional right.[16] Courts do not apply a reasonableness test when ruling on the validity of restrictions found in a declaration. In fact, it is recognized that some restrictions may be seemingly draconian

---

[10] *Wilson v. Rex Quality*, 839 So. 2d 928, 930 (Fla. 2d Dist. Ct. App. 2003).

[11] *Pelican Island Prop. Owners Ass'n v. Murphy*, 554 So. 2d 1179, 1181 (Fla. 2d Dist. Ct. App. 1989) (quoting *Stephl v. Moore*, 94 Fla. 313, 114 So. 455 (Fla. 1927)).

[12] *Wilson v. Rex Quality*, 839 So. 2d 928, 930 (Fla. 2d Dist. Ct. App. 2003).

[13] *Pepe v. Whispering Sands Condo. Ass'n*, 351 So. 2d 755, 757 (Fla. 2d Dist. Ct. App. 1977).

[14] Fla. Stat. § 718.303(1) (2016); Fla. Stat. § 720.305(1) (2016).

[15] *Hidden Harbour Estates v. Basso*, 393 So. 2d 637, 639 (Fla. 4th Dist. Ct. App. 1981).

[16] *Hidden Harbour Estates v. Basso*, 393 So. 2d 637, 640 (Fla. 4th Dist. Ct. App. 1981); *Pines of Boca Barwood Condo. Ass'n v. Cavouti*, 605 So. 2d 984, 985 (Fla. 4th Dist. Ct. App. 1992).

and unreasonable. Nevertheless, such restrictions will survive legal challenge, as owners must be able to count on stability in the restrictions found in the recorded declaration.[17]

2-2:3   Invalid Restrictions

As stated above, however, restrictions contained in a declaration may be invalidated if found to be wholly arbitrary in their application, contrary to public policy, or in violation of a constitutional right. For instance, a provision expressly empowering an association to "arbitrarily, capriciously, or unreasonably" withhold its consent to any sale, lease, assignment, or transfer of a unit has been held invalid as a violation of the public policy against unreasonable restraints on alienation.[18]

While restrictions may contain a certain degree of unreasonableness, they are invalidated when they violate "external public policy or constitutional right[s] of the individual."[19] Essentially, the owner's right to alienate his property must be balanced against the association's right to maintain the community's homogeneity by controlling unit transfer. A declaration that allows the association to reject any unit owner's prospective purchaser for any or no reason is clearly a restraint on alienation and can only be saved from invalidity by obligating the association to purchase or procure a new purchaser at the property's fair market value. Conversely, a reverter clause that binds an association to pay fair market value but is only triggered by a violation of the prohibition against unapproved transfers provides an illusory obligation. Without an unapproved sale, the reverter clause is never triggered,

---

[17.] *Hidden Harbour Estates v. Basso*, 393 So. 2d 637, 640 (Fla. 4th Dist. Ct. App. 1981).

[18.] *Aquarian Found. v. Sholom House*, 448 So. 2d 1166, 1167 (Fla. 3d Dist. Ct. App. 1984) (a board member-unit owner disregarded the declaration's requirement that all sales necessitate the board's written approval and sold her condominium unit without the board's consent; the association sued to set aside the conveyance and to recover damages under a "reverter clause" in the declaration that provided that fee simple title to condominiums immediately reverted to the association, subject to payment of the fair appraised value *in the event of a violation* of any covenant, restriction, or limitation in the declaration; in a non-jury trial, the court found that the owner violated the declaration and entered a judgment for the association, declaring the conveyance null and void, ejecting the new owner, and retaining jurisdiction to award damages, attorneys' fees, and costs; on appeal, the court reversed, holding that the association cannot be given power to arbitrarily, capriciously, or unreasonably withhold its consent to transfer, which represents an unreasonable restraint on alienation).

[19.] *Aquarian Found. v. Sholom House*, 448 So. 2d 1166, 1168 (Fla. 3d Dist. Ct. App. 1984).

meaning that when the association prevents a sale by exercising its right to arbitrarily, capriciously, or unreasonably withhold its consent, it has absolutely no obligation to pay the fair market value for the unit, since the reverter clause has not yet been triggered by an unapproved transfer. In such cases, an association's power to arbitrarily, capriciously, or unreasonably withhold consent to transfers is invalid as a violation of the public policy against unreasonable restraints on alienation.[20]

2-2:4   Required Declaration Provisions for Condominium Associations

Under Chapter 718, certain provisions must be included in a declaration of condominium. For instance, the declaration must include a statement submitting the property to the condominium form of ownership.[21] The declaration must also state the name of the condominium property, "which shall include the word 'condominium' or be followed by the words 'a condominium.'"[22] The declaration must include a legal description of the land, a survey, a graphic description of improvements, a plot plan, and an identification of each unit by letter, name, or number.[23] The declaration shall state if the construction of the condominium is not substantially completed.[24] Upon substantial completion, the developer or the association shall amend the declaration to include a certificate of a surveyor and mapper that the construction of the improvements is substantially complete such that the declaration, survey, graphic description, and plot plan accurately identifies and provides the location and dimensions of the common elements and each unit.[25]

The condominium parcel includes an undivided share in the common elements. The declaration must set forth the undivided share that is appurtenant to each unit as a percentage or fraction of the whole. For residential condominiums created after April 1, 1992, each unit shall share either an equal percentage or fraction

---

[20.] *Aquarian Found. v. Sholom House*, 448 So. 2d 1166, 1170 (Fla. 3d Dist. Ct. App. 1984).

[21.] Fla. Stat. § 718.104(4)(a) (2016).

[22.] Fla. Stat. § 718.104(4)(b) (2016).

[23.] Fla. Stat. § 718.104(4)(c)-(e) (2016).

[24.] Fla. Stat. § 718.104(4)(e) (2016).

[25.] Fla. Stat. § 718.104(4)(e) (2016).

of the common elements, or each unit shall share in a percentage or fraction of the common elements based on the "square footage of each residential unit in uniform relationship to the total square footage of each other residential unit."[26] The declaration must also state the percentage or fractional shares of liability for common expenses, which equals the unit's share in the common elements.[27]

The declaration must include the owners' membership and voting rights,[28] and a copy of the bylaws attached as an exhibit.[29] The declaration must also dedicate the streets, walks, and other rights-of-way to the public, or create a nonexclusive easement for ingress and egress to provide reasonable access to the streets, walks, and other rights-of-way serving the units.[30]

2-3   ARTICLES OF INCORPORATION

"Articles of incorporation" are defined by the Florida Not For Profit Corporation Act to include

> original, amended, and restated articles of incorporation, articles of consolidation, and articles of merger, and all amendments thereto, including documents designated by the laws of this state as charters.[31]

Section 617.0203 provides that corporate existence begins with the filing of the articles of incorporation or on a date specified in the articles of incorporation.[32] The Florida Not For Profit Corporation Act requires that the articles of incorporation contain the following items: (a) the corporate name; (b) the street address of the initial principal office and, if different, the mailing address of the corporation; (c) the purpose of the corporation; (d) a statement of the procedures for electing the directors of the board or reference to the manner of election as set forth in the bylaws; (e) any provision that limits the corporate powers

---

[26] Fla. Stat. § 718.104(4)(f) (2016).
[27] Fla. Stat. § 718.104(4)(g) (2016).
[28] Fla. Stat. § 718.104(4)(j) (2016).
[29] Fla. Stat. § 718.104(4)(l) (2016).
[30] Fla. Stat. § 718.104(4)(n) (2016).
[31] Fla. Stat. § 617.01401(1) (2016).
[32] Fla. Stat. § 617.0203(1) (2016).

authorized under Chapter 617 as permitted by law; (f) the street address of the corporation's initial registered office and the name of its initial registered agent; and (g) the name and address of each incorporator.[33] The Florida Not For Profit Corporation Act also describes the following optional articles of incorporation provisions that may pertain to community associations: (a) the names and addresses of the initial directors; (b) any provision permitted by law, regarding the governance of the corporation, including, for instance, any provision regarding the rights of the members; and (c) a description of the various classes of members.[34]

2-4 BYLAWS

The bylaws govern the community association's corporate rituals. The Condominium Act requires that the bylaws contain certain provisions, the omission of which triggers the inclusion of standard provisions from the Condominium Act. The bylaws are expected to contain a description of the form of administration, including the title of the officers of the board of directors, specifying their powers, duties, manner of selection and removal, and compensation, if any.[35] The bylaws should also set forth the percentage of voting interests required to establish a quorum at a membership meeting and a description of the procedures for noticing and conducting membership meetings and meetings of the board of directors.[36] The method of amendment of the bylaws must also be set forth in the bylaws.[37]

The condominium bylaws may also include certain optional provisions, including procedures for adopting rules and regulations for operation and use of the common elements; restrictions on use, maintenance, and appearance of the units and use of the common elements; provisions for giving email notice of association meetings; and any other provisions which are not inconsistent with the Condominium Act.[38] The bylaws of any residential condominium shall include a provision for mandatory nonbinding arbitration of disputes regarding the board's authority to require owners to take

---

[33] Fla. Stat. § 617.0202(1) (2016).
[34] Fla. Stat. § 617.0202(1) (2016).
[35] Fla. Stat. § 718.112(2)(a) (2016).
[36] Fla. Stat. § 718.112(2) (2016).
[37] Fla. Stat. § 718.112(2)(h) (2016).
[38] Fla. Stat. § 718.112(3) (2016).

or refrain from action involving owners' units, or to alter or add to a common area or element. The mandatory non-binding arbitration provision shall also cover disputes regarding the board's failure to properly conduct elections, give adequate notice of meetings or other actions, properly conduct meetings, or allow inspection of books and records.[39]

Under Chapter 720, governing homeowners' associations, the bylaws must require notice to members of all member meetings[40] and board meetings.[41] While the homeowners' association bylaws are not required to contain provisions regarding meeting quorum requirements, bylaw amendments, and procedures for conducting meetings, Chapter 720 does provide minimum requirements if the bylaws are silent.[42]

2-5   CONFLICTS BETWEEN GOVERNING DOCUMENTS

There is a hierarchy among a community association's governing documents. The declaration is the association's constitution. The articles of incorporation are the documents filed with the Secretary of State as part of the incorporation process. The bylaws are rules adopted by an association for its internal governance. In case a conflict arises between these governing documents, the declaration controls over the articles of incorporation and the bylaws.[43]

2-6   RULES AND REGULATIONS

Boards of directors are permitted to adopt rules and regulations that are "reasonably related to the promotion of the health, happiness and peace of mind of the unit owners."[44] Unlike restrictions in the recorded declaration, there is no presumption of validity for board-made rules. The association may not adopt

---

[39] Fla. Stat. § 718.112(2)(k) (2016).

[40] Fla. Stat. § 720.306(5) (2016).

[41] Fla. Stat. § 720.303(2)(c) (2016).

[42] Fla. Stat. § 720.306 (2016).

[43] *Heron at Destin W. Beach & Bay Resort Condo. Ass'n v. Osprey at Destin W. Beach*, 94 So. 3d 623, 629 (Fla. 1st Dist. Ct. App. 2012) (in a dispute related to the voting procedures for electing officers of a master condominium association composed of five sub-associations, the court held that the voting procedure in the declaration of condominium controls over voting procedures based on an interpretation of the articles of incorporation).

[44] *Hidden Harbour Estates v. Basso*, 393 So. 2d 637, 640 (Fla. 4th Dist. Ct. App. 1981).

"arbitrary or capricious rules bearing no relationship to the health, happiness and enjoyment of life of the various unit owners."[45] The courts apply a reasonableness test in determining the validity of board made rules, examining the unique facts and circumstances pertaining to challenged rules on a case by case basis.[46] This test is applied to board-made rules in both condominium and homeowners' associations.[47]

This same reasonableness standard is applied when the board is given discretion to allow particular uses of the property. When conflicts arise over an owner's proposed use of the property the board must demonstrate a reasonable relationship between property use rules and the legitimate objective sought to be achieved.[48] When a reasonable relationship cannot be demonstrated between a rule and a legitimate objective, the rule is unenforceable.[49]

2-7 PROHIBITED PROVISIONS

2-7:1 Prohibited Provisions for Homeowners' Associations

Florida Statutes prohibit inclusion of certain types of provisions in a homeowners' association's governing documents. For instance, homeowners' associations' governing documents may not give developers the unilateral right to change the documents after control

---

[45.] *Hidden Harbour Estates v. Norman*, 309 So. 2d 180, 182 (Fla. 4th Dist. Ct. App. 1975).

[46.] *Hidden Harbour Estates v. Norman*, 309 So. 2d 180, 182 (Fla. 4th Dist. Ct. App. 1975).

[47.] See *Hidden Harbour Estates v. Basso*, 393 So. 2d 637 (Fla. 4th Dist. Ct. App. 1981); *see Eastpointe Prop. Owners' Ass'n v. Cohen*, 505 So. 2d 518, 520 (Fla. 4th Dist. Ct. App. 1987).

[48.] *Hidden Harbour Estates v. Basso*, 393 So. 2d 637, 640 (Fla. 4th Dist. Ct. App. 1981).

[49.] *Hidden Harbour Estates v. Basso*, 393 So. 2d 637, 640 (Fla. 4th Dist. Ct. App. 1981) (denying condominium board an injunction to prevent maintenance of a well on an owner's property; the board refused permission for the well, which was required under a declaration article that prohibited improvements, alterations, or changes to the exterior of mobile homes or apartments without written board approval; the denial was based on (1) a perceived threat of increased salinity in the association's deeper wells, (2) potential staining of condominium common areas, and (3) potential proliferation of other private wells; after the owner drilled without permission, the association sought injunctive relief alleging that the owner violated the declaration of condominium; the court found that since the board presented no evidence that the owner's well effected salinity, stained common areas, or caused other wells to be drilled, the association "failed to demonstrate a reasonable relationship between its denial of the [owner's] application and the objectives which the denial sought to achieve").

of the homeowners' association is transferred to the membership.[50] In a further effort to protect owners, Chapter 720 also prohibits clauses that prevent homeowners' associations from filing lawsuits against developers.[51] Moreover, developers may not include provisions that entitle them to more than one vote per residential lot after control is turned over to homeowners.[52]

In addition, homeowners' associations' governing documents may not prohibit the display of one portable, removable United States flag, provided that it is "displayed in a respectful manner, consistent with Title 36 U.S.C. chapter 10."[53] Regardless of any covenants or rules and regulations, homeowners are permitted to display one portable, removable United States flag or official flag of the State of Florida, and one portable, removable official flag, not larger than 4.5 feet by 6 feet, which represents any branch of the United States military or a POW-MIA flag. Subject to all building codes, setbacks, and other governmental regulations, homeowners may also erect a flagpole no more than 20 feet high on any portion of their property, displaying any of the aforementioned flags, so long as the flagpole does not obstruct sightlines at intersections and is not erected on an easement.[54] Chapter 720 provides homeowners with a right of action to enjoin any infringement of these rights.[55]

The Florida Legislature promotes "Florida-friendly" landscapes that "conserve water, protect the environment, are adaptable to local conditions, and are drought tolerant" through the use of "efficient watering, appropriate fertilization, mulching, attraction of wildlife, responsible management of yard pests, recycling yard waste, reduction of stormwater runoff, and waterfront protection."[56] Recognizing that homeowners' associations and local governments are essential partners in water conservation and water quality protection and restoration, the Florida Legislature

---

[50.] Fla. Stat. § 720.3075(1)(a) (2016).
[51.] Fla. Stat. § 720.3075(1)(b) (2016).
[52.] Fla. Stat. § 720.3075(1)(c) (2016).
[53.] Fla. Stat. § 720.3075(3) (2016); 36 U.S.C. § 10 (describing in detail the United States flag's proper position and manner of display).
[54.] Fla. Stat. § 720.304(2) (2016).
[55.] Fla. Stat. § 720.304(3) (2016).
[56.] Fla. Stat. § 373.185(1)(b) (2016).

has forbidden homeowners' associations' governing documents from prohibiting Florida-friendly landscaping or from requiring enforcement that prohibits implementation of Florida-friendly landscaping.[57]

2-7:2   Prohibited Provisions for Condominium Associations

For condominiums consisting of both residential and commercial units, the governing documents may not give commercial unit owners veto power over amendments to the governing documents.[58] In addition, a 1995 statute provides that where the number of residential units in the condominium is equal to or greater than 50 percent of the total number of units, the residential owners are entitled to vote for a majority of the members of the association's board of directors.[59] While this was meant to apply retroactively, the Supreme Court of Florida held that retroactively applying the 1995 amendment to change the distribution of voting power in a mixed-use condominium violates the Florida Constitution's prohibition against the enactment of any "law impairing the obligation of contracts," unless there is specific language in the condominium declaration indicating that it is subject to future statutory amendments.[60]

Chapter 718 also invalidates any declaration provision, rule, or regulation that prohibits any unit owner from displaying a

---

[57.] Fla. Stat. § 720.3075(4)(a)-(b) (2016).

[58.] Fla. Stat. § 718.404(1) (2016).

[59.] Fla. Stat. § 718.404(2) (2016).

[60.] *Cohn v. Grand Condo. Ass'n*, 62 So. 3d 1120, 1121 (Fla. 2011) (mixed residential-retail-commercial condominium's 1986 declaration provided that the retail and commercial unit owners had majority vote control over the board versus residential units; a residential unit owner requested that the voting system be amended to comply with Fla. Stat. § 718.404, which was enacted in 1995 and by its terms was to be applied retroactively "as a remedial measure"; condominium sought a declaration that the statute was an unconstitutional impairment of its right to contract with regard to the declaration of condominium, which is a contract that "spell[s] out mutual rights and obligations of the parties thereto"; the Court held that since the 1986 declaration contained no language suggesting that it was subject to future statutory amendments, retroactively applying the 1995 amendment in order to change the distribution of voting power would violate Article I, section 10 of the Florida Constitution, which prohibits the enactment of any "law impairing the obligation of contracts"). Fla. Stat. § 718.404; Fla. Const. art. I, § 10.

portable, removable United States flag and, on Armed Forces Day, Memorial Day, Flag Day, Independence Day, and Veterans Day, a portable, removable official flag, not larger than 4.5 feet by 6 feet, that represents any branch of the United States military.[61]

2-8   AMENDING THE GOVERNING DOCUMENTS

Amendments to an association's governing documents made by the membership are valid and enforceable so long as the amendments are properly adopted in compliance with the association's governing documents.[62] For example, the Supreme Court of Florida upheld an amendment, adopted by owners in compliance with the declaration, which reduced the permissible period of condominium leasing from a period in excess of one year to a period of no more than nine months in a 12-month period.[63]

For amendments imposed by the developer, the Courts inquire into whether the amendment is reasonable such that it does not destroy the scheme of development.[64] The purpose of this test is to protect the character and restrictions contemplated by the developer and each owner at the time of conveyance[65] in order to avoid altering the "mutual benefit or consideration necessary to allow enforcement" of the restrictions contemplated at the time of purchase.[66] Thus, by reading a reasonableness requirement "into the reservation of power to modify," the court "undercuts the grantor's unfettered

---

[61.] Fla. Stat. § 718.113(4) (2016).

[62.] *Woodside Vill. Condo. Ass'n, Inc. v. Jahren*, 806 So. 2d 452 (Fla. 2002).

[63.] *Woodside Vill. Condo. Ass'n, Inc. v. Jahren*, 806 So. 2d 452, 461 (Fla. 2002) (when plaintiffs purchased their condominium, the declaration provided that units could be leased without prior board approval for a period in excess of one year; the Supreme Court held that the amendment to the declaration reducing the lease period to no more than nine months in a 12-month period was entirely valid based on the fact that owners were "on notice that the unique form of ownership they acquired when they purchased their units in the [condominium] was subject to change through the amendment process, and that they would be bound by properly adopted amendments").

[64.] *Flamingo Ranch Estates v. Sunshine Ranches Homeowners*, 303 So. 2d 665 (Fla. 4th Dist. Ct. App. 1974); *Holiday Pines Prop. Owners Ass'n v. Wetherington*, 596 So. 2d 84 (Fla. 4th Dist. Ct. App. 1992).

[65.] *Nelle v. Loch Haven Homeowners' Ass'n*, 413 So. 2d 28, 29 (Fla. 1982) ("Traditionally, reservation of the right to modify restrictions, without some limit, allowed the grantor to entirely change the character of the subdivision at the grantor's whim with no corresponding benefit to the grantee.").

[66.] *Nelle v. Loch Haven Homeowners' Ass'n*, 413 So. 2d 28, 29 (Fla. 1982).

control and provides the mutual burden and benefit to both grantor and grantees necessary to sustain the covenants."[67]

2-8:1   Amending Homeowners' Association Governing Documents

Unless otherwise stated in the governing documents, an amendment to any homeowners' association governing document requires approval of two-thirds of the voting interests of the association.[68] Chapter 720 prohibits any amendment that alters the proportionate voting interest appurtenant to a parcel or increases the proportion by which a parcel shares in the common expenses unless the owner and all record owners of liens on the parcels join in the execution of the amendment.[69] A change in quorum requirements is not an alteration of voting interests that would trigger this rule.[70]

2-8:2   Amending Condominium Governing Documents

Chapter 718 provides that unless otherwise stated in the declaration, the declaration may be amended if approved by not less than two-thirds of the unit owners. No declaration recorded after April 1, 1992, shall require more than four-fifths of the owners to approve amendments.[71] A condominium association may not pass certain types of amendments, however, with a simple unit owner vote unless expressly provided for in the declaration as originally recorded.[72] For instance, unless provided for in the declaration as originally recorded, a simple unit owner vote may not give effect to an amendment that materially changes the configuration of any unit, modifies the appurtenances to the unit, or changes the unit owner's percentage share in the common expenses or common surplus.[73] This would have the effect of divesting owners of their vested rights.

An amendment that materially changes the configuration of any unit, modifies the appurtenances to the unit, or changes the unit

---

[67.] *Nelle v. Loch Haven Homeowners' Ass'n*, 413 So. 2d 28, 29 (Fla. 1982).

[68.] Fla. Stat. § 720.306(1)(b) (2016).

[69.] Fla. Stat. § 720.306(1)(c) (2016).

[70.] Fla. Stat. § 720.306(1)(c) (2016).

[71.] Fla. Stat. § 718.110(1)(a) (2016).

[72.] Fla. Stat. § 718.110(4), (8) (2016).

[73.] Fla. Stat. § 718.110(4) (2016).

owner's percentage share in the common expenses or common surplus requires the affected owner and all record owners of liens on the unit to join in the execution of the amendment and the approval of all other unit owners.[74] A simple majority of the unit owners cannot amend the declaration to add a new provision which permits the common elements to be altered based on a general power to amend contained in the declaration.[75] If such an amendment were validated, unit owners would be deprived of their vested interest in the common elements of the condominium.[76] Public policy dictates that a purchaser of a condominium unit should be able to rely on the governing documents in effect on the date of purchase in anticipating the cost of owning a unit, including the costs associated with the common elements.

In addition, unless otherwise stated in the declaration, a condominium association may not make an amendment allowing for the creation of timeshare estates in any unit of the condominium, unless the record owner of each unit and the record owners of liens on each unit join in the execution of the amendment.[77] Amendments prohibiting owners from renting their units, setting minimum or maximum rental terms, or limiting the number of times a unit can be rented during a period, are only effective against owners who consent to the amendment and owners who acquire title after the effective date of the amendment.[78]

Prior to the enactment of section 718.110(13), however, the Court held that owners *could* adopt an amendment to the declaration that would prohibit rentals during the first 12 months of ownership and limit rentals to nine-month terms in any 12-month period.[79] The Court upheld the validity of such a leasing restriction based on two primary principles: (1) condominium associations are creatures of statute, and neither Chapter 718 nor any provision in the state or federal constitutions barred such a leasing restriction,

---

[74] Fla. Stat. § 718.110(4) (2016).

[75] *Wellington Prop. Mgmt. v. Parc Corniche Condo. Ass'n*, 755 So. 2d 824 (Fla. 5th Dist. Ct. App. 2000).

[76] *Wellington Prop. Mgmt. v. Parc Corniche Condo. Ass'n*, 755 So. 2d 824, 825 (Fla. 5th Dist. Ct. App. 2000).

[77] Fla. Stat. § 718.110(8) (2016).

[78] Fla. Stat. § 718.110(13) (2016).

[79] *Woodside Vill. Condo. Ass'n, Inc. v. Jahren*, 806 So. 2d 452, 464 (Fla. 2002).

and (2) the condominium form of ownership "is unique and involves a greater degree of restrictions upon the rights of the individual unit owners."[80] Since the owners were on notice that the "unique form of ownership they acquired ... was subject to change through the amendment process, and that they would be bound by properly adopted amendments,"[81] and the amendment's purpose of promoting owner occupancy of the condominium units was "a goal certainly consistent with the concept of condominium living as originally contemplated by the legislation authorizing the condominium form," the Court upheld the validity of the amendment.[82]

In its opinion, the Court described the lack of any prohibition against this type of amendment as a "legislative oversight." The Court also expressed concern over owners who purchased their units for investment purposes, who would be restricted in their ability to earn income on their properties because of an amendment imposed by two-thirds of the membership. Both of these issues were later addressed by the enactment of section 718.110(13).

Chapter 718 also prescribes the method of amendment. The proposed amendment must include the full text of the provision, underlining new words, and striking through deletions. Extensive proposed amendments may forego this procedure if it would hinder understanding of the amendment, but must include the following language immediately preceding the proposed amendment: "Substantial rewording of declaration. See provision for present text."[83] Only material deficiencies in the amendment process will invalidate the amendment.[84] An amendment is effective upon recording[85] and shall include a certificate of amendment to evidence the amendment, which is executed in the form required for the execution of a deed and must include the recording data identifying the declaration.[86]

---

[80] *Woodside Vill. Condo. Ass'n, Inc. v. Jahren*, 806 So. 2d 452, 456 (Fla. 2002).
[81] *Woodside Vill. Condo. Ass'n, Inc. v. Jahren*, 806 So. 2d 452, 461 (Fla. 2002).
[82] *Woodside Vill. Condo. Ass'n, Inc. v. Jahren*, 806 So. 2d 452, 462 (Fla. 2002).
[83] Fla. Stat. § 718.110(1)(b) (2016).
[84] Fla. Stat. § 718.110(1)(c) (2016).
[85] Fla. Stat. § 718.110(3) (2016).
[86] Fla. Stat. § 718.110(2) (2016).

Chapter 3

Developer Obligations and Turnover

3-1 INTRODUCTION

The relationship between the developer and the community association is critical to the early development of the community. The interests of the developer and the community association, however, are not necessarily aligned. In fact, they are oftentimes strictly at odds. At no other time is this fact brought more clearly to the forefront than when control of the community is turned over to the non-developer owners. To provide safeguards for both entities, the Florida Legislature included provisions in both the Homeowners' Association Act and the Condominium Act that provide guidance leading up to turnover, through the turnover process, and for the period following turnover during which the developer relinquishes, and the owners accept, control of the community.

3-2 DEVELOPER OBLIGATIONS AND HOMEOWNERS' ASSOCIATIONS

Chapter 720 outlines developers' obligations and prohibited practices, which protect the interests of prospective purchasers and owners in subdivisions subject to developer control. Generally, these provisions apply to any person or entity that "creates the community served by the association" or "succeeds to the rights and liabilities of the person or entity that created the community served by the association."[1]

The developer's first obligation is to create a Florida homeowners' association, which, after October 1, 1995, must be incorporated under Florida law with the initial governing documents recorded in the official records of the county in which the community is located.[2] In addition, the developer is subject to strict bookkeeping requirements, including maintaining all association funds separately in the association's name. Prior to turnover, reserve and operating funds may not be commingled by the developer, nor may the developer commingle association funds with his or her own funds or with the funds of any other homeowners' association or community association.[3] In addition, prior to turnover, the developer-controlled association may not vote to use reserves for purposes other than those for which they were intended. In order to use reserves for purposes other than those initially intended, the association must obtain the approval of a majority of all non-developer voting interests voting in person or by limited proxy at a duly called meeting of the association.[4]

The developer is also prohibited from using association funds to defend a civil or criminal action, administrative proceeding, or arbitration proceeding that has been filed against the developer or directors appointed to the association board by the developer. This is true even if the subject of the proceeding concerns the operation of the developer-controlled association.[5]

Under any circumstances where owners pay mandatory maintenance or amenity fees to the developer, the developer must provide a complete financial report of the actual, total receipts of maintenance or amenity fees, and an itemized listing of the expenditures made using the fees, within 60 days following the end of each fiscal year. The developer must mail the report to each lot or parcel owner in the subdivision, publish the report in a publication regularly distributed within the subdivision, or

---

[1.] Fla. Stat. § 720.301(6) (2016).
[2.] Fla. Stat. § 720.303(1) (2016).
[3.] Fla. Stat. § 720.303(8) (2016).
[4.] Fla. Stat. § 720.303(6)(h) (2016).
[5.] Fla. Stat. § 720.303(8)(c) (2016).

post the report in prominent locations in the subdivision.[6] Before turnover, the developer-controlled board of directors may not levy a special assessment unless approved by a majority of the parcel owners other than the developer at a duly called special meeting of the membership at which a quorum is present.[7]

3-2:1   Developer-Made Contracts

The developer is also restricted in the contracts it may enter into on behalf of the association prior to turnover. Any contract that has a term greater than 10 years, which is made before control of the association is turned over to the members, and that provides for the operation, maintenance, or management of the association or common areas, must be fair and reasonable.[8]

Any lease of recreational or other common facilities serving the association, which is entered into prior to turnover must include specific terms to protect the owners' interests. The facilities may not be offered for sale unless the association has the option to purchase the facilities.[9] The time, unless agreed to otherwise, within which the homeowners' association must execute a contract with the facility owner is within 90 days of notice of intent to sell. The homeowners' association must meet the price, terms, and conditions of the facility owner. If a contract between the facility owner and the association is not executed within the 90-day period, and the owner receives a bona fide offer to purchase the facilities, his or her only obligations shall be to notify the association, disclose the price and material terms and conditions upon which the owner would consider selling the facilities, and consider any offer made by the association. If the association does not consummate its option within 90 days, the owner is under no obligation to sell to the homeowners' association or to interrupt or delay negotiations.[10]

These obligations do not apply to any sale or transfer to a person within the table of descent and distribution if the facility owner were to die intestate; any transfer by gift, devise, or operation of

---

[6.] Fla. Stat. § 720.3086 (2016).
[7.] Fla. Stat. § 720.315 (2016).
[8.] Fla. Stat. § 720.309 (2016).
[9.] Fla. Stat. § 720.31 (2016).
[10.] Fla. Stat. § 720.31(2) (2016).

law; any transfer by a corporation to an affiliate; any transfer to a governmental or quasi-governmental entity; any conveyance of an interest in the facilities for financing; any conveyance resulting from foreclosure or any deed in lieu; any sale or transfer between joint tenants in common owning the facilities; or the purchase of the facilities by a governmental entity under eminent domain.[11]

3-2:2   Disclosures Prior to Sale

Prospective purchasers are also protected by the disclosures of their obligations as future members of a homeowners' association that are required under Florida law. The developer, or the parcel owner if the sale is by a non-developer owner, must supply a disclosure with the following information, which must be incorporated in the purchase and sale contract: (1) as a purchaser of property in the community, the purchaser is required to be a member of a homeowners' association; (2) recorded restrictive covenants govern use of the property in the community; (3) the purchaser will be obligated to pay assessments, which are subject to change, and may be obligated to pay special assessments, which are also subject to change (the disclosure must state the current amount if applicable); (4) the purchaser may be obligated to pay special assessments to the municipality, county, or special district, which are subject to change; (5) failure to pay assessments or special assessment could result in a lien on the purchaser's property; (6) there may be an obligation to pay rent or fees for recreational or other common facilities (the disclosure must state the current amount if applicable); (7) the developer may have the right to amend the restrictive covenants without approval of the membership or parcel owners; (8) the statements in the disclosure are only summary in nature and the purchaser should refer to the covenants and other governing documents before purchasing; and (9) the covenants and governing documents can be obtained from the official records office in the county where the property is located or, if not recorded, from the developer.[12]

Each contract for the sale of property governed by covenants subject to disclosure must contain a clause in conspicuous type

---

[11.] Fla. Stat. § 720.31(4) (2016).
[12.] Fla. Stat. § 720.401(1)(a) (2016).

to the effect that if the disclosure summary is not provided to the prospective purchaser before executing the contract the contract is voidable by the buyer. The clause should instruct the buyer that the contract is voidable by delivering written notice of the buyer's intent to cancel within three days after receipt of the disclosure summary or prior to closing, whichever occurs first. The right to void the contract terminates upon closing.[13] Any waiver of the right to voidability is entirely unenforceable, as the statutory right to void the contract may not be waived.[14] Even if the seller can show that the buyer was aware of all, or substantially all, of the items included in the summary, it does not prevent the buyer from voiding the contract.[15]

Purchasers are also entitled to protection from false and misleading information contained in marketing materials prepared by the developer. Anyone who reasonably relies on material information that is false or misleading and published by or under the authority of the developer, and pays anything toward the purchase of a parcel in a Florida community, has a cause of action to rescind the contract or collect damages from the developer for his or her loss before closing. This includes false or misleading information contained in the purchase contract, the declaration of covenants, exhibits to the declaration of covenants, brochures, and newspaper advertising.[16]

After closing, the purchaser has a statutory cause of action against the developer for damages relating to their reliance on false and misleading information communicated by the developer. This cause of action survives from the time of closing until one year after the date of the last of the following events: closing; the issuance of a certificate of occupancy or other evidence of sufficient

---

[13.] Fla. Stat. § 720.401(b)-(c) (2016).

[14.] *Princeton Homes v. Morgan*, 38 So. 3d 207 (Fla. 4th Dist. Ct. App. 2010).

[15.] *Princeton Homes v. Morgan*, 38 So. 3d 207, 211-212 (Fla. 4th Dist. Ct. App. 2010) (buyer executed a purchase agreement to buy a townhome and never received a disclosure summary from the developer pursuant to section 720.401; before the developer completed construction, buyer demanded a refund of her deposit and advised the developer that she was voiding the contract; developer refused to refund the deposit, maintaining that the buyer could not void the contract because she had knowledge of all or substantially all of the items in the disclosure summary; the court rejected the developer's argument, holding that the statute clearly states that the right to void the contract may not be waived by the purchaser; "[Section 720.401] is a strong anti-waiver provision, evidencing the legislature's intent that if the disclosure summary is never provided, the buyer's right to void the contract is not something that can somehow be waived because of the buyer's knowledge or sophistication."); *see* Fla. Stat. § 720.401.

[16.] Fla. Stat. § 720.402(1) (2016).

completion of construction; or the completion by the developer of the common areas and recreational facilities, whether required by contract or law. This cause of action may not survive for more than five years after closing.[17] A developer may not expend association funds to defend against any such suit, and the prevailing party is entitled to recover reasonable attorney's fees.[18]

3-3   DEVELOPER OBLIGATIONS AND CONDOMINIUM ASSOCIATIONS

The developer of a condominium may create the condominium on land owned in fee simple or held under a lease.[19] For residential condominiums, the lease must have an unexpired term of at least 50 years on the date the first unit is conveyed by the developer to a bona fide purchaser. An unexpired term of only 30 years is required for nonresidential or commercial condominiums.[20]

The developer creates the condominium by recording a declaration in the public records of the county where the land is located. The declaration must be executed and acknowledged with the requirements for a deed. The developer must ensure that all persons who have record title to the land being submitted to condominium ownership, or their lawfully authorized agents, execute the declaration.[21]

Any person with record interest in any mortgage encumbering the land being submitted to condominium ownership must also execute the declaration. Alternatively, they may execute, with the requirements for deed, and record a consent to the declaration or an agreement subordinating their mortgage interest to the declaration.[22] The units described in the declaration come into existence upon the recording of the declaration. The developer then files the recording information with the Division of Florida Condominiums, Timeshares, and Mobile Homes of the

---

17. Fla. Stat. § 720.402(1) (2016).
18. Fla. Stat. § 720.402(2) (2016).
19. Fla. Stat. § 718.104(1) (2016).
20. Fla. Stat. § 718.401(1) (2016).
21. Fla. Stat. § 718.104(2) (2016).
22. Fla. Stat. § 718.104(3) (2016).

Department of Business and Professional Regulation within 120 days on a form provided by the Division.[23]

Prior to turnover, the developer is required to maintain property insurance based on the replacement cost of the property as determined by an independent insurance appraisal or update of a prior appraisal. The replacement cost must be determined at least once every 36 months. Failure to maintain adequate property insurance during the period of developer control constitutes a breach of fiduciary duty by the developer-appointed members of the board of directors, unless the members can show that they made their best efforts to maintain the required coverage.[24]

Before turnover, all unit owners, including the developer, may vote on issues related to the preparation of financial reports for the first two fiscal years of the association's operation. Thereafter, all unit owners except the developer may vote on such issues until control is turned over to the owners.[25] The developer-controlled association may not vote to use reserves for purposes other than their intended purposes without the approval of a majority of all non-developer voting interests, voting in person or by limited proxy at a duly called meeting of the association.[26]

3-3:1   Recreation Facility Leases

Condominium members are also protected against certain recreational or other common facility leases entered into by the developer-controlled board. In the Condominium Act, the legislature expresses concern over leases for use of recreational or other common facilities by residents of condominiums, which were entered into by a party's representative of the interests of the developer when the unit owners did not control their condominium and had no voice in its administration. Such leases often contain obligations on the part of the association and the unit owners with relatively few obligations on the part of the lessor. While these leases may or may not be unconscionable in any given case, the legislature finds that "a combination of certain onerous obligations

---

[23.] Fla. Stat. § 718.104(2) (2016).
[24.] Fla. Stat. § 718.111(11) (2016).
[25.] Fla. Stat. § 718.111(13)(d) (2016).
[26.] Fla. Stat. § 718.112(2)(f)(3) (2016).

and circumstances warrants the establishment of a rebuttable presumption of unconscionability."[27]

If the following elements exist, common facility leases entered into by the developer-controlled board carry a rebuttable presumption of unconscionability: (a) the lease was executed on behalf of the condominium unit owners by persons elected by the developer; (b) the lease requires the association or the unit owners to pay real estate taxes on the subject property; (c) the lease requires the association or the unit owners to insure buildings or other facilities on the property; (d) the lease requires the association or the unit owners to perform maintenance obligations on the property or facilities; (e) the lease requires the association or the unit owners to pay rent for 21 years or more; (f) the lease provides that failure to pay rent either establishes or permits establishment of a lien upon the condominium units; (g) the lease requires an annual rental which exceeds 25 percent of the appraised value of the leased property; (h) the lease provides for a periodic rental increase; and (i) the lease or other condominium documents require that every new owner must assume obligations under the lease.[28] Failure of a lease to contain all these elements neither precludes a determination of unconscionability nor raises a presumption as to its conscionability.[29]

The presumption of unconscionability created by these factors may be rebutted by showing additional facts and circumstances that may justify what appears to be an unconscionable lease. The Condominium Act does not create a statutory cause of action to invalidate such leases, but operates "as a statutory prescription on procedural matters in actions brought on one or more causes of

---

[27] Fla. Stat. § 718.122(2) (2016).

[28] Fla. Stat. § 718.122(1) (2016); *see Beeman v. Island Breakers, A Condo.*, 577 So. 2d 1341, 1346 (Fla. 3d Dist. Ct. App. 1990) opinion corrected sub nom. *Beeman v. Island Breakers*, 591 So. 2d 1031 (Fla. 3d Dist. Ct. App. 1991) (the recreation lease at issue covered a condominium swimming pool and included a rent escalator clause; the initial rent was set at $21,600 per year and at a certain point, and every ten years thereafter, the rent was to be adjusted in accordance with the consumer price index; the trial court found that with the escalator, the developer would receive in excess of $200 million, whereas without the escalator the recreation lease would amount to approximately $2 million, of which the developer had already received nearly $400,000; the court also found that the pending escalation in rent created difficulties in resale of units and depressed prices compared to similar condominiums; the appellate court agreed with the trial court regarding the unconscionability of the recreation lease, opining that the escalated rents were plainly unconscionable, even without any other finding on the other criteria set forth in section 718.122); *see* § 3-3:4.

[29] Fla. Stat. § 718.122(2) (2016).

action existing at the time of the execution of such lease."[30] Unit owners may maintain a cause of action to invalidate what they believe to be unconscionable common facility leases entered into by the developer-controlled board without regard for the statute of limitations or a defense based on laches.[31]

Any lease of recreational or other common facilities entered into by a residential condominium association prior to turnover shall grant to the lessee an option to purchase. The purchase must be made in cash at a price then determined by agreement on any anniversary date of the effective date of the lease after the tenth anniversary.[32] The association may exercise the option by two-thirds vote of the units served by the leased property.[33] If there is no agreement on price, then the price shall be determined by arbitration.[34]

If the lessor wishes to sell the recreational facilities and has received a bona fide offer, the lessor shall send the association and each unit owner a copy of the signed offer. The association or unit owners have the option to purchase on the terms and conditions in the offer for 90 days following receipt of the offer. If the association or unit owners do not exercise the option, the lessor may complete the transaction within 60 days after the 90-day period. If the transaction is not concluded within 60 days, the offer is abandoned, and the option to purchase is reimposed.[35] This does not apply if the lessor is the Government of the United States or Florida or any political subdivision thereof. In addition, in the case of an underlying land lease, the foregoing does not apply to a person or entity which is not the developer, or owned or controlled by the developer, who did not obtain ownership of the leased property from the developer.[36]

3-3:2   Sale Prior to Completion

If a developer contracts to sell a condominium prior to substantial completion of construction, furnishing, and landscaping, the

---

30. Fla. Stat. § 718.122(2) (2016).
31. Fla. Stat. § 718.122(3) (2016).
32. Fla. Stat. § 718.401(1)(f)(1) (2016).
33. Fla. Stat. § 718.401(1)(f)(3) (2016).
34. Fla. Stat. § 718.401(1)(f)(1) (2016).
35. Fla. Stat. § 718.401(1)(f)(2) (2016).
36. Fla. Stat. § 718.401(1)(f)(4) (2016).

developer must pay into escrow all payments up to 10 percent of the sale price received by the developer from the buyer. Alternatively, the developer may provide other assurances, including, but not limited to, a surety bond or an irrevocable letter of credit in an amount equal to the foregoing escrow requirements. Funds held in escrow together with any interest shall be released to the buyer if the buyer properly terminates the contract pursuant to its terms or pursuant to the Condominium Act. Funds held in escrow together with any interest shall be released to the developer if the buyer defaults in the performance of his or her obligations under the contract, or if the funds of the buyer have not been previously disbursed, unless prior to the disbursement the escrow agent receives from the buyer written notice of a dispute.[37]

All payments in excess of 10 percent of the sale price received prior to completion of construction must be held in a special escrow account.[38] If the condominium unit sale contract so provides, the developer may withdraw these escrow funds when the construction of improvements has begun. If permitted by the contract, the developer may use the funds in the construction of the condominium property; however, no part of these funds may be used for salaries, commissions, or expenses of salespersons or for advertising purposes. A contract which permits use of advance payments shall include the following statement in conspicuous type on the first page of the contract and immediately above the place for the signature of the buyer: "ANY PAYMENT IN EXCESS OF 10 PERCENT OF THE PURCHASE PRICE MADE TO DEVELOPER PRIOR TO CLOSING PURSUANT TO THIS CONTRACT MAY BE USED FOR CONSTRUCTION PURPOSES BY THE DEVELOPER."[39]

Failure to comply with the foregoing renders the contract voidable by the buyer. If voided, all sums advanced under the contract shall be refunded with interest "at the highest rate then being paid on savings accounts, excluding certificates of deposit, by savings and loan associations" in the condominium property's

---

[37.] Fla. Stat. § 718.202(1) (2016).
[38.] Fla. Stat. § 718.202(2) (2016).
[39.] Fla. Stat. § 718.202(3) (2016).

area.[40] In addition, any developer who willfully fails to comply with the requirements concerning establishment of an escrow account, deposits of funds into escrow, and withdrawal of funds from escrow is guilty of a third degree felony, and failure to establish or place funds into an escrow account "is prima facie evidence of an intentional and purposeful violation of this section."[41] Developers may raise a good faith defense to this statutory requirement.[42] Read together, sections 718.202 and 718.505 require a developer to make a good faith effort to substantially comply with the disclosure requirements of the Act.

3-3:3   Developer Warranty

Pursuant to the Condominium Act, the developer grants to each purchaser of a condominium unit an implied warranty of fitness and merchantability for the purposes or uses intended. For each unit, the developer is deemed to grant a warranty for three years commencing with the completion of the condominium building. For personal property transferred with, or appurtenant to, each unit, the developer is deemed to grant a warranty which is for the same period as that provided by the manufacturer of the personal property, commencing with the earlier of the date of closing or the date of possession of the unit. For all other personal property for the use of unit owners, the developer is deemed to grant a warranty which shall be the same as that provided by the manufacturer. [43]

For all other improvements for the use of unit owners, the developer is deemed to grant a three-year warranty commencing with the date of completion of the improvements. For the roof, structural components, and mechanical, electrical, and plumbing elements of the building or other improvements, the developer is deemed to grant a warranty beginning at the completion of construction of each building or improvement and continuing for

---

[40.] Fla. Stat. § 718.202(5) (2016).

[41.] Fla. Stat. § 718.202(7) (2016).

[42.] Fla. Stat. § 718.505 (2016) ("If a developer, in good faith, has attempted to comply with the requirements of this part, and if, in fact, he or she has substantially complied with the disclosure requirements of this chapter, nonmaterial errors or omissions in the disclosure materials shall not be actionable."); *In re Mona Lisa at Celebration*, 472 B.R. 582, 627 (Bankr. M.D. Fla. 2012) ("a closer read of the entire Florida Condominium Act as a whole indicates certain errors or omissions ... are excusable upon a showing of good faith").

[43.] Fla. Stat. § 718.203(1) (2016).

three years thereafter or one year after turnover, whichever occurs last. In no event shall the warranty last for more than five years. This does not include mechanical elements serving only one unit. For all other property which is conveyed with a unit, the developer is deemed to grant a warranty to the initial purchaser of each unit for one year from the date of closing or possession, whichever occurs first.[44]

The foregoing warranties inure to the benefit of each owner and his or her successor and to the benefit of the developer.[45] These warranties are conditioned on performance of routine maintenance, unless the maintenance is a developer obligation.[46]

3-3:4   Developer-Made Contracts

The unit owners also benefit from protections against any unfair and unreasonable pre-turnover contracts executed by the developer. Pursuant to section 718.302, "any grant or reservation made by a declaration, lease, or other document, and any contract" made by the developer-controlled association "that provides for operation, maintenance, or management of a condominium association or property serving the unit owners of a condominium shall be fair and reasonable."[47] Such contracts shall not be in conflict with the powers and duties of the association or the rights of the unit owners as provided in the Condominium Act.[48] In addition, the developer must disclose any financial or ownership interest in the company contracting to provide maintenance or management services.[49]

The unit owners may cancel the contract subject to certain procedural requirements. If the association operates only one condominium and the non-developer unit owners have assumed control of the association, or if the non-developer unit owners own at least 75 percent of the voting interests, the contract may be cancelled by a vote of at least 75 percent of the non-developer voting interests. If the contract is cancelled in this manner, but

---

44. Fla. Stat. § 718.203(1) (2016).
45. Fla. Stat. § 718.203(5) (2016).
46. Fla. Stat. § 718.203(4) (2016).
47. Fla. Stat. § 718.302 (2016).
48. Fla. Stat. § 718.302(3) (2016).
49. Fla. Stat. § 718.3025(1)(e) (2016).

turnover has yet to occur, the association shall enter into a new contract or otherwise provide for maintenance, management, or operation, at the direction of at least a majority of the non-developer voting interests.[50]

If the association operates more than one condominium and the non-developer unit owners have not assumed control of the association, and if the non-developer unit owners own at least 75 percent of the voting interests in a condominium operated by the association, the contract providing for maintenance, management, or operation of buildings containing the units in that condominium or of improvements used only by unit owners of that condominium may be canceled by a vote of at least 75 percent of the non-developer voting interests in the condominium.[51] If the non-developer unit owners have assumed control of a multi-condominium association, the contract may be cancelled by a vote of at least 75 percent of the total number of non-developer voting interests in all condominiums operated by the association.[52]

If the unit owners have the right to use recreational areas or other property in common with unit owners in other condominiums and those condominiums are operated by more than one association, no grant, reservation, or contract for maintenance, management, or operation of the recreational areas or other property may be canceled until all of the associations are turned over to non-developer unit owners, after which the contract may be cancelled by the vote of 75 percent of the total number of non-developer voting interests in those condominiums.[53] When developers enter into cable television contracts prior to turnover, such contracts are subject to cancellation by the membership after turnover.[54]

[50.] Fla. Stat. § 718.302(1)(a) (2016).

[51.] Fla. Stat. § 718.302(1)(b) (2016).

[52.] Fla. Stat. § 718.302(1)(c) (2016).

[53.] Fla. Stat. § 718.302(1)(d) (2016).

[54.] *Comcast of Florida v. L'Ambiance Beach Condo. Ass'n*, 17 So. 3d 839, 843 (Fla. 4th Dist. Ct. App. 2009) (prior to the association's incorporation, the developer entered into a cable service contract with Comcast including a bulk rate addendum providing services to residents at a discounted monthly rate; by its terms, the agreement could "be terminated prior to expiration of its term subject to conditions and regulations required under [Chapter] 718" and the developer intended to ensure that after turnover the association would have the right to terminate the contract upon a timely 75 percent vote of the unit owners; following turnover and a unit owner vote, the agreement was terminated in accordance with section 718.302; Comcast filed suit and the court rejected its argument that section 718.302 does not apply to a cable television service contract since it is not an

Any obligation imposed on the association by a declaration, lease, contract, or other document entered into by the developer or association prior to turnover, which requires the association to purchase condominium property or to lease condominium property to another party, is ratified unless rejected by a majority of the non-developer voting interests within 18 months after turnover. This does not apply to any obligation imposed on the association by a declaration, lease, contract, or other document allowing persons other than the developer or the developer's heirs, assigns, affiliates, directors, officers, or employees to use the condominium property, so long as such persons are obligated to pay at least a proportionate share of the cost associated with such property.[55]

Escalation clauses in management contracts for condominiums, which provide that the fee increases at the same percentage rate as a commodity or consumer price index, are void as a matter of public policy.[56] Actions to enforce Condominium Act provisions that protect against pre-turnover contracts entered into by the developer may be brought under section 51.011, which provides for expedited rules of procedure and reasonable attorney's fees for the prevailing party.[57]

3-3:5   Disclosures Prior to Sale

The Condominium Act requires that any contract for the sale of a residential condominium unit or lease of a residential condominium unit for more than five years contain certain information and disclosures.[58] For example, the contract must contain language in conspicuous type stating that the agreement is voidable by the buyer by delivering notice of the buyer's intention to cancel within 15 days of execution of the agreement by the buyer. The contract must also state whether the unit has been occupied by someone

---

agreement "that provides for operation, maintenance, or management of a condominium association or property serving the unit owners of a condominium," on the grounds that since (1) the agreement provided service for all unit owners, (2) the cost was part of the monthly maintenance fee, and (3) the provider was required to service and maintain the cable television, the agreement was one for the "operation, maintenance, or management" of the cable television services and section 718.302 applied).

[55.] Fla. Stat. § 718.302(2) (2016).
[56.] Fla. Stat. § 718.302(5) (2016).
[57.] Fla. Stat. § 718.302(6) (2016).
[58.] Fla. Stat. § 718.503 (2016).

other than the buyer. If the unit is subject to a lease, the contract must include a copy of the executed lease and shall contain the following text in conspicuous type: THE UNIT IS SUBJECT TO A LEASE (OR SUBLEASE). In addition to the foregoing, the contract must contain other disclosures specifically outlined in section 718.503.[59]

The developer is also required to furnish certain documents to prospective buyers or lessees. For residential condominiums which contain more than 20 residential units or which are part of a group of residential condominiums which will be served by property to be used in common by unit owners of more than 20 residential units, the developer shall deliver to the prospective buyer a prospectus or disclosure statement with enumerated exhibits.[60] The prospectus or offering circular must contain a number of specific statements and disclosures set forth in section 718.504. For instance, the front cover or first page must contain only the name of the condominium and the following statements in conspicuous type: 1. THIS PROSPECTUS (OFFERING CIRCULAR) CONTAINS IMPORTANT MATTERS TO BE CONSIDERED IN ACQUIRING A CONDOMINIUM UNIT; 2. THE STATEMENTS CONTAINED HEREIN ARE ONLY SUMMARY IN NATURE. A PROSPECTIVE PURCHASER SHOULD REFER TO ALL REFERENCES, ALL EXHIBITS HERETO, THE CONTRACT DOCUMENTS, AND SALES MATERIALS; and ORAL REPRESENTATIONS CANNOT BE RELIED UPON AS CORRECTLY STATING THE REPRESENTATIONS OF THE DEVELOPER. REFER TO THIS PROSPECTUS (OFFERING CIRCULAR) AND ITS EXHIBITS FOR CORRECT REPRESENTATIONS.[61]

The prospectus or offering circular must contain a description of the condominium on the first page of the text, including the condominium name and location, the number of buildings, the number of units in each building, the number of bathrooms and bedrooms in each unit, and the total number of units, if the condominium is not a phase condominium. If the condominium is

---

[59.] Fla. Stat. § 718.503(1)(a) (2016).
[60.] Fla. Stat. § 718.504 (2016).
[61.] Fla. Stat. § 718.504(1) (2016).

a phase condominium, the description must include the maximum number of buildings, the minimum and maximum numbers of units in each building, the minimum and maximum numbers of bathrooms and bedrooms that may be contained in each unit, and the maximum number of units that may be contained within the condominium.[62]

The prospectus or offering circular must contain an estimated operating budget for the condominium and the association,[63] the identity of the developer and the chief operating officer or principal directing the creation and sale of the condominium, and a statement of his or her experience in this field.[64] The prospectus must contain a schedule of estimated closing expenses to be paid by a buyer or lessee of a unit and a statement of whether a title opinion or title insurance policy is available to the buyer and, if so, at whose expense.[65] In addition to the foregoing, the prospectus or offering circular must contain other disclosures, statements, and exhibits specifically set forth in section 718.504.[66]

In addition to the prospectus or offering circular, each buyer must receive a "Frequently Asked Questions and Answers" sheet (FAQ) and a copy of the financial information required by section 718.111. The FAQ must inform prospective purchasers of their voting rights and unit use restrictions, including restrictions on the leasing of units. It must also indicate whether and in what amount the unit owners or the association are obligated to pay rent or land use fees for recreational facilities. It must contain a statement identifying the amount of assessments which would be levied upon each unit type, exclusive of any special assessments, and shall identify the basis upon which assessments are levied. It must identify any litigation in which the association is currently a party in which it may face liability in excess of $100,000. It shall further state whether membership in a recreational facilities association is mandatory and the fees currently charged per unit type for such mandatory memberships.[67]

For residential condominiums that contain less than 20 residential units, the developer is required to furnish the FAQ sheet. In addition,

---

[62] Fla. Stat. § 718.504(4) (2016).
[63] Fla. Stat. § 718.504(21) (2016).
[64] Fla. Stat. § 718.504(23) (2016).
[65] Fla. Stat. § 718.504(22) (2016).
[66] Fla. Stat. § 718.504 (2016).
[67] Fla. Stat. § 718.504 (2016).

the developer must provide the declaration, the documents creating the association, the bylaws, the ground lease or other underlying lease of the condominium, the management contract and other contracts for management of the association and operation of the condominium and facilities used by the unit owners having a service term in excess of one year, and any management contracts that are renewable. The developer must also furnish the estimated operating budget, a schedule of expenses for each type of unit, the lease of recreational and other facilities that will be used only by unit owners of the subject condominium, and the form unit lease if a leasehold is offered, among other documents specifically listed in section 718.503.[68]

Until the developer has furnished the documents required by the Condominium Act, the contract may be voided, entitling the prospective buyer or lessee to a refund of any deposit together with interest thereon. The prospective buyer or lessee may terminate by written notice delivered to the developer within 15 days after the buyer or lessee receives all of the documents required by the Act. The developer may not close for 15 days following the execution of the agreement and delivery of the documents unless the buyer is informed of the voidability period and agrees to close prior to the expiration of the 15 days.[69]

3-4 TURNOVER OF HOMEOWNERS' ASSOCIATIONS

3-4:1 Conditions Triggering Turnover

Ultimately, control of a Florida community association is relinquished by the developer and given to the owners. At that time, the owners will determine their own course, electing a board of administration to act on behalf of the community in its operation and management. The non-developer owners do not have to wait until the developer leaves the community for turnover to occur. Because developers often retain an ownership interest in parcels long after the association is created, the Florida Legislature designated certain events that automatically trigger turnover.

---

[68] Fla. Stat. § 718.503 (2016).
[69] Fla. Stat. § 718.503(1)(b) (2016).

The members of a homeowners' association can elect at least a majority of the board of directors three months after 90 percent of the parcels have been conveyed to members. This does not include conveyances to builders, contractors, or others who purchase a parcel for construction and resale. Alternatively, the members can elect at least a majority of the board when such other event occurs or upon such other date as set forth in the governing documents. In addition, turnover occurs upon the developer abandoning its responsibility to maintain and complete the amenities as disclosed in the governing documents; upon the developer filing for chapter 7 bankruptcy; upon the developer losing title to the property through a foreclosure action, unless the successor owner has accepted an assignment of the developer's rights; or upon a receiver for the developer being appointed by a circuit court and not being discharged in 30 days, unless the court determines within 30 days that turnover would be detrimental to the association.[70]

The developer does not, however, lose all influence on operation and management. The developer retains the ability to elect at least one member of the board as long as the developer holds for sale at least 5 percent of the parcels. Furthermore, after turnover, the developer may vote developer-owned voting interests just like any other member; however, the developer may not gain control of the homeowners' association or elect a majority of the members of the board.[71] In addition, the developer may not cast votes in an amount that exceeds one vote per residential lot.[72]

3-4:2   Developer Obligations Following Turnover

Within 90 days of the time the owners are entitled to elect at least a majority of the board, the developer must, at the developer's expense, deliver certain documents to the homeowner-controlled board of directors. The developer must deliver to the board the deeds to the association's common property; the original declaration of covenants; a certified copy of the articles of incorporation; a copy of the bylaws; the minute books; the association's books and records; the rules and regulations; resignations of developer-appointed board

---

[70.] Fla. Stat. § 720.307(1) (2016).
[71.] Fla. Stat. § 720.307(2) (2016).
[72.] Fla. Stat. § 720.3075(1)(c) (2016).

members; all association funds and control thereof; all tangible association property; a copy of all operative contracts; the contact information of all contractors, subcontractors, or employees of the association; all effective insurance policies; any permits; all effective warranties; a list of owners with their contact information and lot numbers; and all operative employment and service contracts.[73]

When the developer delivers the financial records to the homeowner-controlled board, the developer must include the financial statements, prepared in accordance with generally accepted accounting principles, and source documents from incorporation through the date of turnover. The financial records must be audited at the developer's expense in accordance with generally accepted auditing standards by an independent certified public accountant. The records must be audited for the period from incorporation or from the period covered by the last audit, if an audit was performed for each fiscal year since incorporation. The certified public accountant performing the audit must determine whether the developer was charged and paid the proper amount of assessments by examining the supporting documents and records, including the cash disbursements and invoices.[74]

Following turnover the developer may not enforce any clause of the governing documents that provides the developer the right to unilaterally make changes to the documents. In addition, the homeowners' association is free to sue the developer following turnover despite any provision of the documents to the contrary.[75]

3-5 TURNOVER OF CONDOMINIUM ASSOCIATIONS

3-5:1 Conditions Triggering Turnover

If the non-developer owners own 15 percent of the units, the unit owners other than the developer are entitled to elect at least one-third of the members of the board of directors. There are, however, several possible events that give the owners the ability to elect at least a majority of the board. Turnover to unit owner

---

73. Fla. Stat. § 720.307(4) (2016).
74. Fla. Stat. § 720.307(4) (2016).
75. Fla. Stat. § 720.3075(1) (2016).

control will occur three years after 50 percent of the units have been conveyed to purchasers. Turnover may also occur three months after 90 percent of the units have been conveyed to purchasers. Turnover will occur when all of the units have been completed, some of them have been conveyed to purchasers, but no other units are being offered for sale by the developer.

Turnover will occur when some of the units have been conveyed and none of the others are being constructed or offered for sale by the developer. Turnover occurs if the developer files a petition for bankruptcy. Turnover will occur when a receiver is appointed by a circuit court and is not discharged within 30 days, "unless the court determines within 30 days after appointment of the receiver that transfer of control would be detrimental to the association or its members." Finally, turnover will occur seven years after the recording of the certificate of a surveyor or mapper or the recording of an instrument transferring title to a unit which is not accompanied by a recorded assignment of developer rights in favor of the grantee; or, if the association operates more than one condominium, seven years after recording of these same documents of the first condominium it operates. The first to occur of any of the foregoing conditions will trigger turnover.[76]

The association must give not less than 60 days notice of the first election of the non-developer board members within 75 days after turnover. Any unit owner may give notice if the association fails to do so.[77]

Turnover is triggered by the developer's conveyance of more than 50 percent of the units notwithstanding the status of title to the units subsequent to conveyance.[78] Once condominium turnover has occurred, a developer may not regain control of the association, whether by reacquiring title through foreclosure proceedings or any other means.[79] As soon as 50 percent of the

---

[76.] Fla. Stat. § 718.301(1) (2016).

[77.] Fla. Stat. § 718.301(2) (2016).

[78.] *Hamptons Dev. Corp. of Dade v. State, Dep't of Bus. Reg., Div. of Florida Land Sales, Condos. & Mobile Homes*, 519 So. 2d 661 (Fla. 3d Dist. Ct. App. 1988).

[79.] *Hamptons Dev. Corp. v. State, Dep't of Bus. Reg., Div. of Florida Land Sales, Condos. & Mobile Homes*, 519 So. 2d 661, 662 (Fla. 3d Dist. Ct. App. 1988) (developer sold 75 units one month after the condominium was established; less than three years later the developer reacquired title to all 75 units by foreclosure and judicial sale, making the developer the owner of more than 50 percent of the condominium units; the court

units are sold, non-developer unit owners are entitled to elect a majority of the board.[80]

In certain circumstances, turnover is even required when 60 percent of the units are held for lease by developers. Specifically, when an entity such as a partnership purchases over 60 percent of an entire condominium as investment properties, it meets the statutory definition of "developer" and may not (1) control the condominium association through ownership of the majority of voting interests, or (2) elect a majority of the board.[81] In this scenario, control of the board must be ceded to non-developer owners, despite the fact that the developer controls 60 percent of the units.[82]

In cases involving developers that are not in the regular business of selling their units, turnover is triggered pursuant to subsections 718.301(1)(c) and (d), which provide that unit owners other than the developers are entitled to elect a majority of the board when all of the units have been completed, some of them have been sold, and none of the others are being offered for sale; or when some of the units have been sold and none of the others are being constructed or offered for sale by the developer in the ordinary course of business, whichever occurs first.[83]

---

rejected the developer's argument that since section 718.301 excludes what the developer characterized as a "temporary" conveyance, its initial sale of units should not have triggered turnover, holding that "once the developer by statute loses the right to elect a majority of the board, that developer may not regain control of the association"; the court opined that interpreting the statute to provide an exception for "temporary" conveyances, where none actually exists, would "generate wholesale uncertainty in the operation of the turnover provisions of Chapter 718").

[80.] *Hamptons Dev. Corp. v. State, Dep't of Bus. Reg., Div. of Florida Land Sales, Condos. & Mobile Homes*, 519 So. 2d 661, 662 (Fla. 3d Dist. Ct. App. 1988).

[81.] *Bishop Assocs. v. Belkin*, 521 So. 2d 158, 161 (Fla. 1st Dist. Ct. App. 1988) (ten separate limited partnerships bought over 60 percent of an entire condominium as investment properties to lease, obtaining control of the association through ownership of the majority of voting interests, which allowed them to elect a majority of the board; the partnerships managed the leasing of their units as their sole business, with intent to profit on their real-estate investment; the court agreed with a non-developer unit owner who requested a declaration that the limited partnerships were developers as defined by the Condominium Act, and as such were obligated to turn over control of the board to the non-developer owners, concluding that the partnerships met the statutory definition of "developer" as one who "creates a condominium or offers condominium parcels for sale or lease"; the court also concluded that the term "developer" is appropriately applied to owners who own more than one unit, and not to individuals who own a unit as their residence).

[82.] *Bishop Assocs. v. Belkin*, 521 So. 2d 158, 161 (Fla. 1st Dist. Ct. App. 1988).

[83.] *Bishop Assocs. v. Belkin*, 521 So. 2d 158, 161 (Fla. 1st Dist. Ct. App. 1988); Fla. Stat. § 718.301(1)(c)-(d) (2013).

While the developer loses the ability to elect a majority of the board following turnover, the developer retains the ability to elect at least one member of the board as long as the developer holds for sale at least 5 percent of the units in condominiums with fewer than 500 units, and 2 percent of the units in condominiums with more than 500 units. After turnover, the developer may vote in the same manner as any other unit owner except for purposes of reacquiring control of the association or selecting a majority of the members of the board.[84]

If the association violates any provision of the Condominium Act or any rule promulgated by the Division before the developer relinquishes control of the association, the developer is (1) responsible for the violation, (2) subject to administrative action provided by the Condominium Act, and (3) may be liable to third parties.[85] Before the developer relinquishes control, actions taken by the developer-controlled board are considered actions of the developer, "and the developer is responsible to the association and its members for all such actions."[86]

3-5:2   Developer Obligations Following Turnover

At the time of turnover, the developer must, at their own expense, deliver certain items to the condominium association. The developer must deliver to the association all property of the unit owners and the association, which may include, but is not limited to, the original or certified copy of the recorded declaration and all amendments thereto, a certified copy of the articles of incorporation, a copy of the bylaws, the minute books, all other books and records of the association, any rules and regulations, and resignations of board members who are required to resign at the time the developer relinquishes control.[87]

The developer must also turn over association funds or control thereof; all tangible personal property of the association, and an inventory of that property; a copy of the plans and specifications; a list of the names and addresses of all contractors, subcontractors,

---

[84] Fla. Stat. § 718.301(1) (2016).
[85] Fla. Stat. § 718.301(5) (2016).
[86] Fla. Stat. § 718.301(6) (2016).
[87] Fla. Stat. § 718.301(4) (2016).

and suppliers used in the construction or remodeling of the condominium; all insurance policies; copies of any certificates of occupancy; any operative permits issued within one year of turnover; all written warranties of any contractors; a roster of unit owners and their addresses and telephone numbers; any leases to which the association is a party; all contracts to which the association is a party; and a turnover inspection report, comprised of a report under seal of an architect or engineer authorized to practice in Florida, attesting to required maintenance, useful life, and replacement costs of the common elements.[88]

Within 90 days of turnover, the developer must deliver the financial records to the association. The financial records include financial statements and source documents from incorporation through turnover. An independent certified public accountant must audit the records at the developer's expense for the period from the incorporation of the association or from the period covered by the last audit, if an audit was performed each fiscal year since incorporation. Financial statements must be prepared in accordance with generally accepted accounting principles and audited in accordance with generally accepted auditing standards. The accountant performing the audit must examine any documents necessary to determine if expenditures were for association purposes and if the developer was charged and paid the appropriate amount of assessments.[89] In disputes relating to the turnover audit, the trial court may consider any prior business relationship between the developer and the certified public accountant in determining whether the accountant is an "independent certified public accountant" under section 718.301(5).[90]

The Condominium Act also provides safeguards to protect the developer's interests after turnover. For instance, the association must obtain the developer's approval in writing before it can pursue an action that might be detrimental to the sale of the developer's units.[91] In addition, the association may not assess the developer as a unit owner for capital improvements. The

---

[88.] Fla. Stat. § 718.301(4) (2016).

[89.] Fla. Stat. § 718.301(4)(c) (2016).

[90.] *Alternative Dev. v. St. Lucie Club & Apartment Homes Condo. Ass'n*, 608 So. 2d 822, 826-27 (Fla. 4th Dist. Ct. App. 1992).

[91.] *Bishop Assocs. v. Belkin*, 521 So. 2d 158, 163 (Fla. 1st Dist. Ct. App. 1988).

association may, however, increase assessments for common expenses against the developer and all other unit owners, so long as the assessments are not increased against the developer in a discriminatory manner.[92]

[92.] Fla. Stat. § 718.301(3) (2016).

Chapter 4

Board of Directors

4-1   INTRODUCTION

Members of a community association's board of directors are typically elected volunteers who give their time to help operate and manage the corporate affairs of the association. They come from all walks of life, with varying levels of education, expertise, and life experience. Many members of the board bring professional and practical skills that aid in operating the community. Many members commit themselves to learning the requirements of Florida law and the association's governing documents. Courts defer to the decisions made by the elected officials of the community association. They are not expected to make the right decision on every occasion. They are simply expected to act within their authority and reasonably use their best business judgment.

4-2   ELECTION OF THE BOARD

4-2:1   Qualification for Board Membership

For both homeowners' and condominium associations, all association members are eligible to serve on the board of directors.[1] This does not include, however, members who are delinquent in the payment of any fee, fine, or other monetary obligation to the association.[2] In addition, a member is not eligible for the board of directors if they were convicted of a felony, unless their civil rights were restored for at least five years as of the date on which they seek

---

[1.] Fla. Stat. §§ 720.306(9), 718.112(2) (2016).
[2.] Fla. Stat. §§ 720.306(9)(b), 718.112(2)(d)(2) (2016).

election to the board.[3] The Homeowners' Association Act provides that actions by the board are not invalidated if it is later determined that a board member is ineligible for board membership.[4] The Condominium Act provides that actions by the board are not invalidated if it is later determined that a board member is ineligible because they were convicted of a felony.[5]

In a condominium association of more than 10 units, or in one that does not include timeshares, unit co-owners may not serve on the board at the same time. There are exceptions to this rule if the co-owners own more than one unit, or if there are not enough eligible candidates to fill the vacancies on the board at the time of the vacancy.[6]

4-2:2   Election Procedures

The election of directors, if one is required, must be held at, or in conjunction with, the annual meeting or as provided in the governing documents.[7] The Condominium Act sets forth certain exceptions to this rule. For instance, a board member may not have to participate in an election if his or her staggered term does not expire until a later annual meeting. Also, an election may be impossible if all the members' terms would otherwise expire but there are no candidates.[8] For both homeowners' and condominium associations, elections of directors must be in accordance with the procedures set forth in the association's governing documents.[9]

4-2:3   Required Condominium Association
Election Procedures

In the event a condominium's bylaws do not set forth board composition and election procedures, the Condominium Act sets forth certain basic requirements. For instance, the members of the board shall be elected by written ballot or voting machine.[10] The

---

[3] Fla. Stat. §§ 720.306(9)(b), 718.112(2)(d)(2) (2016).
[4] Fla. Stat. § 720.306(9)(b) (2016).
[5] Fla. Stat. § 718.112(2)(d)(2) (2016).
[6] Fla. Stat. § 718.112(2)(d)(2) (2016).
[7] Fla. Stat. §§ 720.306(2), 718.112(2)(d)(2) (2016).
[8] Fla. Stat. § 718.112(2)(d)(2) (2016).
[9] Fla. Stat. §§ 720.306(9)(a), 718.112 (2016).
[10] Fla. Stat. § 718.112(2)(d)(4) (2016).

board shall be composed of five members, except in the case of a not-for-profit condominium which has five or fewer units, in which case the board shall consist of no less than three members. The board shall have a president, a secretary, and a treasurer, who shall perform the duties customarily performed by such officers. Unless prohibited in the bylaws, the board may appoint other officers and grant them duties deemed appropriate.[11]

At least 60 days before a scheduled election, the association shall mail, deliver, or electronically transmit to each eligible unit owner a first notice of the election date. Eligible candidates must give written notice of their intent to run for the board at least 40 days before the election. The association shall mail, deliver, or electronically transmit a second notice of the election to all unit owners entitled to vote with a ballot that lists all candidates. Upon a candidate's request, an information sheet must be included with the mailing, delivery, or transmission of the ballot at least 35 days before the election. The association bears the costs of mailing, delivery, or electronic transmission. The association is not liable for the contents of the information sheets prepared by the candidates.[12]

Elections shall be decided by a plurality of ballots cast. At least 20 percent of the eligible voters must cast a ballot in order to have a valid election. Subject to a fine, a unit owner may not permit any other person to vote his or her ballot, and any ballots improperly cast are invalid.[13]

For both homeowners' associations and condominium associations, within 90 days after joining the board, new directors must certify in writing to the secretary of the association that they have read the association's declaration, articles of incorporation, bylaws, and current written policies. New directors must also certify that they will uphold the association's governing documents and policies to

---

[11.] Fla. Stat. § 718.112(2)(a)(1) (2016).

[12.] Fla. Stat. § 718.112(2)(d) (2016).

[13.] Fla. Stat. § 718.112(2)(d)(4) (2016). At the time of the drafting of this update in May 2017, the Florida Legislature is considering Senate Bill 1682, which could go into effect on July 1, 2017, that would amend add a new Fla. Stat. § 718.129, titled "Fraudulent voting activities related to association elections; penalties." This proposed section includes a list of fraudulent voting activities punishable as a third degree felony. This would include willfully, knowingly, and fraudulently changing or attempting to change a vote or ballot cast by an elector in an association election to prevent such elector from voting or casting a ballot as he or she intended.

the best of their ability, and that they will faithfully discharge their fiduciary responsibility to the association's members.[14]

In lieu of a written certification, within 90 days after joining the board, the new directors may submit a certificate of having satisfactorily completed the educational curriculum administered by the Division of Florida Condominiums, Timeshares, and Mobile Homes of the Department of Business and Professional Regulation within one year before or 90 days after the date of election or appointment. The certification or educational certificate is effective until the board member leaves office. A board member who fails to timely file the written certification or educational certificate is suspended until he or she comes into compliance. The association must retain a director's written certification or educational certificate for five years after a director's election or the duration of the director's uninterrupted tenure, whichever is larger. Failure to have the written certification or educational certificate on file does not invalidate any board action.[15] Any challenge to the election process must be commenced within 60 days of announcement of the election results.

4-2:4   Filling Vacancies on the Board

When vacancies on homeowners' association boards occur before the expiration of a term, they may be filled by an affirmative vote of the majority of the remaining directors, even if the remaining directors constitute less than a quorum, or through appointment by the sole remaining director. In the alternative, a board may hold an election to fill the vacancy in accordance with the procedures set forth in the governing documents. Unless otherwise provided in the bylaws, a board member appointed or elected to fill a vacancy stays on the board for the remainder of the previously vacant seat's term.[16]

Unless the condominium bylaws provide otherwise, a vacancy caused by the expiration of a director's term must be filled by electing a new board member by secret ballot. An election is not required if the number of vacancies equals or exceeds the number

---

[14.] Fla. Stat. §§ 718.112(2)(d)(4) (2016), 720.3033(1)(a) (2016).
[15.] Fla. Stat. §§ 718.112(2)(d)(4) (2016), 720.3033 (2016).
[16.] Fla. Stat. § 720.306(9)(c) (2016).

of candidates.[17] If the number of board members whose terms expire at the annual meeting equals or exceeds the number of candidates, the candidates become members of the board upon the adjournment of the annual meeting. Unless the bylaws provide otherwise, any remaining vacancies shall be filled by a vote of the majority of the directors making up the newly constituted board even if the directors constitute less than a quorum.[18]

If a community association fails to fill vacancies on the board of directors sufficient to constitute a quorum, any member may seek the appointment of a receiver. While Florida courts have equitable authority to appoint a receiver,[19] it is a remedy that should only be exercised in drastic circumstances, such as fraud, insolvency, or mismanagement, when there is no other means to protect the applicant.[20]

In the context of Florida community associations, however, receivership is available by statute. If a community association fails to fill vacancies on the board of directors sufficient to constitute a quorum, any member may give notice of their intent to apply to the circuit court for the appointment of a receiver to manage the affairs of the association. The form of the notice must be in accordance with either the Homeowners' Association Act[21] or the Condominium Act,[22] whichever applies. Notice must be provided by the unit owner to the association by certified mail or personal delivery, posted in a conspicuous place on the property, and provided by the unit owner

---

[17.] Fla. Stat. § 718.112(2)(d)(2) (2016). At the time of the drafting of this update in May 2017, the Florida Legislature is considering Senate Bill 1682, which could go into effect on July 1, 2017, and would have the effect of limiting board members to no more than four consecutive two-year terms, unless approved by an affirmative vote of two-thirds of the total voting interests of the association.

[18.] Fla. Stat. § 718.112(2)(d)(2) (2016).

[19.] *Edenfield v. Crisp*, 186 So. 2d 545, 548 (Fla. 2d Dist. Ct. App. 1966).

[20.] *Papazian v. Kullhanjian*, 78 So. 2d 85 (Fla. 1955); *see Lehman v. Trust Co. of Am.*, 57 Fla. 473, 477 (Fla. 1909) (establishing the following guidelines for appointment of a receiver: "(1) That the power of appointment is a delicate one, and to be exercised with great circumspection. (2) That it must appear the claimant has a title to or lien upon the property, and the court must be satisfied by affidavit that a receiver is necessary to preserve the property. (3) That there is no case in which the court appoints a receiver merely because the measure can do no harm. (4) That fraud or imminent danger, if the immediate possession should not be taken by the court, must be clearly proved."); *Mirror Lake Co. v. Kirk Sec. Corp.*, 124 So. 719 (Fla. 1929) (setting forth various parameters to the court's authority to enter the drastic relief of receivership).

[21.] Fla. Stat. § 720.3053 (2016).

[22.] Fla. Stat. § 718.1124 (2016).

to every other unit owner by certified mail or personal delivery. The notice must be posted and mailed or delivered at least 30 days prior to the filing of the petition for receivership. Notice by mail to a unit owner shall be sent to the address used by the county property appraiser for notice to the unit owner.[23] The Condominium Act provides that if the unit owner's address is not publicly available, the notice shall be mailed to the unit.[24]

If the association fails to fill the vacancies within 30 days after the notice is posted and mailed or delivered, the unit owner may proceed with the petition. If a receiver is appointed, the association is responsible for the salary of the receiver, court costs, and attorney's fees. The receiver shall have all the powers and duties of a duly constituted board of directors and shall serve until the association fills vacancies on the board sufficient to constitute a quorum and the court lifts the receivership.[25]

While homeowners' and condominium associations are creatures of statute, the courts do not limit the circumstances under which a receiver may be appointed to those described in applicable governing statutes. Indeed, governing statutes "cite to specific instances when a receiver may be appointed," but do not "restrict a trial court's broad, equitable authority to appoint a receiver."[26]

4-2:5   Election Disputes

Both the Homeowners' Association Act and the Condominium Act require mandatory arbitration of election disputes between members and associations.[27] Mandatory binding arbitration under the Homeowners' Association Act[28] follows the Condominium

---

[23.] Fla. Stat. §§ 720.3053, 718.1124(2) (2016).

[24.] Fla. Stat. § 718.1124(2) (2016).

[25.] Fla. Stat. §§ 720.3053, 718.1124 (2016).

[26.] *Metro-Dade Invs. v. Granada Lakes Villas Condo*, 74 So. 3d 593, 595 (Fla. 2d Dist. Ct. App. 2011) review granted, 97 So. 3d 823 (Fla. 2012) (holding that the trial court erred as a matter of law when it refused to appoint a receiver based on the fact that the circumstance upon which the petition was based, simple condominium mismanagement, was not in the Condominium Act or the Florida Not For Profit Corporation Act; explaining that the right to appoint a receiver "is inherent in a court of equity, [and is] not a statutorily created right").

[27.] Fla. Stat. §§ 720.306(9)(c), 718.1255 (2016) (arbitration under both the Homeowners' Association Act and the Condominium Act is administered by the Division of Florida Condominiums, Timeshares, and Mobile Homes of the Department of Business and Professional Regulation).

[28.] Fla. Stat. § 720.306(9)(c) (2016).

Act arbitration process, under which every arbitration petition regarding election irregularities must be expedited according to the division's Rules of Procedure Governing Recall Arbitration.[29]

A petition for arbitration is a condition precedent to filing suit. The legislative intent of this condition is to level the playing field for unit owners, who are seen as disadvantaged in litigation due to the association's statutory assessment authority and superior ability to bear litigation costs, and to reduce court dockets through alternative dispute resolution.[30]

The Rules of Procedure Governing Recall Arbitration provide for limited discovery following receipt and acceptance of the petition and the respondent's answer.[31] Discovery is to be used sparingly, and only after the arbitrator's approval, following a motion setting out the subject matter and permissible methods of discovery. The only discoverable items are information and documents necessary for the proper disposition of the petition.[32] Parties may obtain discovery, as provided in the Florida Rules of Civil Procedure, through written interrogatories, requests for production, and depositions. However, a member desiring to obtain copies of official records for use in the proceeding shall utilize the owner's right of access to the official records.[33] Parties may serve subpoenas requiring the attendance of witnesses or document production for discovery or for the final hearing.[34]

The rules also provide for motion practice. The arbitrator may conduct proceedings and render orders necessary to dispose of issues raised in the arbitration. Non-moving parties may file written responses to motions within seven business days of service of a written motion.[35] In addition, any disputes that do not involve disputed issues of material fact are subject to summary disposition. If there are no disputed issues of material fact, the arbitrator shall summarily enter a final order denying relief if the arbitrator finds no basis for relief in the petition. The arbitrator may also

---

[29]. Fla. Stat. § 718.1255(5) (2016).
[30]. Fla. Stat. § 718.1255(3) (2016).
[31]. Fla. Admin. Code R. 61B-50.124 (2016).
[32]. Fla. Admin. Code R. 61B-50.124 (2016).
[33]. Fla. Admin. Code R. 61B-50.124 (2016).
[34]. Fla. Admin. Code R. 61B-50.127 (2016).
[35]. Fla. Admin. Code R. 61B-50.117 (2016).

summarily enter a final order awarding relief if the arbitrator finds no meritorious defense or no demonstration of substantial compliance with the requirements of the rules and statutes.

No formal evidentiary hearing is required if the arbitrator disposes of the petition summarily by deciding the dispute solely on the pleadings and evidence filed by the parties. Any party may move for a summary final order whenever there are no disputed issues of material fact. The motion must be accompanied by supporting affidavits if necessary. Non-moving parties may file a response in opposition, with or without supporting affidavits, within seven days of service of the motion.[36]

Hearings are open to the public. Each party may present witnesses, evidence, cross examine the other party's witnesses, enter objections, and rebut the opposing party's evidence. Oral testimony is taken under oath. With regard to evidence rules, arbitration proceedings are less formal than court proceedings; however, the parties are limited to relevant evidence, and hearsay evidence may only be submitted to supplement or explain other evidence, but is not sufficient to support a finding, unless the hearsay evidence would otherwise be admissible in a court of law. The rules of privilege apply.[37]

After the final hearing, the parties may submit proposed findings of fact, conclusions of law, proposed orders, and legal briefs or memoranda, within a time designated by the arbitrator.[38] The parties may waive final orders. If a final order is entered, it must be entered within 30 days of (1) the final hearing, (2) receipt by the arbitrator of the hearing transcript if one is filed, or (3) receipt of the parties' memoranda. The final order takes effect upon mailing.[39] For non-binding arbitrations, the arbitration decision is final if a complaint for a trial de novo is not filed within 30 days.[40]

The prevailing party in a non-binding arbitration pursuant to section 718.1255 is entitled to reasonable attorney's fees and costs as determined by the arbitrator, including reasonable fees

---

[36.] Fla. Admin. Code R. 61B-50.119 (2016).
[37.] Fla. Admin. Code R. 61B-50.131 (2016).
[38.] Fla. Admin. Code R. 61B-50.131 (2016).
[39.] Fla. Admin. Code R. 61B-50.139 (2016).
[40.] Fla. Stat. § 718.1255(4)(k) (2016).

and costs incurred in the arbitration proceeding and in preparing for and attending any scheduled mediation.[41] A party who files a complaint for a trial de novo shall be assessed the other party's reasonable arbitration fees and costs and reasonable court fees and costs if the judgment upon the trial de novo is not more favorable than the arbitration decision. If the judgment is more favorable, the party who filed a complaint for trial de novo shall be awarded reasonable court fees and costs.[42] No party, however, is entitled to recover its fees and costs in a condominium board member recall proceeding[43] initiated pursuant to the Condominium Act.[44]

4-3 DUTIES OF THE MEMBERS OF THE BOARD

The Homeowners' Association Act provides that the association or any member may bring "actions at law or in equity, or both" against directors and officers who "willfully and knowingly" fail to comply with Chapter 720, the governing documents, or the rules of the association.[45] Similarly, a condominium association or the unit owners may sue members of the condominium board of directors for damages, for injunctive relief, or for both, who "willfully and knowingly" fail to comply with the provisions of the Condominium Act, the declaration, the documents creating the association, and the association bylaws.[46] The Condominium Act specifically states that board members may be sued for "damages or for injunctive relief," but does not include Chapter 720's broader language permitting "actions at law or in equity."

Courts construing the Condominium Act's statutory cause of action for injunctive relief, however, have given it broad application. For instance, the court allowed a condominium association to pursue a statutory cause of action to enjoin a unit owner from future acts of violence.[47] The condominium association had standing to proceed because injunctions are authorized by statute to prevent breaches of

---

41. Fla. Stat. § 718.1255(4)(k) (2016).
42. Fla. Stat. § 718.1255(4)(l) (2016).
43. Fla. Admin. Code R. 61B-50.1405 (2016).
44. Fla. Stat. § 718.112 (2016).
45. Fla. Stat. § 720.305 (2016).
46. Fla. Stat. § 718.303 (2016).
47. *Casa Del Mar Condo. Ass'n v. Richartz*, 641 So. 2d 470 (Fla. 3d Dist. Ct. App. 1994).

governing document provisions, such as the provision at issue which prohibited "any use or practice ... which interferes with the peaceful and proper use of the property by its residents."[48]

The statutory cause of action for injunctive relief also eases the burden on the plaintiff in setting forth his or her claim. While a claim for injunctive relief typically requires a showing of irreparable harm, a Chapter 718 violation is considered, in and of itself, sufficient harm to authorize injunctive relief, without any "additional showing of harm."[49]

4-3:1   Fiduciary Duty

Both the Homeowners' Association Act[50] and the Condominium Act[51] impose a fiduciary duty on members of boards of directors. Actions for breach of fiduciary duty against community association directors are subject to a four-year statute of limitations.[52]

Ordinarily, to establish a cause of action for breach of fiduciary duty, a party must plead the existence of a fiduciary relationship and a breach thereof, which results in damage.[53] The existence of the fiduciary relationship is established with evidence of dependency on the fiduciary and an undertaking on the part of the fiduciary "to advise, counsel, and protect the weaker party."[54] In the case of community association board members, however, the fiduciary relationship is statutory.

---

[48] *Casa Del Mar Condo. Ass'n v. Richartz*, 641 So. 2d 470, 471 (Fla. 3d Dist. Ct. App. 1994) (after the condominium association president promised to investigate a unit owner's complaints about ongoing renovation work on the owner's unit, the owner allegedly prevented the president's exit, threw him against the wall and onto the floor, and threatened the association and the president specifically; the association's subsequent injunctive action to prevent future threats of violence or acts of physical violence against the association, its board, association employees, and residents was dismissed by the trial judge on the theory that the association had no standing in a private dispute between the president and the owner; the Third District Court of Appeal reversed).

[49] *Hobbs v. Weinkauf*, 940 So. 2d 1151, 1153 (Fla. 2d Dist. Ct. App. 2006).

[50] Fla. Stat. § 720.303 (2016) ("The officers and directors of an association have a fiduciary relationship to the members who are served by the association.").

[51] Fla. Stat. § 718.111(1)(a) (2016) ("The officers and directors of the association have a fiduciary relationship to the unit owners.").

[52] Fla. Stat. § 95.11(3) (2016).

[53] *Southtrust Bank & Right Equip. Co. of Pinellas Cty. v. Exp. Ins. Servs.*, 190 F. Supp. 2d 1304, 1308 (M.D. Fla. 2002).

[54] *Taylor Woodrow Homes Florida v. 4/46-A*, 850 So. 2d 536, 540 (Fla. 5th Dist. Ct. App. 2003).

The Condominium Act defines the fiduciary duty of board members via reference to the Florida Not For Profit Corporation Act, which requires directors to discharge their duties (1) in good faith; (2) with the care an ordinarily prudent person in a like position would exercise under similar circumstances; and (3) in a manner they reasonably believe to be in the corporation's best interests.[55] While the Condominium Act does not expressly incorporate the entire statute, the Florida Not For Profit Corporation Act further explains that a director may rely on information, opinions, reports, or statements, if prepared or presented by (1) legal counsel, public accountants, other professionals or experts as to matters within their expertise, (2) a committee of the board of directors of which the director is not a member "if the director reasonably believes the committee merits confidence," or (3) others members of the board or employees of the corporation "whom the director reasonably believes to be reliable and competent in the matters presented."[56]

A director does not act in good faith if he or she relies on another despite personal knowledge regarding a matter that makes reliance on that person unwarranted.[57] If the director complies with the foregoing, the director is not liable for "any action taken as a director, or any failure to take action."[58]

The Condominium Act imposes liability on members of the board of directors if their breach constitutes (1) a violation of criminal law; (2) a transaction from which the board member derived an improper personal benefit; or (3) "recklessness or an act or omission ... in bad faith, with malicious purpose, or in a manner exhibiting wanton and willful disregard of human rights, safety, or property."[59] In articulating the circumstances under which directors may be subject to personal liability, the Condominium Act incorporates the Florida Not For Profit Corporation Act's pronouncement that personal liability for a criminal act will be imposed unless the officer or director had reasonable cause to

---

55. Fla. Stat. § 617.0830 (2016).
56. Fla. Stat. § 617.0830 (2016).
57. Fla. Stat. § 617.0830(3) (2016).
58. Fla. Stat. § 617.0830(4) (2016).
59. Fla. Stat. § 718.111(1)(d) (2016).

believe his or her conduct was lawful or had no reasonable cause to believe his or her conduct was unlawful.[60]

While a judgment or other final adjudication for a violation of criminal law prevents a director from contesting that they violated criminal law, it does not prevent the director from establishing that he or she had reasonable cause to believe that his or her conduct was lawful or had no reasonable cause to believe that his or her conduct was unlawful.[61]

Pursuant to the Florida Not For Profit Corporation Act, recklessness for which personal liability may be imposed includes acts or omissions "in conscious disregard" of a risk that is (1) either (a) known to the director, or (b) so obvious that it should have been known, and (2) is "so great as to make it highly probable that harm would follow from such action or omission."[62] For example, directors' deliberate abdication of responsibilities related to the annual budget, the levying of assessments, and the holding of board meetings may represent acts constituting recklessness or acts or omissions in bad faith or with malicious purpose.[63] Finally, board members' fiduciary duty is strictly limited to the unit owners and does not extend to prospective purchasers.[64]

4-3:2   Director Compensation Prohibited

Unless authorized in the governing documents, or approved in advance by a majority of the voting interests voting in person or by proxy at a membership meeting, the homeowners' association may not salary members of its board of directors to compensate

---

[60.] Fla. Stat. § 617.0834 (2016).

[61.] Fla. Stat. § 617.0834(1)(b) (2016).

[62.] Fla. Stat. § 617.0834(2) (2016).

[63.] *Berg v. Wagner*, 935 So. 2d 100, 102 (Fla. 4th Dist. Ct. App. 2006) (owner sought individual liability for homeowners' association board members, alleging that they deliberately abdicated their responsibilities with respect to the annual budget, the levying of assessments, and the holding of board meetings and that such actions were taken in bad faith and with a malicious purpose; appellate court reversed the trial court's entry of summary judgment in favor of the directors, holding that the directors failed to meet their burden of demonstrating with undisputed evidence the owner could not prove actions on the part of the board sufficient to impose personal liability).

[64.] *Maillard v. Dowdell*, 528 So. 2d 512, 514 (Fla. 3d Dist. Ct. App. 1988) (prospective purchasers sued for breach of fiduciary duty based on an alleged pre-sale failure to disclose information concerning the defective condition of a condominium building; the Third District Court of Appeal affirmed the trial court's decision that the statutory fiduciary duty pursuant to subsection 718.111(1)(a) extends only to unit owners and does not protect prospective purchasers).

them for their service as directors, officers, or committee members, nor may board members "in any other way benefit financially from service to the association."[65] Board members may, however, enjoy benefits that all or a significant number of members receive from a lawful action by the board or a committee, including maintenance of community property. A board member may also be reimbursed for approved out-of-pocket expenses and may receive proceeds from an insurance claim made on an association policy maintained for the members' benefit. In addition, a developer or its representative may serve as a director, officer, or committee member even though they benefit financially from service to the association.[66]

Similarly, condominium association directors are prohibited from accepting compensation for their service on the board, unless permitted by the bylaws.[67] In addition, directors are prohibited from accepting compensation from vendors who provide goods or services to the association.[68] Directors are subject to a civil penalty if they knowingly solicit or accept compensation for their own benefit or that of their immediate family from vendors who provide goods or services to the association, for which consideration has not been provided.[69]

4-3:3 Business Judgment Rule as Applied to Board Members

The business judgment rule, as codified in the Florida Business Corporation Act,[70] applies to homeowners' association and

---

[65] Fla. Stat. § 720.303(12) (2016).

[66] Fla. Stat. § 720.303(12) (2016).

[67] Fla. Stat. § 718.112(2) (2016).

[68] Fla. Stat. § 718.111(1)(a) (2016).

[69] Fla. Stat. § 718.111(1)(a) (2016). At the time of the drafting of this update in May 2017, the Florida Legislature is considering Senate Bill 1682, which could go into effect on July 1, 2017. It would amend Fla. Stat. § 718.112(2) to prohibit an association that is not a timeshare condominium association from employing or contracting with any service provider that is owned or operated by a board member or with any person who has a financial relationship with a board member or officer.

[70] Fla. Stat. § 607.0831 (2016) (setting forth a version of the business judgment rule that protects corporate directors from personal liability and damages for any "statement, vote, decision, or failure to act, regarding corporate management or policy," unless the director breached his or her duties as a director in one of the following ways: a violation of the criminal law, unless the director had reasonable cause to believe his or her conduct was lawful; a transaction from which the director derived an improper personal benefit; recklessness; "or an act or omission which was committed in bad faith or with malicious

condominium association board members. This means that if board members act within their authority and reasonably use their best business judgment, Florida courts will shield them from personal liability. The simple policy behind this rule is that individual board members do not serve as insurance or personal guarantors against losses sustained by the community association. Requiring them to serve this purpose would make it difficult, if not impossible, to obtain volunteers needed to form the board.

When directors and officers commit acts of fraud, self-dealing, unjust enrichment, or betrayal of trust, courts suspend the general rule that their role as corporate agents shields them from personal liability for official corporate acts.[71] Under this standard, the failure of a condominium association board of directors member to pay for and maintain the association's insurance does not rise to a level that justifies imposing personal liability.[72]

Negligence alone is also not sufficient to impose personal liability.[73] For example, a director's negligent failure to administer insurance proceeds does not represent a breach of corporate duties sufficient to impose personal liability, since it does not qualify as "fraud, criminal activity or self-dealing/unjust enrichment."[74]

In addition, the court has rejected attempts to hold developer-appointed directors to a higher standard than owner-elected directors.[75] Indeed, courts will not impose personal liability on developer-appointed directors who breach their fiduciary duty to maintain and repair common areas absent a showing of fraud/self-dealing/unjust enrichment, as they are held to the same standard as owner-elected directors.[76]

---

purpose or in a manner exhibiting wanton and willful disregard of human rights, safety, or property").

[71] *Munder v. Circle One Condo.*, 596 So. 2d 144, 145 (Fla. 4th Dist. Ct. App. 1992).

[72] *Munder v. Circle One Condo.*, 596 So. 2d 144, 145 (Fla. 4th Dist. Ct. App. 1992).

[73] *Perlow v. Goldberg*, 700 So. 2d 148, 149 (Fla. 3d Dist. Ct. App. 1997).

[74] *Perlow v. Goldberg*, 700 So. 2d 148, 149 (Fla. 3d Dist. Ct. App. 1997).

[75] *Sonny Boy v. Asnani*, 879 So. 2d 25 (Fla. 5th Dist. Ct. App. 2004).

[76] *Sonny Boy v. Asnani*, 879 So. 2d 25, 27 (Fla. 5th Dist. Ct. App. 2004) (unit owner sued developer-appointed directors personally for alleged breach of fiduciary duty relating to failure to maintain and repair common areas; the appeals court affirmed the trial court's decision (1) granting the directors' motion for judgment on the pleadings, since the owner's pleadings failed to allege fraud, self-dealing, or betrayal of trust, and (2) denying the owner's motion to amend his pleadings to allege that the directors' breach was "willful," rejecting the owner's argument that developer-appointed directors should be held to a stricter standard than owner-elected directors; unit owner's argument was based

4-3:4   Self-Dealing and Unjust Enrichment

When a director derives improper "personal benefit"[77] from their role as a board member, this represents self-dealing for which the courts may impose personal liability. Members of homeowners' and condominium association boards, however, are not prohibited from receiving compensation for their services as board members if permitted by the association's governing documents.[78] In addition, the Homeowners' Associations Act expressly permits board members to receive benefits enjoyed by all or a significant number of members resulting from a lawful action by the board or a committee, including maintenance of community property.[79] This does not constitute an improper personal benefit sufficient to show self-dealing or unjust enrichment. The same holds true in the context of condominium associations.[80]

---

on the language of section 718.303(1), which states that unit owners may bring suit against condominium board directors "designated by the developer, for actions taken by them prior to the time control of the association is assumed by unit owners other than the developer" *and* any director who "willfully and knowingly" fails to comply with the provisions of the association's governing documents and the Condominium Act; the court explicitly rejected the owner's argument that the legislature intended to distinguish between owner-elected directors and developer-appointed directors by including a willfulness requirement *only* for owner-elected directors, while holding developer-appointed directors to a higher standard; the court noted, "[i]f a higher standard was intended to apply to directors designated by the developer, that standard was not included in the statute"; as a result, merely alleging simple willfulness was insufficient to impose personal liability without some indication of fraud, self-dealing, or unjust enrichment, and the developer-appointed directors could not be held personally liable); *see* Fla. Stat. § 718.303(1) (2013).

[77] *Raphael v. Silverman*, 22 So. 3d 837, 839 (Fla. 4th Dist. Ct. App. 2009).

[78] Fla. Stat. §§ 720.303(12), 718.112(2) (2014). At the time of the drafting of this update in May 2017, the Florida Legislature is considering Senate Bill 1682, which could go into effect on July 1, 2017, that would add a new Fla. Stat. § 718.3027. This section, titled "conflicts of interest," would require board members to disclose to the board any activity that may reasonably be construed to be a conflict of interest. The new statute would create a rebuttable presumption of a conflict of interest under certain circumstances if a board members fails to give prior notice, such as when any director, officer, or relative of any director or officer enters into a contract for goods or services with the association.

[79] Fla. Stat. § 720.303(12) (2016).

[80] *Raphael v. Silverman*, 22 So. 3d 837, 839 (Fla. 4th Dist. Ct. App. 2009) (unit owners sued the condominium association and individual board members alleging self-dealing based on improper improvements to the condominium common areas which benefited the directors, since they lived in the condominium; the court held that these allegations were insufficient to overcome the immunity afforded condominium board members who simply participate in a benefit enjoyed by all or a significant number of the condominium members).

4-3:5   Business Judgment Rule as Applied to Community Associations

In addition to protecting members of the board of directors from personal liability, an adaptation of the business judgment rule applies to decisions made by the community association itself. In other words, the business judgment rule applies even in suits against the community association as a corporate entity, not only in suits against board members in their individual capacity. For instance, the rule was used to protect a condominium association's decision to lease common element parking spots. The court held that the rule protects association decisions provided that the association "act[ed] in a reasonable manner."[81]

The rule has been developed further in Florida through the adoption of California's *Lamden* test,[82] under which courts defer to a duly constituted community association board when it (1) exercises discretion within its authority, as set forth in the relevant statutes and the association's governing documents, and (2) acts "upon reasonable investigation, in good faith and with regard for the best interests of the community association and its members."[83] Under the Florida formulation of the *Lamden* test, courts defer to decisions that are (a) within the scope of the association's authority, and (b) "reasonable," meaning that the association has not "acted arbitrarily, capriciously, or in bad faith."[84]

To avoid second-guessing an association in its decision to amend its governing documents, Florida courts also apply the *Hollywood Towers* version of the *Lamden* reasonableness test to amendments to governing documents. Under this test, a "reasonable" amendment

---

[81.] *Garcia v. Crescent Plaza Condo. Ass'n*, 813 So. 2d 975, 978 (Fla. 2d Dist. Ct. App. 2002).

[82.] *Hollywood Towers Condo. Ass'n v. Hampton*, 40 So. 3d 784 (Fla. 4th Dist. Ct. App. 2010).

[83.] *Lamden v. La Jolla Shores Clubdominium Homeowners Ass'n*, 21 Cal. 4th 249, 980 P.2d 940, 942 (1999).

[84.] *Hollywood Towers Condo. Ass'n v. Hampton*, 40 So. 3d 784 (Fla. 4th Dist. Ct. App. 2010) (trial court granted a permanent injunction requiring an owner to allow the association access to her unit to perform repair work, despite testimony from the owner's expert that exterior work was sufficient; on appeal, the court held (1) that the business judgment rule applies not only to immunize directors and officers from personal liability, but also to immunize the association itself, (2) that courts defer to associations' decisions that are reasonable and within the scope of the association's authority, and (3) decisions are "reasonable" as long as the association has not "acted arbitrarily, capriciously, or in bad faith"; the appeal court remanded to the trial court to apply the *Lamden* test to determine whether the association acted appropriately in demanding access to the owner's unit).

is one that is "not arbitrary, capricious, or in bad faith," meaning that it does not destroy the general plan of development.[85]

It is important to note that the business judgment rule only protects an association and its board from a member suit. It does not protect against suits brought to enforce the association's obligations to third-parties, and is thus "not a weapon permitting the [a]ssociation to renege on statutory, contractual, and other obligations on a whim (or even after solemn deliberation)."[86] In other words, while the business judgment rule applies to disputes instigated by members, it "does not empower a corporation to escape the consequences of the corporation's actions toward the outside world."[87]

4-4   BOARD MEMBER DISCIPLINE AND REMOVAL

4-4:1   Civil Penalty for Condominium Board Members

A civil penalty may be imposed by the Division of Florida Condominiums, Timeshares, and Mobile Homes on condominium directors who willfully and knowingly violate a provision of the Condominium Act, or an adopted rule or final order of the division. The division may remove directors and may prohibit them from serving on the board for a period of time. For these purposes, "willfully and knowingly" means that the director refused to comply with the division after being informed that his or her action or intended action violates the Condominium Act or an adopted rule or final order of the division. Before imposing the penalty, the division must afford the director 10 days to comply. The penalty is imposed for each day of a continuing violation, but may not exceed $5,000.[88]

[85.] *Klinow v. Island Court at Boca W. Prop. Owners' Ass'n*, 64 So. 3d 177, 180 (Fla. 4th Dist. Ct. App. 2011) (owners challenged an amendment to the original governing documents passed by two-thirds approval of the voting members, which allowed the homeowners' associations to replace privately owned driveway and walkway materials; since the amendment benefited the association and the owners equally, resulting in a more aesthetically pleasing community "without fundamentally changing any homeowner's personal property or community plans," the court held that "no radical change of plan would occur as to make the changes unreasonable" and permitted the amendment).

[86.] *In re Colony Beach & Tennis Club Ass'n*, 456 B.R. 545, 559 (M.D. Fla. 2011).

[87.] *In re Colony Beach & Tennis Club Ass'n*, 456 B.R. 545, 559 (M.D. Fla. 2011).

[88.] Fla. Stat. § 718.501(1)(d) (2016).

The Florida Administrative Code sets forth a detailed list of minor and major violations. The division may impose a civil penalty between $1 and $5, per unit, for each minor violation. The penalty may be adjusted either up or down based upon any aggravating or mitigating factors. An occurrence of six or more aggravating factors or five or more mitigating factors will result in a penalty being assessed outside of the specified range. The total penalty to be assessed shall be calculated according to the guidelines or $100, whichever amount is greater. In no event shall a penalty of more than $2,500 be imposed for a single violation.[89] Examples of minor violations include the following: failure to maintain corporate status; improper use of secret ballot, or use of proxy, by board members at a board meeting; failure to provide a timely or substantive response to a written inquiry received by certified mail; improper quorum at unit owner meeting; failure to properly notice and conduct board of administration or committee meetings; failure to provide notice of the annual meeting not less than 14 days prior to the meeting; and failure to allow unit owners to speak at meetings.[90]

The Florida Administrative Code provides for two categories of major violations. The division may impose a civil penalty for Category 1 violations of between $6 and $10 per unit.[91] The division may impose a civil penalty for Category 2 violations of between $12 and $20 per unit.[92] The penalty is assessed beginning with the middle of the range and adjusted either up or down based upon aggravating or mitigating factors. An occurrence of six or more aggravating factors or five or more mitigating factors will result in a penalty outside the specified range. The total penalty to be assessed shall be calculated according to the guidelines or $100,

---

[89] Fla. Admin. Code R. 61B-21.003 (2016).

[90] Fla. Admin. Code R. 61B-21.003 (2016).

[91] Fla. Admin. Code R. 61B-21.003 (2016) (Category 1 major violations include: failure to assess at sufficient amounts; improper compensation of officers or directors; commingling reserve funds with operating funds; failure to include all timely submitted names of eligible candidates on the ballot; failure to maintain election materials for one year; and failure to maintain minutes of meetings).

[92] Fla. Admin. Code R. 61B-21.003 (2016) (Category 2 major violations include: insufficient detail in the accounting records; failure to maintain sufficient accounting records; failure to assess based upon proportionate share or as stated in the declaration of condominium; failure to hold annual meeting; failure to propose/adopt budget for a given year; commingling association funds with non-association funds; failure to maintain records within Florida; and using association funds for other than common expenses).

whichever amount is greater. In no event shall a penalty of more than $5,000 be imposed for a single violation.[93]

4-4:2   Recall of Board Members

Any member of a community association board of directors may be recalled and removed from office with or without cause by written agreement of a majority of the total voting interests.[94] Members of a homeowners' association may also recall board members by vote at a meeting if the declaration, articles of incorporation, or bylaws so provide.[95] Members of a condominium association may recall board members by vote at a meeting pursuant to statute.[96] For both homeowners' associations and condominium associations, recall disputes are subject to arbitration with the Division of Florida Condominiums, Timeshares, and Mobile Homes of the Department of Business and Professional Regulation.[97]

If the recall is by an agreement in writing, the agreement or a copy thereof, shall be served on the association by certified mail or by personal service pursuant to the Florida Rules of Civil Procedure.[98] The written agreement shall provide for a separate vote for each board director sought to be recalled.[99] After receipt of the agreement, the board shall duly notice and hold a meeting of the board within five business days. At the meeting, the board may certify the written agreement, in which case the board member or members shall be recalled immediately and shall turn over to the board within five business days any records and property of the association in their possession.[100]

For homeowners' associations, if it is determined by the Department of Business and Professional Regulation pursuant to binding arbitration proceedings that an initial recall was defective,

---

[93.] Fla. Admin. Code R. 61B-21.003 (2016).

[94.] Fla. Stat. §§ 720.303(10)(a), 718.112(2)(j) (2016).

[95.] Fla. Stat. § 720.303(10)(c) (2016).

[96.] Fla. Stat. § 718.112(2)(j) (2016).

[97.] Fla. Stat. §§ 720.303(10), 718.1255 (2016).

[98.] Fla. Stat. §§ 720.303(10), 718.112(2)(j) (2016).

[99.] Fla. Stat. § 720.303(10)(i) (2016); Fla. Admin. Code R. 61B-23.0028 (2016).

[100.] Fla. Stat. §§ 720.303(10), 718.112(2)(j) (2016). At the time of the drafting of this update in May 2017, the Florida Legislature is considering Senate Bill 1682, which could go into effect on July 1, 2017, that would amend Fla. Stat. § 718.112(2)(j) to take away the board's right to certify or not certify the recall. The recall would be automatic.

for up to 120 days written recall agreements or written ballots used in the first recall effort and not found to be defective may be reused in one subsequent recall.[101] For condominium associations, written recall ballots in a recall by written agreement may be reused in one subsequent recall effort. In the context of condominium associations, written recall ballots do not expire through the passage of time, but they become void with respect to the board member sought to be recalled where that board member is elected during a regularly scheduled election.[102]

Any rescission or revocation of a member's written recall ballot or agreement must be in writing and delivered to the association before the association is served with the written recall agreements or ballots.[103] The agreement in writing or ballot shall list at least as many possible replacement directors as there are directors subject to the recall, when at least a majority of the board is sought to be recalled.[104]

If the recall of a director or directors is by vote at a meeting, the special meeting may be called by 10 percent of the voting interests giving notice of the meeting, and the notice shall state the purpose of the meeting. Email notice is not an appropriate method of giving notice of a meeting called in whole or in part for this purpose.[105] For homeowners' associations, the vote at the meeting shall allow for a separate vote for each board director sought to be recalled.[106] For condominium associations, the Florida Administrative Code calls for the voting interests to vote to recall each board member separately, unless otherwise provided in the declaration or bylaws.[107]

If the recall is approved by a vote of the majority of all voting interests at a meeting, the board shall notice and hold a board meeting within five business days after the adjournment of the member meeting. If the board certifies the recall, the recalled member or members shall be recalled effective immediately and shall turn over to the board within five business days any records

---

[101] Fla. Stat. § 720.303(10)(b) (2016).

[102] Fla. Admin. Code R. 61B-23.0028 (2016).

[103] Fla. Stat. § 720.303(10)(b) (2016); Fla. Admin. Code R. 61B-23.0028 (2016).

[104] Fla. Stat. § 720.303(10)(b) (2016); Fla. Admin. Code R. 61B-23.0028 (2016).

[105] Fla. Stat. §§ 720.303(10)(c), 718.112(2)(j) (2016).

[106] Fla. Stat. § 720.303(10)(j) (2016).

[107] Fla. Admin. Code R. 61B-23.0027 (2016).

and property of the association in their possession.[108] If the board fails to notice and hold a meeting within five days after service of an agreement in writing or adjournment of the member recall meeting, the recall shall be deemed effective and the directors so recalled shall immediately turn over to the board all records and property of the association.[109]

If a homeowners' association board decides not to certify the recall, the board must file a petition for binding arbitration with the Department of Business and Professional Regulation within five business days after the meeting.[110] If a condominium association board decides not to certify the recall, the board shall file a petition for arbitration with the Department of Business and Professional Regulation within five business days after the meeting.[111] The condominium board may seek binding or nonbinding arbitration.[112] If the arbitrator certifies the recall, the recall will be effective upon mailing of the final order to the association. The recalled director or directors shall deliver to the board any records of the association in their possession within five business days after the effective date of the recall.[113]

For homeowners' associations, if a recalled director fails to leave office or turn over records and property of the association, the association may petition the circuit court to order the director to leave office and turn over all association records and property.[114]

If the recall results in a vacancy on the board and less than a majority of the board members are removed, the remaining directors may vote to fill the vacancy. For homeowners' associations, if more than a majority of the board members is removed, the vacancies shall be filled by votes of the members voting in favor of the recall.[115] For condominium associations, if more than a majority of the board members is removed, the association shall conduct an election to fill vacancies on the board. The voting interests may vote

---

[108] Fla. Stat. §§ 720.303 (10)(c), 718.112(2)(j) (2016).
[109] Fla. Stat. §§ 720.303(10)(f), 718.112(2)(j) (2016).
[110] Fla. Stat. § 720.303(10)(d) (2016).
[111] Fla. Stat. § 718.112(2)(j)(3) (2016).
[112] Fla. Stat. § 718.1255 (2016).
[113] Fla. Stat. § 720.303(10)(d) (2016).
[114] Fla. Stat. § 720.303(10)(h) (2016).
[115] Fla. Stat. § 720.303(10)(e) (2016).

in person or by limited proxy to elect replacement board members in an amount equal to the number of recalled board members.[116]

The Condominium Act also sets forth certain circumstances under which a director may be removed from office. Condominium association board members who are more than 90 days delinquent in the payment of any monetary obligation due to the association shall be deemed to have abandoned their office.[117] In addition, a condominium director charged by information or indictment with a felony theft or embezzlement involving the association's funds or property must be removed from office. If the charges are resolved without a finding of guilt, the director or officer shall be reinstated for the remainder of his or her term of office. A person otherwise eligible for directorship may not be appointed or elected while charges of felony theft or embezzlement involving the association's funds or property are pending.[118]

[116.] Fla. Admin. Code R. 61B-23.0027 (2016).
[117.] Fla. Stat. § 718.112(2)(n) (2016).
[118.] Fla. Stat. § 718.112(2)(0) (2016).

Chapter 5

Operation of the Community Association

5-1   INTRODUCTION

As corporate entities, community associations operate by and through their board of directors. The association and its board are responsible for safeguarding the health, safety, welfare, and property values in the community. The association must act as a good shepherd of the community's finances, ensuring that members' assessments are used properly. This requires transparency in the adoption of the budget and levying of assessments, as well as regular financial reporting. The association should also set aside funds for capital improvements and deferred maintenance.

Property maintenance is one of the community association's primary functions and includes maintenance of common areas held in the homeowners' association name and elements owned in common by condominium unit owners. A condominium association may also be responsible for any real or personal property owned or leased by the association for the use and benefit of its members.

To ensure transparency, the Florida Legislature requires associations to maintain official records that are open to members for inspection and copying. In fact, there are penalties for failure to make the records available to owners in a timely manner and in a reasonably accessible place. Condominium owners also benefit from a statutory right to make written inquiries to the board of directors regarding community operations. These requirements illustrate that serving community members is the only function of the board of directors and the corporate entity that operates the community.

To assist it in carrying out this function, the association is permitted to hire office staff, maintenance personnel, managers, contractors, engineers, accountants, attorneys, and any other tradesmen or professionals needed to serve the community. To obtain certain goods and services, however, the association must solicit competitive bids and maintain them in official records. While the association is not required by statute to choose the lowest bidder, soliciting bids ensures that the membership has the information it needs to determine whether the board of directors is operating the community using good business judgment.

Despite their many obligations, neither the board of directors nor the association itself is a guarantor of the safety, welfare, and property values of the membership. As such, Florida community associations may obtain insurance against casualty, liability insurance for directors and officers, insurance for the benefit of association employees, and flood insurance for the common elements, association property, and units. Florida community associations also have a right to sue on behalf of their membership, and may maintain class action suits on behalf of all association members without satisfying all of the Florida Rules of Civil Procedure requirements for pleading and maintaining class actions.

5-2   HOMEOWNERS' ASSOCIATION FINANCES

5-2:1   Homeowners' Association Budgets

Homeowners' associations must prepare annual budgets setting forth the upcoming year's estimated revenues and expenses and the current year's estimated surplus or deficit. In addition to annual operating expenses, the budget may include reserve accounts for capital expenditures and deferred maintenance. The budget must also state all fees paid by the association for recreational amenities. The association must provide each member with a copy of the annual budget or a written notice that it is available upon request at no charge.[1]

[1.] Fla. Stat. § 720.303(6) (2016).

5-2:2   Homeowners' Association Reserves

The homeowners' association budget may include reserve accounts for capital expenditures and deferred maintenance. If reserve accounts are initially established by the developer, or if the membership elects to provide reserves, the association may maintain, waive, or terminate the reserve in accordance with the provisions of Chapter 720. If reserve accounts are not initially established by the developer, the membership may elect by a majority of the voting interests to provide reserves.[2]

Members must approve reserve accounts either via a vote at a duly called membership meeting or by the written consent of a majority of the total voting interests. The approval action must state that reserve accounts shall be provided for in the budget and must designate the reserve accounts' purpose. Upon membership approval, the board of directors must include the required reserve accounts in the budget in the next fiscal year following the approval and each year thereafter, unless waived or terminated.[3] If a reserve is terminated, it is removed from the budget.[4]

The amount placed in the reserve is determined based on the "estimated remaining useful life and estimated replacement cost or deferred maintenance expense" of each item for which the reserve is created.[5] Replacement reserve assessments may be adjusted on an annual basis to account for any change in estimated useful life, replacement cost, or deferred maintenance cost.[6] The funding formula must be based on the analysis of each asset as set forth section 720.303(6)(g).[7]

Reserve funds and any interest shall remain in the reserve account and may only be used for intended purposes. A majority of the voting interests, however, may vote in advance to approve their use for other purposes. Prior to turnover, a developer-controlled association may not make unauthorized reserve expenditures

[2] Fla. Stat. § 720.303(6)(d) (2016).
[3] Fla. Stat. § 720.303(6)(d) (2016).
[4] Fla. Stat. § 720.303(6)(b) (2016).
[5] Fla. Stat. § 720.303(6)(e) (2016).
[6] Fla. Stat. § 720.303(6)(e) (2016).
[7] Fla. Stat. § 720.303(6)(g) (2016).

unless the use is approved by a majority of all non-developer voting interests voting in person or by limited proxy.[8]

After a reserve account is established, the membership may eliminate or decrease reserves by a majority vote at a meeting at which a quorum is present, and the developer may vote its interest to waive or reduce the funding of reserves after turnover.[9] Any section 720.303(6)(f) membership or developer vote to waive or reduce reserves is applicable to only one budget year.[10]

If the budget's failure to provide for reserve accounts creates the possibility that the association may need to specially assess for capital improvements, each financial report must contain the following statement in conspicuous type:

> THE BUDGET OF THE ASSOCIATION DOES NOT PROVIDE FOR RESERVE ACCOUNTS FOR CAPITAL EXPENDITURES AND DEFERRED MAINTENANCE THAT MAY RESULT IN SPECIAL ASSESSMENTS. OWNERS MAY ELECT TO PROVIDE FOR RESERVE ACCOUNTS PURSUANT TO SECTION 720.303(6), FLORIDA STATUTES, UPON OBTAINING THE APPROVAL OF A MAJORITY OF THE TOTAL VOTING INTERESTS OF THE ASSOCIATION BY VOTE OF THE MEMBERS AT A MEETING OR BY WRITTEN CONSENT.[11]

If reserve accounts are not initially established by the developer or if the membership does not elect to provide for reserves, the association may maintain limited voluntary deferred expenditure accounts. Funding is limited to the extent that the governing documents limit increases in assessments, including reserves. For associations maintaining limited voluntary deferred expenditure accounts, each financial report must contain the following statement in conspicuous type:

---

8. Fla. Stat. § 720.303(6)(h) (2016).
9. Fla. Stat. § 720.303 (6)(f) (2016).
10. Fla. Stat. § 720.303(6)(f) (2016).
11. Fla. Stat. § 720.303(6)(c) (2016).

THE BUDGET OF THE ASSOCIATION PROVIDES FOR LIMITED VOLUNTARY DEFERRED EXPENDITURE ACCOUNTS, INCLUDING CAPITAL EXPENDITURES AND DEFERRED MAINTENANCE, SUBJECT TO LIMITS ON FUNDING CONTAINED IN OUR GOVERNING DOCUMENTS. BECAUSE THE OWNERS HAVE NOT ELECTED TO PROVIDE FOR RESERVE ACCOUNTS PURSUANT TO SECTION 720.303(6), FLORIDA STATUTES, THESE FUNDS ARE NOT SUBJECT TO THE RESTRICTIONS ON USE OF SUCH FUNDS SET FORTH IN THAT STATUTE, NOR ARE RESERVES CALCULATED IN ACCORDANCE WITH THAT STATUTE.[12]

5-2:3   Homeowners' Association Assessments

A homeowners' association by definition is a "Florida corporation responsible for the operation of a community ... authorized to impose assessments that, if unpaid, may become a lien on the parcel."[13] "Assessment" is defined as

a sum or sums of money payable to the association ... by the owners of one or more parcels as authorized in the governing documents, which if not paid by the owner of a parcel, can result in a lien against the parcel.[14]

Assessments levied pursuant to the annual budget must be in the member's proportional share of common expenses. For any homeowners' association created after October 1, 1995, the governing documents must specify the member's proportional share.[15] Shares may differ by "class," which is based on levels of services received by the owner or other relevant factors.[16]

[12.] Fla. Stat. § 720.303(6)(c) (2016).
[13.] Fla. Stat. § 720.301(9) (2016).
[14.] Fla. Stat. § 720.301(1) (2016).
[15.] Fla. Stat. § 720.308(1) (2016).
[16.] Fla. Stat. § 720.308(1)(a) (2016).

Regardless of how title to property has been acquired, an owner "is liable for all assessments that come due while he or she is the parcel owner."[17] The owner may not avoid assessments because they are not using the common areas, or by abandoning their parcel.[18] In addition, a unit owner is "jointly and severally liable with the previous parcel owner for all unpaid assessments that came due up to the time of transfer of title."[19]

Delinquent assessments bear interest at the rate set forth in the governing documents. If the governing documents are silent, interest accrues at the rate of 18 percent per year.[20] If provided for in the governing documents, the association may charge a late fee "not to exceed the greater of $25 or 5 percent of the amount of each installment that is paid past the due date."[21] Payments accepted by the association are applied first to interest, then to any late fee, then to any costs and reasonable attorney's fees incurred in collection, and then to the delinquent assessment.[22]

5-3   CONDOMINIUM ASSOCIATION FINANCES

5-3:1   Condominium Association Budgets

The annual budget for a condominium association must set forth estimated revenues and expenses. It must detail the amounts budgeted by accounts and specific expense classifications, including, but not limited to, expenses for administration, management fees, maintenance, rent for recreational facilities, taxes upon association property, taxes upon leased areas, insurance, and security.[23]

A multicondominium association must adopt separate budgets for each condominium it operates and a separate common expense budget for the multicondominium association itself. If the association maintains limited common elements, the use and cost of which is limited by the declaration to specific owner classes,

---

17. Fla. Stat. § 720.3085(2)(a) (2016).
18. Fla. Stat. § 720.3085(2)(a) (2016).
19. Fla. Stat. § 720.3085(2)(b) (2016).
20. Fla. Stat. § 720.3085(3) (2016).
21. Fla. Stat. § 720.3085(3)(a) (2016).
22. Fla. Stat. § 720.3085(3)(b) (2016).
23. Fla. Stat. § 718.112(2)(f) (2016).

then the budget must delineate the specific amounts designated for their maintenance.[24]

5-3:2   Condominium Association Reserves

For condominium associations, reserve accounts must be included in the budget pursuant to statute. The Condominium Act requires condominium associations to maintain reserves for capital expenditures and deferred maintenance, which must include, but are not limited to, roof replacement, building painting, pavement resurfacing, and any other item for which the deferred maintenance expense or replacement cost exceeds $10,000.[25]

Reserve funds may be commingled with association operating funds for investment purposes only, but they must be accounted for separately. In addition, for investment purposes only, a multicondominium association may commingle the operating funds and reserve funds of separate condominiums. A commingled account may not contain an amount less than the amount identified as reserve funds.[26]

The amount in the reserve is determined based on the "estimated remaining useful life and estimated replacement cost or deferred maintenance expense" of each item for which the reserve is created. Replacement reserve assessments may be adjusted on an annual basis to account for any changes in estimates of the useful life of a reserve item caused by deferred maintenance.[27]

Condominium association members may by majority vote at a duly called association meeting elect to provide no reserves or less reserves than the Condominium Act requires. In addition, prior to turnover, the developer may vote to waive the reserves or reduce the funding of reserves for two fiscal years after the recording of the certificate of a surveyor and mapper or an instrument that transfers title to a unit which is not accompanied by a recorded assignment of developer rights in favor of the grantee, whichever occurs first. After this period, reserves may be waived or reduced only upon a majority vote of all non-developer voting interests

---

[24.] Fla. Stat. § 718.112(2)(f) (2016).
[25.] Fla. Stat. § 718.112(2)(f) (2016).
[26.] Fla. Stat. § 718.111(14) (2016).
[27.] Fla. Stat. § 718.112(2)(f) (2016).

voting in person or by limited proxy at a duly called meeting. After turnover, the developer may use its voting interests to waive or reduce the funding of reserves.[28]

Reserve funds and any interest shall remain in the reserve account and may only be used for intended purposes. The members may vote to use the reserve funds for other purposes if the use is approved in advance by a majority vote of the members at a duly called meeting of the association. Prior to turnover, the developer-controlled association may not vote to use reserves for unintended purposes without the approval of a majority of all non-developer voting interests, voting in person or by limited proxy at a duly called meeting.[29]

Only voting interests subject to assessments for funding the reserves in question may vote to waive or reduce reserves or use reserves for unintended purposes. Proxy questions submitted for votes to waive or reduce reserves, or use reserves for unintended purposes, must contain the following statement in capitalized, bold letters in a larger font size than any other used on the face of the proxy:

> WAIVING OF RESERVES, IN WHOLE OR IN PART, OR ALLOWING ALTERNATIVE USES OF EXISTING RESERVES MAY RESULT IN UNIT OWNER LIABILITY FOR PAYMENT OF UNANTICIPATED SPECIAL ASSESSMENTS REGARDING THOSE ITEMS.[30]

5-3:3   Condominium Association Assessments

The Condominium Act defines "assessment" as "a share of the funds which are required for the payment of common expenses, which from time to time is assessed against the unit owner."[31] For residential or mixed-use condominiums created after January 1, 1996, each unit's share of the common expenses of the condominium shall be the same as the unit's "appurtenant ownership interest

---

[28] Fla. Stat. § 718.112(2)(f) (2016).
[29] Fla. Stat. § 718.112(2)(f) (2016).
[30] Fla. Stat. § 718.112(2)(f)(4) (2016).
[31] Fla. Stat. § 718.103(1) (2016).

in the common elements."[32] Common expenses are defined by statute to include expenses incurred in the

> operation, maintenance, repair, replacement, or protection of the common elements and association property ... and any other expense ... designated as common expense by this chapter, the declaration, the documents creating the association, or the bylaws.[33]

A "special assessment" is "any assessment levied against a unit owner other than the assessment required by a budget adopted annually."[34] The association must deliver a written notice to each owner of the specific purpose of any special assessment approved in accordance with the governing documents. The association may only use the special assessments for the specific purpose set forth in the notice. Any excess funds available upon completion of the specific purpose of the special assessment, however, are common surplus that may be returned to the unit owners or applied as a credit toward future assessments.[35]

The condominium association's bylaws must provide for the manner of collecting assessments from unit owners. The association shall levy assessments at least quarterly to pay in advance for "all of the anticipated current operating expenses and for all of the unpaid operating expenses previously incurred."[36] A unit owner may not be excused from payment of assessments "unless all other unit owners are likewise proportionately excluded from payment."[37]

5-4 FINANCIAL REPORTING

Homeowners' associations and condominium associations are subject to similar financial reporting requirements. Both Chapter 720 and the Condominium Act impose strict guidelines to ensure financial transparency for the protection of the owners. The association must complete a financial report every year within

---

[32.] Fla. Stat. § 718.115(2) (2016).
[33.] Fla. Stat. § 718.115(1)(a) (2016).
[34.] Fla. Stat. § 718.103(24) (2016).
[35.] Fla. Stat. § 718.116(10) (2016).
[36.] Fla. Stat. § 718.112(2)(g) (2016).
[37.] Fla. Stat. § 718.116(9)(a) (2016).

90 days after the end of the fiscal year or annually on the date provided in the bylaws. The association must provide the members with a copy of the financial report, or written notice that a copy of the financial report is available upon request at no charge, within 21 days after the final financial report is completed. The copy of the financial report or written notice of its availability must be provided to the members no later than 120 days after the end of the fiscal year or such other date as the bylaws provide.[38]

Depending on the association's total annual reserves, it may have to prepare compiled financial statements, reviewed financial statements, or audited financial statements. The financial statements must be prepared in accordance with generally accepted accounting principles.[39]

If a homeowner's association has less than $150,000 in annual revenues, it must prepare a report of cash receipts and expenditures.[40] If a condominium association has less than $150,000 in annual revenues, it shall prepare a report of cash receipts and expenditures.[41] If a homeowners' association has fewer than 50 parcels, it may prepare a report of cash receipts and expenditures unless the governing documents require a financial statement.[42] A condominium association with fewer than 50 units, regardless of annual revenues, must prepare a report of cash receipts and expenditures.[43] A report of cash receipts and disbursements must disclose the amount of receipts and expenses by accounts and classifications. For instance, the report must disclose taxes; reserves; costs for security, management, recreation facilities, building maintenance, and insurance; and expenses for landscaping, refuse collection, and salaries.[44]

By submitting to the board a petition of 20 percent of the owners, homeowners' association members may request a higher level of financial reporting than is statutorily required. Within 30 days of receipt of the petition, the board must notice and hold a

---

[38] Fla. Stat. § 720.303(7) (2016); Fla. Stat. § 718.111(13) (2016).
[39] Fla. Stat. § 720.303(7)(a) (2016); Fla. Stat. § 718.111(13)(a) (2016).
[40] Fla. Stat. § 720.303(7)(b) (2016).
[41] Fla. Stat. § 718.111(13)(b) (2016).
[42] Fla. Stat. § 720.303(7)(b) (2016).
[43] Fla. Stat. § 718.111(13)(b) (2016).
[44] Fla. Stat. § 720.303(7)(b) (2016); Fla. Stat. § 718.111(13)(b) (2016).

members meeting to vote on increasing that year's reporting level. If a majority of the total voting interests approve, the association must amend the budget or adopt a special assessment to pay for the increased level of financial reporting regardless of any contrary provision in the governing documents. Within 90 days of the meeting, or the end of the fiscal year, whichever occurs later, the association must provide (1) compiled, reviewed, or audited financial statements, if the association is otherwise required to prepare a report of cash receipts and expenditures; (2) reviewed or audited financial statements, if the association is otherwise required to prepare compiled financial statements; or (3) audited financial statements if the association is otherwise required to prepare reviewed financial statements.[45] A condominium association also may prepare a higher-level financial report without owner approval.[46]

The members of both homeowners' and condominium associations may also approve by a majority of the voting interests at a duly noticed meeting a lower level of financial reporting.[47] The Condominium Act restricts unit owners' ability to vote for lower-level financial reporting in the following ways. The meeting held to vote for lower-level reporting must occur before the end of the fiscal year. In addition, the resolution is only effective for the fiscal year in which the vote is taken, unless approval is made for the following fiscal year as well. A condominium association may not waive financial reporting requirements for more than three consecutive years. Before turnover, all unit owners, including the developer, may vote on issues related to the preparation of financial reports for the first two fiscal years following the recording of the certificate of a

---

[45] Fla. Stat. § 720.303(7)(c) (2016).

[46] Fla. Stat. § 718.111(13)(c) (2016) (associations required to prepare a report of cash receipts and expenditures may prepare compiled, reviewed, or audited financial statements; associations required to prepare compiled financial statements may prepare reviewed or audited financial statements; associations required to prepare reviewed financial statements may prepare audited financial statements).

[47] Fla. Stat. § 720.303(7)(d) (2016); Fla. Stat. § 718.111(14)(d) (2016) (under these respective subsections, a homeowners' or condominium association may prepare (1) a report of cash receipts and expenditures instead of a compiled, reviewed, or audited financial statement; (2) a report of cash receipts and expenditures or a compiled financial statement instead of a reviewed or audited financial statement; or (3) a report of cash receipts and expenditures, a compiled financial statement, or a reviewed financial statement instead of an audited financial statement).

surveyor and mapper or an instrument that transfers title to a unit which is not accompanied by a recorded assignment of developer rights in favor of the grantee, whichever occurs first, after which the developer may not vote on such issues until turnover. Before turnover, the developer pays for any audit or review.[48]

5-5   COMMON PROPERTY MAINTENANCE, REPLACEMENT, AND IMPROVEMENT

5-5:1   Homeowners' Association Common Areas

Generally, in homeowners' associations the members own their parcels and the association owns the common areas,[49] which the association maintains and operates for use by the homeowners. Common area rights and privileges are generally part of the purchase of a home within the community.[50] Common areas in homeowners' associations are defined as "real property within a community which is owned or leased by an association or dedicated for use or maintenance by the association or its members."[51]

Chapter 720 discusses homeowners' associations' authority to acquire leaseholds, memberships, and other possessory or use interests in lands or facilities. A homeowners association can acquire an interest in country clubs, golf courses, marinas, submerged land, parking areas, conservation areas, and other recreational facilities. If more than 12 months have passed since the declaration's recording, any agreement to acquire leaseholds, memberships, and other possessory or use interests must be authorized by the declaration as a material alteration or substantial addition to the common areas or association property. If the declaration does not address the association's authority to enter into this type of transaction, 75 percent of the total voting interests must approve. The declaration may delineate as common expenses those costs related to the association's possessory or use interests. The

---

[48.] Fla. Stat. § 718.111(13)(d) (2016).

[49.] *Florida Farm, LLC v. 360 Developers*, 45 So. 3d 810, 815 (Fla. 3d Dist. Ct. App. 2010) ("Homeowners' associations differ from condominium associations in that homeowners' associations own the common property used by the property owners, whereas condominium associations do not own any real property.").

[50.] *Savanna Club Worship Serv., Inc. v. Savanna Club Homeowners' Ass'n*, 456 F. Supp. 2d 1223, 1229-30 (S.D. Fla. 2005).

[51.] Fla. Stat. § 720.301(2) (2016).

association may also impose covenants and restrictions concerning use of the lands or facilities.[52]

5-5:2   Condominium Association Common Elements

In condominiums, the unit owners own an undivided share of the common elements, which include condominium property not included in the units; easements through units for wiring, ducts, plumbing, and other facilities for utilities; an easement of support in every portion of the unit which contributes to support of the condominium building; and all property and installations required to furnish utilities and other services to more than one unit or to the common elements.[53] The declaration may also designate other parts of the condominium as common elements.[54]

An undivided share in the common elements passes with title to the unit.[55] This is what distinguishes the condominium form of ownership. While units themselves are subject to exclusive ownership,[56] they are just one part of the condominium parcel, which includes both the unit and an undivided share in the common elements.[57] The common elements are by definition "those portions of the condominium property not included in the units."[58] The unit, by definition, is "subject to exclusive ownership," and "may be in improvements, land, or land and improvements together, as specified in the declaration."[59]

The condominium may also include limited common elements, which are portions of the common elements that are intended for specific unit owners' exclusive use. This may include elements like lanais and patios connected to a unit. Courts will look to the condominium documents for the definition of the unit boundaries in determining what elements of the condominium property constitute the unit, the common elements, and the limited common elements.

---

52. Fla. Stat. § 720.31(6) (2016).
53. Fla. Stat. § 718.108(1) (2016).
54. Fla. Stat. § 718.108(2) (2016).
55. Fla. Stat. § 718.106(2) (2016).
56. Fla. Stat. § 718.103(27) (2016).
57. Fla. Stat. § 718.103(12) (2016).
58. Fla. Stat. § 718.103(8) (2016).
59. Fla. Stat. § 718.103(27) (2016).

The following is an example of a typical description of unit boundaries found in a declaration of condominium:

> Unit Boundaries. Each unit shall include that part of the building that lies within the following boundaries: (A) Upper and Lower Boundaries. The upper and lower boundaries of the unit shall be the following boundaries extended to their intersections with the perimeter boundaries: (1) Upper Boundaries. The horizontal plane of the unfinished lower surface of the ceiling of the unit. (2) Lower Boundaries. The horizontal plane of the unfinished upper surface of the concrete floor of the unit. (B) Perimeter Boundaries. The perimeter boundaries of the unit shall be the vertical planes of the unfinished interior surfaces of the walls bounding the unit as shown in the survey and plot plan incorporated by reference herein, extended to the intersections with each other and with the upper and lower boundaries.

Condominium documents are subject to basic rules of interpretation. Words of common usage in the declaration, such as the description of the unit boundaries above, are construed in their ordinary sense.[60] Moreover, the parol evidence rule applies, dictating that "the terms of a valid written contract or instrument cannot be varied by a verbal agreement or other extrinsic evidence" and prohibiting the use of parol evidence "to contradict, vary, defeat, or modify a complete and unambiguous written instrument" or "to charge, add to, or subtract from it, or affect its construction."[61]

The condominium association is responsible for the operation of the common elements.[62] While owners typically may not improve condominium property outside of their units, they also are not obligated to maintain the common elements. The association is authorized to maintain the condominium's aesthetics, including the building exterior, and is protected by the "business judgment rule," which shields it from liability as long as it acts in a reasonable

---

[60.] *Koplowitz v. Imperial Towers Condo.*, 478 So. 2d 504 (Fla. 4th Dist. Ct. App. 1985).

[61.] *J. M. Montgomery Roofing Co. v. Fred Howland*, 98 So. 2d 484, 485-86 (Fla. 1957).

[62.] Fla. Stat. § 718.103(2) (2016).

manner.[63] Therefore, if "in [its] good business judgment" an association determines that an alteration or improvement is "necessary or beneficial" to maintain, repair, or replace common elements, "all unit owners should equally bear the cost as provided in the declaration, by-laws and statutes."[64]

Common elements are different than "association property," which is real or personal property "owned or leased by, or … dedicated by a recorded plat to, the association for the use and benefit of its members."[65] The association may acquire title to property or hold, convey, lease, and mortgage association property for the members' use and benefit. The association can only acquire, convey, lease, or mortgage association real property in the manner provided in the declaration. If the declaration does not specify the procedure, then the association must obtain approval of 75 percent of the total voting interests.[66]

The association has the power to lease common elements or association property. The association may not, however, charge unit owners use fees for the use of common elements or association property unless otherwise provided for in the declaration or unless approved by a majority vote of the owners, unless the charges relate to expenses incurred by an owner having exclusive use of the common elements or association property.[67]

Unit owners are entitled to exclusive possession of their unit, and use of the common elements in accordance with their intended purposes. A unit owner's use of the common elements may not infringe on other unit owners' lawful rights.[68] Tenants also have full use rights in the common elements. Generally, when a unit is leased, the tenant takes on the owner's use rights, and the owner takes on the use rights of a guest. The Condominium Act permits association rules that specifically prohibit owner-tenant dual usage of association property and common elements. This does not prohibit a unit owner from exercising his or her right to access the

---

[63.] *Farrington v. Casa Solana Condo. Ass'n*, 517 So. 2d 70 (Fla. 3d Dist. Ct. App. 1987).
[64.] *Tiffany Plaza Condo. v. Spencer*, 416 So. 2d 823, 826 (Fla. 2d Dist. Ct. App. 1982).
[65.] Fla. Stat. § 718.103(3) (2016).
[66.] Fla. Stat. § 718.111(7) (2016).
[67.] Fla. Stat. § 718.111(4) (2016).
[68.] Fla. Stat. § 718.106(3) (2016).

unit as a landlord as provided by the Florida Residential Landlord and Tenant Act.[69]

A unit owner's undivided share in the common elements may not be separated from the unit. The undivided share passes with title to the unit. The owner's share in the common elements can only be conveyed or encumbered with the owner's unit and must remain undivided. A party may not file a court action to divide the common elements.[70] A condominium association, however, has limited power to convey the common elements. For condominiums created on or after October 1, 1994, the bylaws must include a provision granting the association a limited power to convey a portion of the common elements to condemning authorities for utility easements, right-of-way expansions, or other public purposes. If the bylaws are silent on this issue, they are deemed to include this limited power to convey.[71]

The condominium association is obligated to maintain the common elements, with the exception of limited common elements used by specific owners whom the governing documents obligate to maintain such elements.[72] Unit owners may not do anything to adversely affect the safety or soundness of the common elements or any portion of association maintained property.[73] The association is also authorized to improve the common elements. Any material alterations or substantial additions to the common elements must be made in accordance with the declaration. If the declaration is silent as to material alteration or substantial addition approval procedures, then the association must obtain approval of 75 percent of the total voting interests.[74]

For multicondominium associations, material alterations or substantial additions to the common elements require approval in compliance with the affected condominium or condominiums' declaration. If the declaration is silent, material alterations or substantial additions to the common elements require approval of 75 percent of the total voting interests of each affected

---

[69.] Fla. Stat. § 718.106(4) (2016); Fla. Stat. § 83.001 et seq. (2016).

[70.] Fla. Stat. § 718.107 (2016).

[71.] Fla. Stat. § 718.112(2)(m) (2016).

[72.] Fla. Stat. § 718.113(1) (2016).

[73.] Fla. Stat. § 718.113(3) (2016).

[74.] Fla. Stat. § 718.113(2)(a) (2016).

condominium. This rule does not prohibit governing document provisions granting unit owners in any condominium operated by the same association, or the board, the right to approve material alterations or substantial additions to the common elements.[75]

The board must adopt hurricane shutter specifications for the condominium building. This includes specifications for color, style, and any other relevant factors. Hurricane shutter specifications must comply with all applicable building codes. The board may not refuse to approve hurricane shutter installation or replacement by a unit owner that conforms to board-adopted specifications, even if the documents require approval.[76]

If it receives majority voting interest approval, the association may install hurricane shutters, impact glass or other code-compliant windows, or hurricane protection that complies with or exceeds the applicable building code. Installation of hurricane shutters is not a material alteration of the common elements requiring approval of 75 percent of the owners. An owner vote is not required at all if maintenance, repair, and replacement of hurricane shutters, impact glass, or other code-compliant windows are the association's responsibility pursuant to the declaration. If hurricane protection was already installed, the board may not install hurricane shutters, impact glass, or other hurricane protection without approval by a majority of the voting interests.[77]

The declaration determines whether hurricane protection maintenance is the association or the owner's responsibility. If necessary to protect the condominium property, the association may operate hurricane shutters installed by the association without permission of the unit owners.[78]

A condominium association may not refuse a unit owner's request to attach a religious object not to exceed 3 inches wide, 6 inches high, and 1.5 inches deep on the unit owner's door frame or mantel.[79] In addition, regardless of the governing documents, the board of directors may, without unit owner approval, install

---

[75] Fla. Stat. § 718.113(2)(b) (2016).
[76] Fla. Stat. § 718.113(5) (2016).
[77] Fla. Stat. § 718.113(5) (2016).
[78] Fla. Stat. § 718.113(5) (2016).
[79] Fla. Stat. § 718.113(6) (2016).

on the common elements or association property solar collectors, clotheslines, or other energy-efficient devices based on renewable resources for the benefit of the unit owners.[80]

Condominium associations can purchase any land or recreation lease subject to the same manner of approval for the acquisition of leaseholds discussed below.[81] Unless prohibited by the governing documents, condominium associations can also purchase condominium units and lease, mortgage, and convey them. There is no limitation on the association's right to purchase a unit at a foreclosure sale when the association forecloses a lien for unpaid assessments, or its right to take title by deed in lieu of foreclosure.[82]

Unless prohibited by the declaration, the board of directors can grant, modify, or move any easement that is part of or crosses the common elements or association property. The association cannot, however, modify or vacate easements created for the use or benefit of anyone who is not a unit owner, or crossing the property of anyone who is not a unit owner, without the consent or approval of those other persons, as required by law or the easement instrument.[83]

A condominium association may acquire leaseholds, memberships, and other possessory or use interests in lands or facilities such as country clubs, golf courses, marinas, and other recreational facilities to provide recreation or other use or benefit to the unit owners. If more than 12 months have passed since the recording of a certificate of a surveyor and mapper or the recording of an instrument that transfers title to a unit which is not accompanied by a recorded assignment of developer rights in favor of the grantee, any agreement to acquire leaseholds, memberships, and other possessory or use interests in lands or facilities is considered a material alteration or substantial addition to association property. This requires the vote of, or written consent by, a majority of the total voting interests or declaration sanctioned authorization. The declaration may designate associated fees as common expenses.

[80.] Fla. Stat. § 718.113(7) (2016).
[81.] Fla. Stat. § 718.111(8) (2016).
[82.] Fla. Stat. § 718.111(9) (2016).
[83.] Fla. Stat. § 718.111(10) (2016).

The association may also impose covenants and restrictions concerning facility use.[84]

5-5:3   Limited Common Elements

Under the Condominium Act, condominium declarations may designate portions of the common elements, known as limited common elements, for particular unit owners' exclusive use. Limited common elements usually consist of parking spaces, balconies, patios or other such property which the unit owners use individually but in which they share a common interest in maintaining. For instance, to ensure the uniform quality of appearance of all the exterior balconies, they might be designated as limited common elements for the exclusive use of the unit owner but subject to maintenance by all the unit owners through the condominium association. Usually, however, every unit owner has the exclusive use of a similar item. If this were not the case, unit owners without balconies would be unjustly obligated help to pay for the maintenance of a balconies used exclusively by other unit owners.

Exclusive rights in the declaration to use limited common elements pass with title to the unit. This includes the right to transfer exclusive use rights to other units or unit owners if authorized by the declaration. A condominium declaration may be amended to provide for the transfer of limited common element use rights.[85] This type of amendment does not materially modify unit appurtenances, which would require approval of all unit owners and record owners of liens on the units.[86] The transfer of limited common element use rights must be made in accordance with the declaration's procedures.[87]

The Act's definition of "limited common elements" implies that they are a subset of "common elements" and therefore a "common expense" properly within the scope of the association's authority.[88] The declaration, however, may provide that unit owners with rights to use the limited common elements are the only owners

---

[84.] Fla. Stat. § 718.114 (2016).

[85.] Fla. Stat. § 718.106(2) (2016).

[86.] Fla. Stat. § 718.110(4) (2016).

[87.] Fla. Stat. § 718.106(2) (2016).

[88.] *Cedar Cove Efficiency Condo. Ass'n v. Cedar Cove Props.*, 558 So. 2d 475, 479 (Fla. 5th Dist. Ct. App. 1990).

obligated to maintain them. Alternatively, the declaration may obligate the association to maintain the limited common elements as a cost shared only by those entitled to use the limited common elements. If the association provides maintenance of limited common elements as a cost shared only by those entitled to use the limited common elements, then the declaration must describe the method of apportioning the costs among users. The association may enforce payment with all its lien and collection rights.[89]

The association is also empowered to regulate common element and limited common element use, so long as the association's regulation is reasonable and does not violate the governing documents. The reasonableness of the association's common element regulation is assessed on a case-by-case basis, examining all the facts of a given set of circumstances. In general, associations may exercise their broad statutory and contractual authority to regulate common element and limited common element use, provided they exercise such power in a manner that is "reasonable," "not violative of any constitutional restrictions," and does "not exceed any specific limitations set out in the statutes or condominium documents."[90]

5-6   THE CONDOMINIUM ACT AND INSURANCE

Unlike Chapter 720, the Condominium Act provides extensive guidelines for insurance. In providing uniform regulation of

---

[89]. Fla. Stat. § 718.113(1) (2016).

[90]. *Juno By The Sea N. Condo. Ass'n v. Manfredonia*, 397 So. 2d 297, 302-304 (Fla. 4th Dist. Ct. App. 1980) (assessing the reasonableness of regulations related to a parking scheme with limited common elements (garage parking spaces) and regular common elements (an outdoor parking lot); the plan required all owners to share equally in the maintenance costs for both garage and outdoor parking, despite the fact that garage parkers paid a premium in advance for their spaces and were prohibited from using the common elements (outdoor parking) to which all owners were ostensibly entitled; the court held that the rules were entirely reasonable because (1) the detriment to outdoor parkers (the cost of maintaining garage parking from which they were prohibited) was offset by the benefit they received (exclusive use of outdoor parking), and (2) the detriment to garage parkers (the cost of maintaining the outdoor parking from which they were prohibited) was offset by the benefit they received (exclusive use of garage parking); the court held that the association exercised its broad statutory and contractual authority to regulate common element and limited common element use in a manner that was "reasonable," "not violative of any constitutional restrictions," and did "not exceed any specific limitations set out in the statutes or condominium documents"; under the circumstances, the court held that the condominium association's plan made good sense, and was the only reasonable alternative).

condominium insurance, the Florida Legislature's express intent is "to protect the safety, health, and welfare of the people of the State of Florida," "to ensure consistency in the provision of insurance coverage to condominiums and their unit owners," and to "encourage lower or stable insurance premiums for associations."[91]

5-6:1   Condominium Property Insurance Coverage

Condominium property insurance policies must provide primary coverage for condominium property as originally installed or replacement of like kind and quality, and all alterations or additions made to condominium property in accordance with the Condominium Act and the association's governing documents. The coverage must exclude owners' personal property within the unit or limited common elements; floor, wall, and ceiling coverings; electrical fixtures; appliances; water heaters; water filters; built-in cabinets and countertops; and window treatments. Personal property and any insurance on it is the owner's responsibility.[92]

Items such as Jacuzzis, trellises, and screen enclosures that are purchased, installed, removable, and usable only by individual unit owners are not condominium property that the association must insure. Indeed, the law does not require association members to take responsibility for insuring property "which they do not and cannot use, and from which they derive no benefit ... [and] have no insurable interest ... even permit[ing] their maintenance of valid insurance."[93] An item's location outside a unit, rather than inside, does not automatically delineate it as condominium property for which all owners are obligated to pay for insurance.[94]

Condominium associations must obtain adequate property insurance based on the replacement cost of the insured property, as determined by an independent insurance appraisal which must be

---

[91] Fla. Stat. § 718.111(11) (2016).

[92] Fla. Stat. § 718.111(11)(f) (2016).

[93] *Costa Del Sol Ass'n v. State, Dep't of Bus. & Prof'l Regulation, Div. of Florida Land Sales, Condos., & Mobile Homes*, 987 So. 2d 734, 736 (Fla. 3d Dist. Ct. App. 2008) (holding that items on condominium patios are not deemed condominium property that the association must insure simply because they are outside units, rather than inside units, since there is no basis in law for a strict inside-outside distinction to determine ownership of items on condominium property).

[94] *Costa Del Sol Ass'n v. State, Dep't of Bus. & Prof'l Regulation, Div. of Florida Land Sales, Condos., & Mobile Homes*, 987 So. 2d 734, 736 (Fla. 3d Dist. Ct. App. 2008).

updated at least once every 36 months.[95] In determining the adequate amount of coverage, the association may consider deductibles,[96] provided they are "consistent with industry standards and prevailing practice" for communities of similar size, age, construction, facilities, and location.[97] Deductibles may be based on available funds, including reserve accounts, or predetermined assessment authority.[98]

5-6:2   Failure to Maintain Condominium Property Insurance

Before turnover, failure to maintain adequate property insurance is a breach of the developer-appointed board members' fiduciary duty, unless the members can show that they made their best efforts to maintain required coverage.[99] After turnover, owner-controlled residential condominium associations must use their best efforts to obtain and maintain adequate property insurance to protect the association, association property, common elements, and the condominium property.[100] A condominium association may provide property insurance through a self-insurance fund pursuant to Florida's Commercial Self-Insurance Fund Act.[101]

5-6:3   Other Types of Condominium Association Insurance

Condominium associations may also obtain liability insurance for directors and officers, insurance for the benefit of association employees, and flood insurance for the common elements, association property, and units.[102] The association must maintain insurance or fidelity bonding for anyone with the authority to control or disburse association funds, including individuals authorized to sign checks on behalf of the association, as well as the president, secretary, and treasurer. This must cover the maximum funds that will be in the custody of the association

---

[95.] Fla. Stat. § 718.111(11)(a) (2016).
[96.] Fla. Stat. § 718.111(11)(a) (2016).
[97.] Fla. Stat. § 718.111(11)(c)(1) (2016).
[98.] Fla. Stat. § 718.111(11)(c)(2) (2016).
[99.] Fla. Stat. § 718.111(11)(b) (2016).
[100.] Fla. Stat. § 718.111(11)(d) (2016).
[101.] Fla. Stat. § 718.111(11) (a) (2016).
[102.] Fla. Stat. § 718.111(11)(e) (2016).

or its management agent at any one time. The association bears the cost of any such bonding.[103] The Homeowners' Association Act includes a parallel requirement; however, the Homeowners' Association Act allows the membership to waive this requirement if annually approved by a majority of the voting interests.[104] The Condominium Act does not allow waiver.

5-6:4 Condominium Owners' Residential Property Insurance

A condominium unit owner's residential property policy must conform to section 627.714's requirements.[105] For policies issued or renewed on or after July 1, 2010, this requires at least $2,000 in property loss assessment coverage for all assessments made as a result of the same direct loss to common elements if the loss is covered by the unit owner's residential property insurance policy, to which a deductible of no more than $250 per direct property loss applies. If a deductible is applied to other property loss sustained by the unit owner resulting from the same direct loss to the property, no deductible applies to the loss assessment coverage. The coverage afforded by this policy is excess over the amount recoverable under any other policy covering the same property.[106]

5-6:5 Reconstruction Work After Property Loss

All reconstruction work after a property loss is the association's responsibility. A unit owner may perform reconstruction on their unit with the board's written consent, which may be conditioned upon repair method approval, contractor qualifications, and the construction contract. Before commencing construction, the unit owner is required to obtain all appropriate permits.[107]

Unit owners are responsible for the reconstruction costs of any portions of the condominium property for which they are required to carry property insurance. The cost of any reconstruction work

---

[103.] Fla. Stat. § 718.111(11)(h) (2016).
[104.] Fla. Stat. § 720.3033(5) (2016).
[105.] Fla. Stat. § 718.111(11)(g) (2016); Fla. Stat. § 627.714 (2016).
[106.] Fla. Stat. § 627.714(12) (2016).
[107.] Fla. Stat. § 718.111(11)(g) (2016).

undertaken by the association on any portion of the condominium property for which the unit owner is required to carry property insurance is chargeable to the unit owner and enforceable with all of the association's lien rights.[108]

The association must reconstruct, repair, or replace as necessary portions of damaged condominium property that it is obligated to insure. The owners share the cost of such reconstruction as a common expense. Deductibles, uninsured losses, and any damage in excess of coverage are a common expense of the association.[109]

Unit owners are responsible for the costs of repair or replacement of the condominium property not paid for by insurance proceeds if the damage is caused by the owners' intentional conduct, negligence, or failure to comply with the terms of the declaration or the rules and regulations. This includes damage caused by owners' family members, unit occupants, tenants, guests, or invitees. The insurer retains all subrogation rights. This rule also applies to the costs of repairing or replacing other unit owners' or the association's property, as well any other real or personal property which the unit owners are required to insure.[110]

With majority approval of the association's total voting interests, an association may opt out of Condominium Act provisions for the allocation of repair or reconstruction expenses, and may instead allocate repair or reconstruction expenses in the manner provided in the declaration. The consent of any mortgagees is not required.[111] An association that opts out of the Condominium Act's guidelines for repair or reconstruction expenses must record a notice setting forth the opt-out vote date and the page of the official records book on which the declaration is recorded. The decision to opt out is effective upon the date of recording. An "opt out" association may also reverse that decision with approval of a majority of the total voting interests without consent of any mortgagees. Notice thereof must be recorded in the official records.[112]

[108.] Fla. Stat. § 718.111(11)(g) (2016).
[109.] Fla. Stat. § 718.111(11)(j) (2016).
[110.] Fla. Stat. § 718.111(11)(j) (2016).
[111.] Fla. Stat. § 718.111(11)(k) (2016).
[112.] Fla. Stat. § 718.111(11)(m) (2016).

If the cost of repair or reconstruction for which the unit owner is responsible is reimbursed to the association by insurance proceeds, the association must reimburse the unit owner for any payments made. The association is not obligated to pay for reconstruction or repairs of property losses if the unit owner knew or should have known about the losses and did not report them to the association until after the association's insurance claim was settled, resolved, or denied for untimely filing. With respect to all of the foregoing, the insurer retains all subrogation rights.[113]

The association is not obligated to pay for reconstruction or repair of any improvements if the improvement benefits only a single unit and is not part of the standard improvements installed by the developer on all units during original construction, whether or not the improvement is located within the unit. This provision "does not relieve any party of its obligations regarding recovery due under any insurance implemented specifically for such improvements," including the association's obligation to reimburse the unit owner for any payments made if the cost of repair or reconstruction for which the unit owner is responsible is reimbursed to the association by insurance proceeds.[114]

5-6:6   Multicondominium Associations

By a majority vote of members of the individual condominiums in a multicondominium association, the association may operate the condominiums as a single condominium for insurance matters, including purchasing property insurance and apportionment of deductibles and damages in excess of coverage. The costs of insurance must be stated in the association budget. The decision to operate as a single condominium for insurance matters constitutes an amendment to the declaration of all condominiums in the multicondominium association, and the amendments must be recorded in the public records of the county where the declaration is recorded.[115] The association may amend the declaration of condominium so that it conforms to

---

[113.] Fla. Stat. § 718.111(11)(j) (2016).
[114.] Fla. Stat. § 718.111(11)(n) (2016).
[115.] Fla. Stat. § 718.111(11)(g) (2016).

the Condominium Act's coverage requirements without approval by mortgagees.[116]

5-7   OFFICIAL RECORDS

5-7:1   Homeowners' Association Official Records

Community associations must maintain their official records and make them available for inspection by the owners. For homeowners' associations this includes copies of any plans, specifications, permits, and warranties related to association property; a copy of the governing documents and the amendments thereto; a copy of the current rules and regulations; the minutes of all board and member meetings; a current roster of all members, including their mailing addresses, parcel identifications, and email addresses if the owners consented to notice by electronic transmission; the association's insurance policies; a copy of all contracts to which the association is a party; bids received by the association for work to be performed; the financial and accounting records; a copy of the section 720.401(1) disclosure; and "all other written records of the association not specifically included in the foregoing which are related to the operation of the association."[117]

The meeting minutes and insurance policies must be retained for at least seven years. Work bids received by the association must be kept for one year. If the owners revoke their consent to receive notices by electronic transmission, unit owners' email addresses and numbers must be removed from the official records. The association is not liable for any erroneous information disclosure.[118]

The association must keep all financial and accounting records in accordance with good accounting practices. The financial and accounting records include "accurate, itemized, and detailed" records of all receipts and expenditures; a current account and a periodic statement of the account for each member, including the name and address of each member who is obligated to pay assessments, the due date and amount of each assessment or other charge, the date and amount of each payment, and the balance due;

[116.] Fla. Stat. § 718.111(11)(i) (2016).
[117.] Fla. Stat. § 720.303(4) (2016).
[118.] Fla. Stat. § 720.303(4) (2016).

all tax returns, financial statements, and financial reports; and any other financial records. The financial records must be maintained for at least seven years.[119]

A homeowners' association's official records must be maintained in Florida and open to members or their authorized agents for inspection and photocopying. Members must request in writing access to inspect and copy records. The association must provide access to the member within 45 miles of the community or within the county in which the association is located within 10 business days after receipt of the written request.[120]

Failure to provide access to the records within 10 business days after receipt of a written request by certified mail, return receipt requested, creates a rebuttable presumption that the association willfully failed to comply.[121] If the association willfully denies access to the official records, it is liable for any actual damages that a member incurs as a result. Alternatively, the association is liable for minimum damages of $50 per calendar day up to ten days. The calculation of minimum damages begins on the eleventh business day after receipt of the written request.[122]

The association may adopt reasonable written rules governing the frequency, time, location, notice, and manner of inspections. The association may not, however, require a parcel owner to demonstrate a proper purpose for the inspection, state any reason for the inspection, or limit a parcel owner's right to inspect records to less than one eight hour business day per month.[123]

If the association has a photocopier available at the location where the records are maintained, it must provide the owner with up to 25 pages of copies on request during the inspection. The association must allow an owner to use a portable device to scan or take photographs of official records in lieu of the association providing copies.[124] The association may impose fees to cover the costs of providing copies. The association may charge up to 25 cents per page for copies made on the association's photocopier.

---

[119] Fla. Stat. § 720.303(4) (2016).
[120] Fla. Stat. § 720.303(5) (2016).
[121] Fla. Stat. § 720.303(5)(a) (2016).
[122] Fla. Stat. § 720.303(5)(b) (2016).
[123] Fla. Stat. § 720.303(5)(c) (2016).
[124] Fla. Stat. § 720.303(5) (2016).

If the association does not have a photocopier available, or if the requested copies exceed 25 pages in length, the association may use an outside vendor or association management company personnel. In this case, the association may charge the actual cost of copying, if the time spent to retrieve and copy the records exceeds one-half hour and if the personnel costs do not exceed $20 per hour. The association must maintain enough copies of the governing documents to ensure they are available to members and prospective members.[125]

Certain records are not accessible to owners, including documentation typically deemed privileged and confidential. This includes documents protected by the attorney-client privilege and the work-product doctrine.[126] The attorney-client privilege extends to any communication between a lawyer and a client that "is not intended to be disclosed to third persons."[127] This is subject to certain exceptions enumerated in section 90.502.[128] Work-product privileged documents include, but are not limited to, records prepared by an association attorney which reflect mental impressions, conclusions, litigation strategies, or legal theories. To benefit from protection under this doctrine, the records must have been prepared for, or in anticipation of, litigation or adversarial administrative proceedings.[129]

The association must keep confidential the following information and documentation and refuse to allow inspection and copying by association members: information obtained in connection with the approval of a lease, sale, or other transfer; personnel records of the association's employees, including disciplinary, payroll, health, and insurance records; medical records of owners or residents; social security numbers; driver license numbers; credit card numbers; email addresses; telephone numbers; facsimile numbers; emergency contact information; addresses other than those provided for association notice requirements; and other personal information, excluding names, parcel designations, mailing addresses, and

---

[125.] Fla. Stat. § 720.303(5)(c) (2016).
[126.] Fla. Stat. § 720.303(5)(c) (2016).
[127.] Fla. Stat. § 90.502(1)(c) (2016).
[128.] Fla. Stat. § 90.502 (2016).
[129.] Fla. Stat. § 720.303(5)(c) (2016).

property addresses. Notwithstanding the restrictions, the association may print and distribute to owners a directory of owners' contact information. However, an owner may exclude his or her telephone number by written request. The association must also implement electronic security measures, including computer passwords. The association need not provide access to software used by the association to organize and manage data.[130]

Protected personnel records do not include employment contracts and financial records that indicate employee compensation. An owner may consent in writing to disclosure of their personal identifying information. The association is not liable for disclosing owners' personal identifying information if the owner voluntarily provided it, it was included in an official association record, and if the association did not request it.[131]

The association must provide prospective purchasers and lienholders access to any official records that it is required to disclose to owners. Unless it is required by law to provide the information, the association may charge a reasonable fee to the prospective purchaser or lienholder, or the current parcel owner or member, for providing good faith responses to information requests. In no event, however, may the association charge more than $150 plus the reasonable cost of photocopying and any attorney's fees incurred by the association in connection with the response.[132]

5-7:2   Condominium Association Official Records

The Condominium Act requires associations to maintain their official records in Florida for at least seven years. This includes the following: a copy of the plans, permits, warranties, and other items provided by the developer; a photocopy of the recorded declaration, bylaws, and amendments thereto; a certified copy of the articles of incorporation and amendments thereto; a copy of the rules and regulations; a book of meeting minutes; a current list of unit owners, including their addresses, unit identifications, voting certifications, and, if known, telephone numbers; all current insurance policies; a current copy of any management agreement,

---

130. Fla. Stat. § 720.303(5)(c) (2016).
131. Fla. Stat. § 720.303(5)(c) (2016).
132. Fla. Stat. § 720.303(5)(d) (2016).

lease, or other contract to which the association is a party; bills of sale or transfer for all association property; accounting records; ballots, sign-in sheets, voting proxies, and all other papers relating to voting; all rental records if the association is acting as rental agent for condominium units; a copy of the current question and answer sheet as described in section 718.504; a copy of the turnover inspection report; and all other records which are related to the operation of the association. Papers relating to voting by unit owners, including ballots and voting proxies, need only be maintained for one year from the date of the election, vote, or meeting to which the document relates.[133]

The accounting records must include, but are not limited to, accurate, itemized, and detailed records of all receipts and expenditures; a current account and a monthly, bimonthly, or quarterly statement of the account for each unit stating the name of the unit owner, the due date and amount of each assessment, the amount paid on the account, and the balance due; all audits, reviews, accounting statements, and financial reports; and all bids and contracts for work to be performed. The Condominium Act imposes a civil penalty on any person who knowingly or intentionally defaces or destroys the accounting records, or who knowingly or intentionally fails to create or maintain the accounting records, with the intent of causing harm to the association or its members.[134] Undifferentiated summary records of unit owner accounts do not satisfy the statutory requirements[135] because the purpose of the statute is "to ensure that condominium associations maintain readily understood and accessible accounting records with respect to individual condominium units."[136]

[133.] Fla. Stat. § 718.111(12)(a) (2016).

[134.] Fla. Stat. § 718.111(12)(a) (2016).

[135.] Fla. Stat. § 718.111 (requiring the association to maintain a "current account and a monthly, bimonthly, or quarterly statement of the account for each unit designating the name of the unit owner, the due date and amount of each assessment, the amount paid on the account, and the balance due").

[136.] *Hobbs v. Weinkauf*, 940 So. 2d 1151, 1152 (Fla. 2d Dist. Ct. App. 2006) (holding that a condominium association that maintained account statements for each owner, but failed to maintain account statements for each unit, did not comply with section 718.111 requirements to maintain account statements "for each unit," and that the potential to deduce individual unit information from a multi-unit owner's summary accounting records does not satisfy the statute).

The association must also maintain the email addresses and facsimile numbers of unit owners consenting to electronic notice. If an owner does not consent in writing to the disclosure of this protected information, their email addresses and facsimile numbers are not accessible to the other members; however, the association is not liable for an inadvertent disclosure if the information is included in an official record of the association and is voluntarily provided by an owner and not requested by the association.[137]

The association's official records must be available for inspection by any member or authorized representative at all reasonable times.[138] Within five business days of receipt of a unit owner's request to inspect the official records, the association must make the records available to the owner within 45 miles of the condominium property or within the county in which the condominium property is located. This distance requirement does not apply to an association operating a timeshare condominium. The association may comply by having a copy of the records available for inspection on the condominium property. Alternatively, the association may offer to make the records available electronically via the Internet or by allowing the owner to view the records in electronic format that is printable upon request. Barring an affirmative statutory duty not to disclose unit owner information, the association is not responsible for the use or misuse of information provided to an association member or their authorized representative "pursuant to the compliance requirements of this chapter."[139]

Any condominium association member has the right to make copies of official records, subject to reasonable association rules regarding the frequency, time, location, notice, and manner of inspections and copying. The association must keep enough copies on the condominium property for unit owners and prospective purchasers of the following documents: governing documents, rules and regulations, all amendments thereto, the section 718.504 question and answer sheet, and year-end financial reports. The association may charge for the actual costs of preparing and furnishing these documents. In addition, the association must

---

[137.] Fla. Stat. § 718.111(12)(a)-(c) (2016).
[138.] Fla. Stat. § 718.111(12)(c) (2016).
[139.] Fla. Stat. § 718.111(12)(b) (2016).

allow the member to scan or photocopy records with portable devices in lieu of providing the member with a copy of such records.[140]

An association's failure to provide access to its official records within 10 business days after receipt of a written request creates a rebuttable presumption that the association willfully failed to comply with the Condominium Act's requirements. If the association willfully denies access to the official records, it is liable for any actual damages a member incurs as a result. Alternatively, the association is liable for minimum damages of $50 per calendar day up to ten days. The calculation of minimum damages begins on the eleventh business day after receipt of the written request. Any person prevailing in an action to enforce their right to inspect the official records is entitled to recover reasonable attorney's fees from the person in control of the records who, directly or indirectly, knowingly denied access.[141]

A unit owner may contact the Division of Florida Land Sales, Condominiums, and Mobile Homes (Division) directly to obtain assistance in obtaining access to condominium association records. If a unit owner provides proof to the Division that he or she requested access to official records in writing by certified mail, and that after 10 days the unit owner again made the same request for access to official records in writing by certified mail, and that more than 10 days elapsed since the second request and the association failed to provide access, the Division will issue a subpoena requiring production where the records are kept.[142]

A condominium association need not provide access to confidential or privileged records, including documents protected by the attorney-client privilege and the work-product doctrine.[143] To benefit from protection under this doctrine, the records must have been prepared for, or in anticipation of, litigation or adversarial administrative proceedings.[144]

[140.] Fla. Stat. § 718.111(12)(c) (2016).
[141.] Fla. Stat. § 718.111(12)(c) (2016).
[142.] Fla. Stat. § 718.501(1)(d) (2016).
[143.] Fla. Stat. § 718.111(12)(c) (2016).
[144.] Fla. Stat. § 718.111(12)(c) (2016).

The association must keep the following information and documentation confidential and refuse to allow inspection and copying by association members: information obtained in connection with the approval of the lease, sale, or other transfer of a unit; personnel records of association or management company employees; medical records of unit owners; electronic security measures used by the association to safeguard data, including passwords; and the software and operating system used by the association to manage data. This does not include written employment agreements with an association employee or management company, or financial records showing the compensation paid to an association employee.[145]

The condominium must also safeguard owners' personal identifying information, including social security numbers, driver's license numbers, credit card numbers, email addresses, telephone numbers, facsimile numbers, emergency contact information, and addresses. This does not include information provided by the owner to fulfill the association's notice requirements. Notwithstanding the restrictions, the association may print and distribute to owners a directory of owners' contact information. However, an owner may exclude his or her telephone number by written request. The association is not liable for inadvertent disclosure of personal identifying information included in association official records that an owner voluntarily provided, unsolicited by the association.[146]

The association must provide prospective purchasers and lienholders access to any official records that it is required to disclose to owners. Unless it is required by law to provide certain information, the association may charge a reasonable fee to the prospective purchaser or lienholder, or the current parcel owner or member, for providing good faith responses to information requests. In no event, however, may the association charge more than $150 plus the reasonable cost of photocopying and any attorney's fees incurred by the association in connection with the response. An association and its authorized agent are not liable for providing information to prospective purchasers and lienholders in good faith pursuant to a written request. To help avoid liability,

---

[145.] Fla. Stat. § 718.111(12)(c) (2016).
[146.] Fla. Stat. § 718.111(12)(c) (2016).

the person providing the information should include the following written statement: "The responses herein are made in good faith and to the best of my ability as to their accuracy."[147]

5-8   WRITTEN INQUIRIES

The Condominium Act provides unit owners with a mechanism for requesting information about the operation of the community. A unit owner may send a written inquiry by certified mail to the board of directors. In response, the board must respond in writing within 30 days with a substantive response, a notification that a legal opinion was requested, or a notification that the board is seeking advice from the Division.[148]

If the board seeks a legal opinion, it must provide a substantive response to the owner within 60 days after receipt of the inquiry. If the board seeks advice from the Division in response to the written inquiry, the board must provide a substantive response to the owner within 10 days of receipt of the advice. If the association fails to provide a substantive response to the unit owner, the board may not recover attorney's fees and costs if it prevails in litigation arising from the inquiry's subject matter. The association may adopt reasonable rules and regulations regarding written inquiries, including reasonable restrictions on the frequency and manner of responses. The association is permitted to adopt a rule that it will only respond to one written inquiry per unit every 30 days. If the association adopts this type of rule, it must respond to any additional inquiries in the next 30-day period.[149]

5-9   HIRING MANAGERS, CONTRACTORS, ATTORNEYS, AND ACCOUNTANTS

While board of directors members are often elected because of the professional backgrounds and unique skills they bring to community governance, they are simply volunteers who may not have the expertise needed to operate and manage the community association. As such, both homeowners' associations and condominium associations are authorized to enter into agreements with licensed community

---

[147.] Fla. Stat. § 718.111(12)(e) (2016).

[148.] Fla. Stat. § 718.112(2)(a) (2016).

[149.] Fla. Stat. § 718.112(2)(a) (2016).

association managers and professionals, such as accountants and attorneys, to provide specialized services. To protect the community and ensure transparency and fiscal responsibility, the statutes governing Florida community associations set forth guidelines for certain types of professional contracts.

Both Chapter 720 and the Condominium Act effectuate the policy consideration underlying the statute of frauds and apply it to Florida community associations. Specifically, they provide that any association contract for services or for the purchase, lease, or renting of materials or equipment must be in writing if it may not be fully performed within one year.[150] This is a restatement of Florida's statute of frauds, which states,

> No action shall be brought ... upon any agreement
> that is not to be performed within the space of 1 year
> from the making thereof ... unless the agreement
> or promise, or some note or memorandum thereof
> shall be in writing and signed by the party to be
> charged therewith.[151]

The Condominium Act takes this one step further and provides that all contracts for the provision of services must be in writing. Condominium associations with 10 or fewer units may opt out of this requirement by an affirmative vote of two-thirds of the unit owners.[152]

The Condominium Act also sets forth specific criteria for certain types of agreements. To be valid and enforceable, maintenance or management services contracts must contain specific provisions. The Condominium Act distinguishes between (a) maintenance or management services for which the association pays vendors directly, and (b) services related to equipment or property provided for the unit owners' convenience, such as laundry services/equipment, food services, telephone vendors, cable television operators, retail stores, businesses, "or similar vendors."[153] Valid maintenance or management contracts must specify the services

---

150. Fla. Stat. § 720.3055(1) (2016); Fla. Stat. § 718.3026(1) (2016).
151. Fla. Stat. § 725.01 (2016).
152. Fla. Stat. § 718.3026(1) (2016).
153. Fla. Stat. § 718.3025(4) (2016).

and obligations to which the parties agree.[154] Any services not stated on the face of the contract are unenforceable.[155]

The contract must specify the reimbursable costs that the party providing maintenance or management services may incur. The contract must indicate the frequency of each service and specify a minimum number of personnel to be employed. Pre-turnover contracts must disclose any financial or ownership interest between the developer and maintenance or management service provider. Finally, the contract must disclose any financial or ownership interest between board members and the maintenance or management service provider.[156]

The Condominium Act provides a remedy for condominium associations when the maintenance or management service provider fails to perform in accordance with the contract. In such cases, the association may procure services from some other party, and the breaching maintenance or management service provider is liable to the association for the costs and fees expended in procuring substitute services.[157]

The Condominium Act also provides strict regulations for contracts or transactions between the association and board members or entities in which board members may have a financial interest. For any such contracts, the association must comply with section 617.0832, which requires that (a) the board member's interest is disclosed or known to the board of directors, which approves the contract or transaction by a vote without counting the votes of the interested directors; (b) the board member's interest is disclosed or known to the members entitled to vote on the contract, if any, and they approve it by vote or written consent; or (c) the contract is fair and reasonable as to the corporation at the time it is authorized by the board, a committee, or the members.[158]

The foregoing disclosures must be written into the condominium association minutes.[159] In addition, the members are entitled to cancel the contract at the next regular members meeting after

---

[154.] Fla. Stat. § 718.3025(1) (2016).
[155.] Fla. Stat. § 718.3025(3) (2016).
[156.] Fla. Stat. § 718.3025(1) (2016).
[157.] Fla. Stat. § 718.3025(2) (2016).
[158.] Fla. Stat. § 617.0832(1) (2016).
[159.] Fla. Stat. § 718.3026(3) (2016).

the contract is executed. At that meeting, the existence of the contract or other transaction must be disclosed to the members. Upon any member's motion, contract cancellation must be set for referendum, with a majority vote by present members sufficing for cancellation. If the members cancel the contract, the association is only liable for the reasonable value of goods and services provided until cancellation. The association is not liable for any termination fee, liquidated damages, or other penalty for early termination.[160]

5-9:1   Competitive Bids

A homeowners' association must obtain competitive bids for materials, equipment, or services before it enters into a contract that requires payment exceeding 10 percent of the annual budget, including reserves. This includes service contracts and contracts for purchase, lease, or renting of materials or equipment. It does not include employment contracts; contracts with community association managers; contracts with attorneys, architects, or engineers; contracts for landscape architect services; and contracts for materials, equipment, or services provided to the association under a local government franchise agreement by a franchise holder.[161] In addition, this rule does not apply if the contracting party is the only source of the goods, materials, equipment, or services.[162] This rule also does not require the association to accept the lowest bid.[163]

If a contract is awarded following a competitive bid, and the contract allows the board to cancel on 30 days' notice, a renewal of the contract is not subject to the competitive bid requirements. Contracts with managers, if made by a competitive bid, may be made for up to three years.[164]

Condominium associations must obtain competitive bids if a contract will cost the association more than 5 percent of the total annual budget, including reserves. This includes any contract for

---

160. Fla. Stat. § 718.3026(3) (2016).
161. Fla. Stat. § 720.3055(2)(a) (2016).
162. Fla. Stat. § 720.3055(2)(c) (2016).
163. Fla. Stat. § 720.3055(1) (2016).
164. Fla. Stat. § 720.3055(2)(a) (2016).

services, as well as contracts for purchase or lease of materials or equipment. This rule does not require the association to accept the lowest bid,[165] and does not apply to employment contracts; contracts for landscape architect services; and contracts with attorneys, accountants, architects, managers, timeshare management firms, and engineers.[166] A condominium association need not obtain a competitive bid in emergency cases in which the association would be prevented from obtaining needed goods or services. In addition, the rule does not apply if only one business entity is capable of supplying the goods or services.[167] Condominium associations with 10 or fewer units may opt out of this requirement by an affirmative vote of two-thirds of the unit owners.[168]

5-10   CONDOMINIUM ASSOCIATION
EMERGENCY POWERS

Under the Condominium Act, condominium associations have certain powers to respond to damages from events giving rise to a Governor's state of emergency proclamation. When an emergency causes damage, a condominium association may generally conduct necessary business without the corporate rituals required by the Condominium Act and the governing documents, unless the governing documents specifically prohibit the association from such actions. In such cases, the board members have a duty to act in good faith, with the care an ordinarily prudent person in a like position would exercise under similar circumstances, and in a manner reasonably believed to be in the association's best interests.[169] These emergency powers are limited to the time reasonably necessary to mitigate further damage, make emergency repairs, and protect the health, safety, and welfare of the association, the unit owners, and their family members, tenants, guests, agents, or invitees.[170]

In response to state-of-emergency damages, the board of directors may take the following actions: conduct meetings with

---

[165.] Fla. Stat. § 718.3026(1) (2016).
[166.] Fla. Stat. § 718.3026(2) (2016).
[167.] Fla. Stat. § 718.3026(2) (2016).
[168.] Fla. Stat. § 718.3026 (2016).
[169.] Fla. Stat. § 718.1265(1) (2016).
[170.] Fla. Stat. § 718.1265(2) (2016).

notice given as is practicable; cancel and reschedule any meeting; name non-directors as assistant officers to fill in for incapacitated or unavailable executive officers during the emergency; relocate the association's principal office; enter into agreements with local counties and municipalities to assist with debris removal; and implement a disaster plan, including shutting down elevators, electricity, water, sewer, security systems, or air conditioners.[171]

The association may also designate any portion of the condominium property unavailable for entry based upon advice of emergency management officials or licensed professionals, and subsequently determine whether such property can be safely inhabited or occupied. The association may require condominium property evacuation in the event of a mandatory evacuation order. The association shall be immune from liability for injury to persons or property arising from an owner or occupant's failure to evacuate during a board-required evacuation. The association may take steps to mitigate further damage, including removing debris and preventing the spread of fungus by removal of wet drywall, insulation, carpet, cabinetry, personal property, or other fixtures on or within the condominium property, even if the unit owner is obligated by the declaration or law to insure or replace those items.[172]

The association may contract, on behalf of any unit owner, for items or services for which the owners are typically responsible, but which are necessary to prevent further damage to condominium property, including drying units, boarding broken windows or doors, and the replacement of damaged air conditioners or air handlers to provide climate control in the units or other portions of the property. The unit owner is ultimately responsible for reimbursing the association for the items or services' actual costs, and the association may use its lien authority to enforce collection of the charges. The association may also levy special assessments without a vote of the owners, as well as borrow money and pledge association assets as collateral to fund emergency repairs without unit owner approval.[173]

[171.] Fla. Stat. § 718.1265(1) (2016).

[172.] Fla. Stat. § 718.1265(1) (2016).

[173.] Fla. Stat. § 718.1265(1) (2016).

5-11   RIGHT TO SUE AND BE SUED

Both homeowners' and condominium associations have the right to sue and be sued on any issue regarding community association operation. After turnover, the association may also litigate disputes in its name on behalf of all unit owners regarding matters of common interest. The right to sue and be sued includes the right to settle disputes. Settlement of a dispute regarding the community's management and operation is within the board of directors' discretion and does not need court approval.[174]

5-11:1   Homeowners' Associations' Right to Sue and Be Sued

After turnover, the association may institute, settle, or appeal legal actions in its name on the members' behalf. The association may litigate and settle disputes regarding matters of common interest, including, but not limited to, common areas; any buildings or improvements for which the association is responsible; mechanical, electrical, or plumbing elements serving a building or improvement for which the association is responsible; and representations of the developer pertaining to commonly used facilities. The association may also protest ad valorem taxes on commonly used facilities. The association may defend eminent domain actions or bring inverse condemnation actions.[175]

Approval by a majority of the voting interests at a membership meeting at which a quorum is present is a precondition to filing actions in which the association intends to litigate amounts in excess of $100,000.[176] This statutory limitation on the association's authority to commit resources to litigation is designed to protect association members.[177]

---

[174] *Ocean Trail Unit Owners Ass'n v. Mead*, 650 So. 2d 4, 8 (Fla. 1994).

[175] Fla. Stat. § 720.303(1) (2016).

[176] Fla. Stat. § 720.303(1) (2016).

[177] *Lake Forest Master Cmty. Ass'n v. Orlando Lake Forest Joint Venture*, 10 So. 3d 1187, 1195 (Fla. 5th Dist. Ct. App. 2009).

5-11:2   Condominium Associations' Right to Sue and Be Sued

A condominium association may sue or be sued on any issue respecting maintenance, management, and operation of the condominium property. After turnover, the association may litigate and settle disputes in its name on behalf of all unit owners regarding matters of common interest, including the common elements; any buildings or improvements for which the association is responsible; mechanical, electrical, or plumbing elements serving a building or improvement for which the association is responsible; and representations of the developer pertaining to commonly used facilities. The association may also protest ad valorem taxes on commonly used facilities. The association may defend eminent domain actions or bring inverse condemnation actions. If the association has the authority, it may bring a class action or be joined in an action as a class representative.[178]

5-11:3   Class Action Suits

After turnover, Rule 1.221 of the Florida Rules of Civil Procedure permits both homeowners' associations and condominium associations to institute class actions on behalf of all association members regarding matters of common interest, *without* satisfying the following Rule 1.220 prerequisites[179] for pleading and maintaining class actions: (1) class size that makes separate joinder impracticable, (2) common questions of law and fact, (3) typicality of the class representative's claims or defenses, and (4) capability of the class representative to fairly and adequately represent class member interests.[180] A homeowners' association or condominium association may also be joined in an action as representative of

---

178. Fla. Stat. § 718.111(3) (2016).

179. Fla. R. Civ. P. Rule 1.220 (2017) (requiring the court to make the following conclusions before any claim or defense may be maintained on behalf of a class by one or more parties suing or being sued as the class representative: (1) the members of the class must be so numerous that separate joinder of each member is impracticable; (2) the representative party's claim or defense must raise questions of law or fact common to those of each class member; (3) the class representative's claim or defense must be typical of the claim or defense of each class member; and (4) the court must conclude that the class representative can "fairly and adequately protect and represent the interests of each member of the class").

180. Fla. R. Civ. P. Rule 1.221 (2017).

all association members regarding matters of common interest. This rule does not limit any statutory or common law right of any owner, or class of owners, to bring an action that is otherwise available.[181]

To maintain a class action on behalf of its members, the only requirement for a community association is that the action concern matters of common interest. In cases involving master homeowners' associations comprised of distinct subdivision associations, subdivision associations have the right to maintain class actions on behalf of their members against the master association, provided subdivision members have a common interest in obligations that are (1) distinct from their interests as members of the master association, and (2) distinct from the interests of homeowners in other subdivisions in the master association.[182]

[181.] Fla. R. Civ. P. Rule 1.221 (2017).

[182.] *Homeowner's Ass'n of Overlook v. Seabrooke Homeowners' Ass'n*, 62 So. 3d 667, 670 (Fla. 2d Dist. Ct. App. 2011) (a subdivision homeowners' association filed a class action against its multi-subdivision master association for declaratory relief regarding obligations to maintain the other subdivisions' roadways; the action was based on a provision in the master association's declaration that members are only obligated to maintain their own subdivision's roads; the court rejected the master association's argument that the subdivision had no standing to maintain an action on behalf of its members, holding that "the sole requirement for the bundling of a class is that the members of the association have a common interest regarding the common elements of the property"; the court held this requirement was met since subdivision members had a common interest in their obligation to pay the costs of maintaining the roads in other subdivisions, which was distinct from any interest as members in the master association and from the interests of other subdivision homeowners).

Chapter 6

Member and Board Meetings

6-1 INTRODUCTION

The community association's purpose is to protect its members, from whom it derives its authority and income. Thus, the association is held fully accountable for the actions it takes on the community's behalf. To this end, the community association must transact business in properly noticed open meetings, to which members must have full access and the opportunity to participate. To ensure transparency, the Florida Legislature requires that association bylaws provide procedures for noticing and conducting board and member meetings. To the extent that the bylaws are silent, minimum requirements are set forth in the Homeowners' Associations Act and the Condominium Act.

6-2 BOARD MEETINGS

6-2:1 Homeowners' Associations

A board of directors meeting occurs whenever a quorum of the board meets to discuss homeowners' association business.[1] At any such meeting, the board members must comply with the pertinent Chapter 720 requirements for noticing and conducting board meetings. All meetings of the board must be open to all members. The only exceptions are board meetings with an attorney, to hold attorney-client privileged discussions about proposed or pending litigation, and board meetings to discuss personnel matters.[2]

[1.] Fla. Stat. § 720.303(2)(a) (2016).
[2.] Fla. Stat. § 720.303(2) (2016).

In addition to board of directors meetings, members have access to (1) meetings of any committee or other body when a final decision will be made regarding the expenditure of association funds, and (2) meetings of any architectural review board or similar body with respect to parcel improvement applications.[3]

The right to attend board meetings includes the right to speak on all agenda items. The association may adopt reasonable written rules governing member comments at board meetings, such as a sign-up requirement for those who wish to speak and rules on member statement frequency and duration.[4]

The bylaws must include procedures for giving notice of all board meetings. If they do not, Chapter 720 requires at a minimum (a) posting notices in a conspicuous place in the community at least 48 hours in advance of meetings, barring an emergency, or (b) mailing or delivering notices to each member at least 7 days before the meeting.[5]

For communities with more than 100 members, the bylaws may provide a reasonable alternative to posting or mailing, including publication or conspicuous posting and repeated broadcasting of the notice on a closed-circuit cable television system. If the association broadcasts notice instead of physical posting in the community, the broadcast must occur at least four times every broadcast hour of each day that a posted notice is otherwise required. The notice and agenda must broadcast for a sufficient length of time and in a manner so as to allow an average reader to read and comprehend the entire content of the notice and agenda. In lieu of posting, mailing, or television broadcast, the association may also provide the members with a schedule of upcoming board meetings. If authorized by the bylaws, and if a member consents in writing, the association may give notice of meetings by electronic transmission, which may include facsimile transmission and email.[6]

If the association intends to levy an assessment at a board meeting, the notice must include a statement that assessments

---

[3.] Fla. Stat. § 720.303(2)(a) (2016).
[4.] Fla. Stat. § 720.303(2)(b) (2016).
[5.] Fla. Stat. § 720.303(2)(c) (2016).
[6.] Fla. Stat. § 720.303(2)(c) (2016).

will be considered. The notice must also discuss the nature of the assessments. If the association wishes to consider special assessments or amendments to rules regarding parcel use, the notice must be mailed, delivered, or transmitted electronically to the members and owners and posted conspicuously on the property or broadcast on closed-circuit cable television at least 14 days before the meeting.[7]

By a petition of 20 percent of the total voting interests, the membership may add an item of business to the agenda at the next regular board meeting or at a special meeting of the board. Notwithstanding the schedule of board meetings, the board must address the item of business within 60 days of receipt of the petition. The board must give 14 days' notice to all members of the meeting at which it will address the petition. Each member may speak for at least three minutes on each matter placed on the agenda by petition, provided that the member signs the sign-up sheet, if one is provided, or submits a written request to speak. The board is only obligated to address the petitioned item and need not take any other action requested by the petition.[8]

Any owner may tape record or videotape board of directors meetings. The board of directors may adopt reasonable taping rules.[9] The association must take minutes of all meetings of the board of directors, which must be reduced to written form within a reasonable time after the meeting. The minutes must record each director's vote or abstention for every agenda item upon which there is a vote.[10]

6-2:2 Condominium Associations

All condominium unit owners may attend condominium board meetings at which a quorum of the board is present.[11] Members are also entitled to attend committee meetings at which final action will be taken on behalf of the board and to make recommendations to the board regarding the association budget. Unless the bylaws

---

7. Fla. Stat. § 720.303(2)(c) (2016).
8. Fla. Stat. § 720.303(2)(d) (2016).
9. Fla. Stat. § 720.306(10) (2016).
10. Fla. Stat. § 720.303(3)(d) (2016).
11. Fla. Stat. § 718.112(2)(c) (2016).

provide otherwise, the members are also entitled to attend all other association committee meetings.[12] Unit owners may not attend attorney-client privileged meetings between the board or a committee and the association's attorney regarding proposed or pending litigation, or board meetings regarding personnel matters.[13]

Board or committee members who attend meetings by telephone conference are counted toward a quorum. A telephone speaker must be used so that they can be heard by the board or committee members and unit owners attending the meeting in person.[14]

Unit owners may tape record or videotape board meetings, committee meetings, and membership meetings. Tape recording and videotaping is subject to several restrictions. For instance, the audio and video equipment may not produce distracting sound or light emissions. In advance of the meeting, the board may adopt requirements that: (a) audio and video equipment be assembled and placed in position before the meeting; (b) those videotaping or recording a meeting may not move about the meeting room to facilitate the recording; and (c) unit owners shall give advance notice of their desire to use any audio or video equipment.[15]

While the unit owners may speak at any board meeting on any and all designated agenda items, the association may adopt reasonable written rules governing the frequency, duration, and manner of unit owner comments on agenda items.[16]

The condominium association must post notice of all board meetings conspicuously on the condominium property at least 48 continuous hours before the meeting, except in an emergency. The notice must identify all agenda items. Notice of any meeting at which regular or special assessments are to be considered must specifically state that assessments will be considered and provide the nature, estimated cost, and purposes of the assessments. If

---

[12.] Fla. Stat. § 718.112(2)(c)(2) (2016).

[13.] Fla. Stat. § 718.112(2)(c)(3) (2016).

[14.] Fla. Stat. § 718.112(2)(b)(5) (2016).

[15.] Fla. Admin. Code R. 61B-23.002(10) (2016).

[16.] Fla. Stat. § 718.112(2)(c) (2016).

the board plans to consider nonemergency special assessments, or amendments to unit use rules, the association must mail, deliver, or electronically transmit notice to the unit owners and post the notice conspicuously on the condominium property at least 14 days before the meeting. An affidavit of compliance with this requirement, executed by the notice provider, must be filed in the association's official records.[17]

The board must adopt a rule designating a specific location on the condominium property for posting all board meeting notices. If there is no condominium property where notices can be posted, notices shall be mailed, delivered, or emailed at least 14 days before the meeting to each unit owner. In lieu of or in addition to physical posting, the association may adopt a rule allowing for conspicuous posting and repeatedly broadcasting the notice and the agenda on a closed-circuit cable television system. If broadcast notice is used instead of physical posting, the notice and agenda must broadcast at least four times every broadcast hour of each day that a posted notice is otherwise required. The notice and agenda must broadcast for the length of time sufficient for an average reader to observe, read, and comprehend the entire content of the notice and agenda.[18]

By petition of 20 percent of the voting interests, members may require the board to address an item of business at the next regular or special board meeting. The board must address the proposed item of business no later than 60 days after the receipt of the petition.[19]

Items of business not listed on the notice may be taken up on an emergency basis. The board may only discuss emergency items upon agreement of at least a majority plus one of the board members. The board may ratify emergency actions upon notice at the next regularly scheduled board meeting.[20]

[17.] Fla. Stat. § 718.112(2)(c)(1) (2016).
[18.] Fla. Stat. § 718.112(2)(c)(1) (2016).
[19.] Fla. Stat. § 718.112(2)(c)(1) (2016).
[20.] Fla. Stat. § 718.112(2)(c)(1) (2016).

6-3   MEMBER MEETINGS

6-3:1   Homeowners' Associations

Homeowners' associations must hold an annual members meeting at a time, date, and place stated in the bylaws. Unless the bylaws state otherwise, any requisite directors' elections must be held at, or in conjunction with, the annual meeting.[21] At least 30 percent of the total voting interests must be present to constitute a quorum, unless the bylaws provide a lower number. Decisions that require a member vote must be made at a meeting at which there is a quorum by a vote of at least a majority of the voting interests present, in person or by proxy, provided that no statutory or contractual exceptions apply.[22]

The board of directors may also call special meetings, notice of which must include a description of the meeting's purpose.[23] At a special meeting, the association may only conduct business described in the meeting's notice.[24] Ten percent of the association's total voting interests may also call a special meeting, unless the bylaws require a different percentage.[25]

The bylaws must require notice of all membership meetings to all parcel owners and members. If the bylaws are silent, the association may mail, deliver, or electronically transmit notice to the members no less than 14 days prior to the meeting. The association must evidence compliance with this 14-day notice requirement via affidavit executed by the notice provider filed in the association's official records. In addition to mailing, delivering, or electronically transmitting the notice, the association may adopt a procedure for conspicuously posting and repeatedly broadcasting the notice and the agenda on a closed-circuit cable television system. The notice and agenda must be broadcast in a manner and for a sufficient length of time to allow an average reader to observe, read, and comprehend the entire content of the notice and the agenda.[26]

[21.] Fla. Stat. § 720.306(2) (2016).
[22.] Fla. Stat. § 720.306(1)(a) (2016).
[23.] Fla. Stat. § 720.306(4) (2016).
[24.] Fla. Stat. § 720.306(3) (2016).
[25.] Fla. Stat. § 720.306(3) (2016).
[26.] Fla. Stat. § 720.306(5) (2016).

Members and parcel owners have the right to attend all membership meetings and speak on all items opened for discussion or included on the agenda. Notwithstanding any governing document rule or provision to the contrary, a member and a parcel owner have the right to speak for at least three minutes on any item. The association may adopt rules on the frequency and duration of member statements consistent with Chapter 720.[27]

Any owner may tape record or videotape member meetings. The board of directors may adopt reasonable taping rules.[28] In addition, the association must take minutes of all membership meetings, which must be reduced to written form within a reasonable time after the meeting.[29]

The association may adjourn an annual or special meeting to a different date, time, or place, and then conduct at the adjourned meeting any business that might have been transacted on the meeting's original date. Only if the adjournment is not announced before it is taken must proper notice be given of the new date, time, or place.[30] However, if the bylaws require fixing a new record date for the adjourned meeting in order to establish voting rights for one or more groups, notice of the adjourned meeting must be given to members entitled to vote via the new record date, even if they were not members as of the previous record date.[31]

6-3:2 Condominium Associations

An annual meeting of the unit owners shall be held at the location provided in the bylaws. If the bylaws are silent, the meeting shall be held within 45 miles of the condominium property. This distance

---

[27] Fla. Stat. § 720.306(6) (2016).

[28] Fla. Stat. § 720.306(10) (2016).

[29] Fla. Stat. § 720.303(3) (2016).

[30] Fla. Stat. § 720.306(7) (2016); *Lake Forest Master Cmty. Ass'n v. Orlando Lake Forest Joint Venture*, 10 So. 3d 1187, 1192 (Fla. 5th Dist. Ct. App. 2009) (in a homeowners' association suit, the developer filed for summary judgment because the meeting at which the association's majority approved litigation, a statutory condition precedent under section 720.303(1), was a reconvened meeting whose date and time was simply announced at the prior meeting, but not separately noticed; the court rejected the developer's argument that the litigation was unapproved since the meeting at which approval was given was an improperly noticed reconvened meeting, in contravention of the association's governing document's requirement of written notice for all meetings, holding that section 720.306(7) recognizes "the propriety of [adjourning] meetings to a different date, time or place without mailed notice if such information is announced prior to adjournment").

[31] Fla. Stat. § 720.306(7) (2016).

requirement does not apply to an association governing a timeshare condominium.[32] The bylaws must set forth the notice requirements for member meetings, including the annual meeting. The notice must include an agenda, and it must be mailed, hand delivered, or emailed to each unit owner at least 14 days before the annual meeting. In addition, the notice must be posted in a conspicuous place on the condominium property at least 14 days before the annual meeting.[33]

The board must adopt a rule designating a specific location on condominium property for posting notices, unless there is no condominium property available for posting notices. In lieu of, or in addition to, physical posting, the association may adopt a rule allowing for conspicuous posting and repeatedly broadcasting the notice and the agenda on a closed-circuit cable television system. The rules for broadcasting board meeting notices apply to broadcasting member meeting notices.[34]

Unless the right to receive notice of the annual meeting is waived in writing, the notice must be hand delivered, mailed, or electronically transmitted to each unit owner. Notices for all purposes must be mailed to each unit owner at the address last provided to the association by the unit owner, or hand delivered to each unit owner. If a unit is owned by more than one person, the association must send notice to the address that the developer identifies for that purpose and thereafter to the address provided by one or more of the owners in writing. If no address is given or the owners of the unit do not agree, the association may send notice to the address on the deed of record. The notice provider must prepare an affidavit or United States Postal Service certificate of mailing, to be included in the association's official records affirming that the notice was mailed or hand delivered in accordance with the Condominium Act.[35]

If permitted by the governing documents, unit owners may waive the right to receive notice of special meetings. Unit owners may also agree in writing to email notice of board meetings, committee

---

[32]. Fla. Stat. § 718.112(2)(d)(1) (2016).
[33]. Fla. Stat. § 718.112(2)(d)(3) (2016).
[34]. Fla. Stat. § 718.112(2)(d)(3) (2016).
[35]. Fla. Stat. § 718.112(2)(d)(3) (2016).

meetings, and unit owner meetings, with the exception of unit owner meetings to recall board members.[36]

Unit owners have the right to participate in all membership meetings regarding all agenda items. The board may adopt rules governing the manner of unit owner participation.[37] Unit owners may tape record or videotape unit owner meetings subject to the same restrictions applicable to videotaping board meetings.[38]

6-4 VOTING PROCEDURES

6-4:1 Homeowners' Associations

Directors may not vote by proxy or by secret ballot at board meetings. The only exception is that board members may vote by secret ballot in officer elections. This also applies to the meetings of any committee or other similar body, when a final decision will be made regarding the expenditure of association funds, and to architectural review boards or similar bodies with respect to parcel improvement applications.[39]

Decisions that require a member vote must be made at a meeting at which there is a quorum by a vote of at least a majority of the voting interests present, in person or by proxy.[40] Unless otherwise provided in the governing documents, members have a right to vote in person or by proxy.[41]

A proxy must be dated and must state the date, time, and place of the meeting for which it was given. It must be signed by the person authorized to execute the proxy, and it is revocable at any time. A proxy is only effective at the meeting for which it was originally given, or at the date, time, and place of the original meeting's lawful adjournment. A proxy automatically expires 90 days after the date of the meeting for which it was originally given. If the proxy form so provides, any proxy holder may appoint, in writing, a substitute to act in his or her place.[42]

---

36. Fla. Stat. § 718.112(2)(d)(6) (2016).
37. Fla. Stat. § 718.112(2)(d)(7) (2016).
38. Fla. Stat. § 718.112(2)(d)(8) (2016).
39. Fla. Stat. § 720.303(2)(c) (2016).
40. Fla. Stat. § 720.306(1)(a) (2016).
41. Fla. Stat. § 720.306(8) (2016).
42. Fla. Stat. § 720.306(8)(a) (2016).

If permitted under the governing documents, those not attending the member meeting for director elections may vote by mailed secret ballot. The ballot must be placed in an inner envelope with no identifying markings and mailed or delivered to the association in an outer envelope bearing the member's name, the lot or parcel for which the vote is being cast, and the signature of the lot or parcel owner casting the ballot. After confirming the member's eligibility to vote and the absence of a ballot for that parcel, the inner envelope shall be removed and counted among the personally-cast ballots. The association may not consider votes received after balloting closes.[43]

6-4:2   Condominium Associations

Association business for which the governing documents or the Condominium Act require unit owner approval must be conducted at a duly noticed unit owners meeting. The only exceptions are those circumstances set forth in the governing documents or Florida law in which unit owners' may take action by written agreement without a meeting, such as a proposed recall of board members.[44]

Unless the bylaws provide otherwise, the majority of voting interests constitute a quorum sufficient to conduct business at a membership meeting. Decisions are made by a majority of the voting interests at a meeting at which a quorum is present, except as otherwise provided in the governing documents, and except as described in the provisions of the Condominium Act detailing board election procedures.[45] An association-owned unit's voting interest may not be considered for any purpose, including establishment of a quorum. Proxies, however, may be used to establish a quorum.[46]

Board or committee members who attend meetings by telephone conference may vote and may be counted toward a quorum. A telephone speaker must be used so that in-person attendees can hear the conversation of those on the telephone.[47]

[43.] Fla. Stat. § 720.306(8)(b) (2016).
[44.] Fla. Stat. § 718.112(2)(d)(5) (2016).
[45.] Fla. Stat. § 718.112(2)(b)(1) (2016).
[46.] Fla. Stat. § 718.112(2)(b)(2) (2016).
[47.] Fla. Stat. § 718.112(2)(b)(5) (2016).

For matters on which the Condominium Act requires or permits a unit owner vote, owners may vote in person at member meetings or via limited proxies conforming to the form adopted by the Division of Florida Condominiums, Timeshares, and Mobile Homes of the Department of Business and Professional Regulation. While proxies may not usually be used to elect board members, general proxies may be used for all other matters, including voting for non-substantive changes to items for which a limited proxy is required.[48] Proxies are revocable at any time and are only effective for the specific meeting for which they were originally given and any lawfully adjourned meetings thereof. A proxy expires 90 days after the date of the first meeting for which it was given.[49]

A condominium association with 10 or fewer units may, by affirmative vote of a majority of the total voting interests, institute in its bylaws different voting procedures for board member elections, including voting by limited or general proxy.[50] The adoption of different voting and election procedures requires an affirmative vote of a majority of the total voting interests, even if the association's bylaws contain different amendment procedures.[51]

6-4:3   Electronic Voting

Both homeowners' and condominium associations may conduct elections and other membership votes through online voting systems if a member consents, in writing, to online voting.[52] The association must provide for and authorize an online voting system by a board resolution. The resolution must provide that owners receive notice of the opportunity to vote through an online system, establish reasonable procedures and deadlines for unit owners to consent, and establish reasonable procedures and deadlines for unit owners to opt out of online voting after giving consent. Written notice of a meeting at which the resolution will be considered must be mailed, delivered, or electronically transmitted to the unit owners and posted conspicuously on the condominium or

---

[48.] Fla. Stat. § 718.112(2)(b)(2) (2016).
[49.] Fla. Stat. § 718.112(2)(b)(3) (2016).
[50.] Fla. Stat. § 718.112(2)(d)(10) (2016).
[51.] Fla. Admin. Code R. 61B-23.0021(1)(c) (2015).
[52.] Fla. Stat. § 720.317; Fla. Stat. § 718.128 (2016).

association property at least 14 days before the meeting. Evidence of compliance with the 14-day notice requirement must be made by an affidavit executed by the person providing the notice and filed among the official records.[53] An owner's consent to online voting is valid until the owner opts out according to the procedures established by the board.[54]

The association must meet certain statutory requirements, including providing each member with a method to authenticate the member's identity to the online voting system, and a method to confirm, at least 14 days before the voting deadline, that the unit owner's electronic device can successfully communicate with the online voting system.[55] The association may only use an online voting system that is able to authenticate the unit owner's identity, authenticate the validity of each electronic vote to ensure that the vote is not altered in transit, transmit a receipt from the online voting system to each unit owner who casts an electronic vote, and store electronic votes for access by election officials for recount and review purposes.[56]

For condominium associations, the method for transmission of electronic ballots must ensure the secrecy and integrity of each ballot, and the online voting system must separate any identifying information from the electronic election ballot, rendering it impossible to tie an election ballot to a specific unit owner.[57] For homeowners' associations, this is only required if the association's bylaws provide for secret ballots for the election of directors.[58] A member voting electronically shall be counted as being in attendance at the meeting for quorum purposes.[59]

[53.] Fla. Stat. § 720.317(4); Fla. Stat. § 718.128(4) (2016).
[54.] Fla. Stat. § 720.317(5); Fla. Stat. § 718.128(5) (2016).
[55.] Fla. Stat. § 720.317(1); Fla. Stat. § 718.128(1) (2016).
[56.] Fla. Stat. § 720.317(2); Fla. Stat. § 718.128(2) (2016).
[57.] Fla. Stat. § 718.128(1), (2) (2016).
[58.] Fla. Stat. § 720.317(1), (2) (2016).
[59.] Fla. Stat. § 720.317(3); Fla. Stat. § 718.128(3) (2016).

Chapter 7

Covenant Enforcement

7-1 INTRODUCTION

By purchasing property in a community governed by a homeowners' or condominium association, owners agree to comply with the association's governing documents, rules, and regulations. Chapter 720 and the Condominium Act require each member of a Florida community association, as well as their tenants, guests, and invitees, to comply with the governing documents and rules of the community. This is not a one-way street, however, since the association is also bound to comply with its rules and governing documents,[1] which are contracts between the association and the property owners "circumscribing the extent and limits of the enjoyment and use of real property."[2]

Restrictions found in a declaration are presumptively valid. Since each purchaser has notice that the property is subject to restrictions in the community association's declaration, which is recorded in the public records, knowledge and willing acceptance of the restrictions are imputed to property owners.[3] Such restrictions have attributes of covenants running with the land and will only be invalidated if shown to be "wholly arbitrary in their application," in violation of public policy, or repugnant to a fundamental constitutional right.[4]

[1.] Fla. Stat. § 720.305(1) (2016); Fla. Stat. § 718.303(1) (2016).

[2.] *Woodside Vill. Condo. Ass'n v. Jahren*, 806 So. 2d 452, 456 (Fla. 2002) (quoting *Pepe v. Whispering Sands Condo. Ass'n*, 351 So. 2d 755, 757 (Fla. 2d 1977)).

[3.] *Hidden Harbour Estates v. Basso*, 393 So. 2d 637, 639 (Fla. 4th Dist. Ct. App. 1981).

[4.] *Hidden Harbour Estates v. Basso*, 393 So. 2d 637, 640 (Fla. 4th Dist. Ct. App. 1981); *Pines of Boca Barwood Condo. Ass'n v. Cavouti*, 605 So. 2d 984, 985 (Fla. 4th Dist. Ct. App. 1992).

The association's governing documents typically set forth prohibited uses, architectural controls, and the association's assessment rights. Such restrictions on property use reflect the basic precept of community association living: individuals sacrifice personal freedom to promote the health, happiness, and welfare of the community's majority, which is a necessity for owners who live in close proximity and share facilities.

Courts treat the declaration as the association's private constitution and strictly enforce its restrictions to "protect[] the members' reliance interests in a document which they have knowingly accepted."[5] In addition, strict enforcement furthers the public policy in favor of establishing and protecting the stability of community types to provide diverse choices in living arrangements.[6]

7-2   USE RESTRICTIONS

Restrictions on the use of property under the community association's control are set forth in the governing documents, including the declaration, articles of incorporation, bylaws, and rules and regulations. The declaration operates as the association's constitution, while the articles establish the association during the incorporation process and the bylaws serve as rules for internal governance. In any conflicts between governing documents, the established hierarchy dictates that the declaration controls.[7]

Since all declaration restrictions are presumptively valid, courts do not apply a reasonableness test when ruling on their validity. In fact, even unreasonable restrictions will survive legal challenge, as owners must be able to count on stability in the recorded declaration's restrictions.[8] This is true unless the restriction is wholly arbitrary in its application, contrary to public policy, or a violation of a constitutional right.

Boards of directors may also adopt use restrictions in the form of board-made rules and regulations, provided they are "reasonably related to the promotion of the health, happiness,

---

[5.] *Aquarian Found. v. Sholom House*, 448 So. 2d 1166, 1168 (Fla. 3d Dist. Ct. App. 1984).

[6.] *Aquarian Found. v. Sholom House*, 448 So. 2d 1166, 1168 (Fla. 3d Dist. Ct. App. 1984).

[7.] *Heron at Destin W. Beach & Bay Resort Condo. Ass'n v. Osprey at Destin W. Beach*, 94 So. 3d 623, 629 (Fla. 1st Dist. Ct. App. 2012).

[8.] *Hidden Harbour Estates v. Basso*, 393 So. 2d 637, 640 (Fla. 4th Dist. Ct. App. 1981).

and peace of mind of the unit owners."[9] Boards may not adopt "arbitrary or capricious rules bearing no relationship to the health, happiness and enjoyment of life of the various unit owners."[10] Board-made rules are also not presumptively valid and are subject to a reasonableness test "to somewhat fetter the discretion of the board of directors."[11] Courts examine challenged rules on a case by case basis[12] in the context of both condominium and homeowners' associations.[13]

7-2:1 Homeowners' Association Use Restrictions

Chapter 720 defines the declaration as "a recorded written instrument or instruments in the nature of covenants running with the land which subject the land comprising the community to" the association's jurisdiction and control.[14] While the declaration of covenants' restrictions are presumptively valid, and the board is free to adopt reasonable rules regarding common areas and recreational facilities use, the homeowners' association's ability to restrict property use is subject to certain statutory limitations. For instance, a homeowners' association may not prevent parcel owners and their invited guests from using common areas and recreational facilities for their intended purpose. In addition, a homeowners' association may not unreasonably restrict an owner's right to peaceably assemble or invite public officers or candidates for public office to appear and speak in common areas and recreational facilities.[15]

7-2:2 Condominium Association Use Restrictions

Under the Condominium Act, the declaration "may include covenants and restrictions concerning the use, occupancy, and transfer of the units permitted by law."[16] Declarations of

---

9. *Hidden Harbour Estates v. Basso*, 393 So. 2d 637, 640 (Fla. 4th Dist. Ct. App. 1981).

10. *Hidden Harbour Estates v. Norman*, 309 So. 2d 180, 182 (Fla. 4th Dist. Ct. App. 1975).

11. *Hidden Harbour Estates v. Basso*, 393 So. 2d 637, 640 (Fla. 4th Dist. Ct. App. 1981).

12. *Hidden Harbour Estates v. Norman*, 309 So. 2d 180, 182 (Fla. 4th Dist. Ct. App. 1975).

13. *See Hidden Harbour Estates v. Basso*, 393 So. 2d 637 (Fla. 4th Dist. Ct. App. 1981); *see Eastpointe Prop. Owners' Ass'n v. Cohen*, 505 So. 2d 518, 520 (Fla. 4th Dist. Ct. App. 1987).

14. Fla. Stat. § 720.301(4) (2016).

15. Fla. Stat. § 720.304(1) (2016).

16. Fla. Stat. § 718.104(5) (2016).

condominium are strictly construed to preclude any use not explicitly authorized by the declaration.[17] A person who consents to the declaration's execution subjects his or her condominium interest to the declaration's provisions.[18] By virtue of purchasing a unit in a condominium, owners are on notice of, and thus accept, the provisions restricting their property use,[19] which are "enforceable equitable servitudes, [that] run with the land, and are effective until the condominium is terminated."[20]

Similar to Chapter 720, the Condominium Act limits an association's right to restrict property use. The association may not prevent unit owners and their invited guests from using for their intended purpose all common elements, common areas, and recreational facilities serving the condominium. Additionally, a condominium association may not unreasonably restrict an owner's right to peaceably assemble or invite public officers or candidates for public office to appear and speak in the common elements, common areas, and recreational facilities.[21] In fact, the Condominium Act provides owners with a statutory cause of action to enjoin the association from enforcing any restrictions that infringe on these rights.[22]

When the members' right to peaceably assemble conflicts with the condominium association's right to restrict common element use, the restriction will be upheld provided it is reasonable and does not violate specific statutory limitations.[23] For example, a condominium association rule banning religious services in the auditorium was deemed reasonable because the services had a divisive effect on the community and a majority voted for the restriction.[24] Likewise,

---

[17] *Brickell Bay Club Condo. Ass'n v. Hernstadt*, 512 So. 2d 994, 996 (Fla. 3d Dist. Ct. App. 1987).

[18] Fla. Stat. § 718.104(6) (2016).

[19] *Wilshire Condo. Ass'n v. Kohlbrand*, 368 So. 2d 629, 630-31 (Fla. 4th Dist. Ct. App. 1979).

[20] Fla. Stat. § 718.104(7) (2016).

[21] Fla. Stat. § 718.123(1) (2016).

[22] Fla. Stat. § 718.123(2) (2016).

[23] *Neuman v. Grandview At Emerald Hills*, 861 So. 2d 494 (Fla. 4th Dist. Ct. App. 2003).

[24] *Neuman v. Grandview At Emerald Hills*, 861 So. 2d 494, 498 (Fla. 4th Dist. Ct. App. 2003) (following community protest over auditorium use for religious services, the condominium association passed a rule banning such services, overriding a previous provision that permitted services when 80 percent of the attendants were residents; two members sued on the grounds that (1) the rule violated their constitutional rights or statutory

the Condominium Act was not violated by the rule because (a) the restriction did not completely prohibit members' use of the auditorium, and (b) the statutory right of peaceable assembly does not necessarily include the right to conduct religious services.[25] Since the rule was reasonable and did not violate statutory limitations, it was a valid restriction on common element use.[26]

In addition to owners, the association must also allow owners' tenants to use the association property and those common elements otherwise readily available to unit owners. A condominium association may, however, adopt rules to prohibit dual usage of association property and common elements by unit owners and their tenants.[27]

7-3 ARCHITECTURAL CONTROL

7-3:1 Homeowners' Association Architectural Controls

A homeowners' association may adopt written standards to control the external aesthetics of the property within its purview. To be enforceable, architectural controls must be set forth in the declaration or other published guidelines authorized by the declaration. The board of directors, or any architectural committee, derives its authority to review and approve parcel improvement plans and specifications from these published standards. If set forth in a declaration or other publication, the board or other review committee may review and approve plans and specifications for the location, size, type, or external appearance of any structure or other improvement on an owner's parcel.[28]

---

entitlements under the Condominium Act, which prohibits unreasonable restrictions on an owner's right to peaceably assemble, and (2) the board arbitrarily and capriciously enacted the rule; the court agreed with the association that it had the right to restrict the common element use and that the right of peaceable assembly does not necessarily include a right to conduct religious services; the court held that since (a) the association's rule banned only one form of assembly, but not all rights to assemble, and (b) the majority voted for the restriction due to the services' disruptive nature, the enactment of the rule was reasonable).

[25.] *Neuman v. Grandview At Emerald Hills*, 861 So. 2d 494, 497-98 (Fla. 4th Dist. Ct. App. 2003).

[26.] *Neuman v. Grandview At Emerald Hills*, 861 So. 2d 494, 498 (Fla. 4th Dist. Ct. App. 2003).

[27.] Fla. Stat. § 718.106(4) (2016).

[28.] Fla. Stat. § 720.3035(1) (2016).

The declaration of covenants or other published guidelines may also provide (1) options for materials that may be used in planned improvements, (2) the size and design of the improvement, and (3) the location of the improvement on the parcel. If the declaration or published guidelines provide such options, the association may not restrict the parcel owner's right to select from the available options.[29] The declaration or published guidelines and standards may also provide specific setback limitations. If they do not, the county or municipal setback limitations apply, and the association may not enforce any setback limitation inconsistent with such standards.[30]

Under Chapter 720, parcel owners are entitled to the rights and privileges in the architectural controls of the declaration or other published guidelines. A homeowners' association may not unreasonably infringe or impair owners' rights to improve their property in accordance with written standards. If the association or any architectural committee "unreasonably, knowingly, and willfully" infringes on an owner's right to improve his or her property in accordance with the written architectural controls, the owner has a statutory cause of action for damages, costs, and reasonable attorney's fees.[31]

Chapter 720 prohibits certain types of aesthetic controls. For instance, parcel owners may not be prevented from displaying a reasonably sized sign showing that the owner has contracted for security services within 10 feet of the entrance to the home.[32] The owner may also display one removable United States flag or official flag of the State of Florida in a respectful manner. Parcels owners can also display, in a respectful manner, one removable official flag, not larger than 4.5 feet by 6 feet, which represents the United States Army, Navy, Air Force, Marine Corps, or Coast Guard, or a POW-MIA flag.[33]

Subject to all building codes, zoning setbacks, and other governmental regulations, homeowners are also allowed to erect a freestanding flagpole up to 20 feet high on any portion of their

---

[29] Fla. Stat. § 720.3035(2) (2016).
[30] Fla. Stat. § 720.3035(3) (2016).
[31] Fla. Stat. § 720.3035(4) (2016).
[32] Fla. Stat. § 720.304(6) (2016).
[33] Fla. Stat. § 720.304(2)(a) (2016).

property, so long as the flagpole does not obstruct sightlines at intersections and is not erected within or upon an easement. The homeowner may display from the flagpole one official United States flag, not larger than 4.5 feet by 6 feet, and one additional official flag of the State of Florida or the United States Army, Navy, Air Force, Marines, or Coast Guard, or a POW-MIA flag. The additional flag must be equal in size or smaller than the United States flag.[34] Owners have a statutory cause of action to file suit to enjoin the enforcement of any covenant or rule that operates to deprive the owner of these rights.[35]

A homeowners' association is also prohibited from enforcing any covenant or rule that infringes an owner's right to install "Florida-friendly landscaping."[36] This includes "landscapes that conserve water, protect the environment, are adaptable to local conditions, and are drought tolerant." Florida-friendly landscaping employs methods aimed at "efficient watering, appropriate fertilization, mulching, attraction of wildlife, responsible management of yard pests, recycling yard waste, reduction of stormwater runoff, and waterfront protection."[37]

In addition, any parcel owner may construct an access ramp to accommodate an occupant with a medical necessity or disability that requires a ramp for egress and ingress. This is subject to the following guidelines: (1) the ramp must be as unobtrusive as possible; (2) the ramp must blend in with the existing aesthetics of the parcel; (3) the ramp must be reasonably sized for the intended use; (4) the plans for the ramp must be submitted to the homeowners' association in advance; and (5) the association may request reasonable modifications to achieve architectural consistency with the surroundings. The parcel owner must submit either an affidavit from a physician attesting to the medical necessity of the access ramp or the certification of disability required for disabled parking permits pursuant to section 320.0848.[38]

---

34. Fla. Stat. § 720.304(2)(b) (2016).
35. Fla. Stat. § 720.304(3) (2016).
36. Fla. Stat. § 720.3075(4) (2016).
37. Fla. Stat. § 373.185(1)(b) (2016).
38. Fla. Stat. § 720.304(5) (2016).

7-3:2   Condominium Association Aesthetic Controls

In condominiums, the owners typically have no options for improving the common elements or other condominium property outside the walls of their units, since the condominium association controls external aesthetics. They are also typically free from having to maintain the external elements of the condominium building, landscaping, common elements, and condominium property.

Certain decorations, however, are permitted by statute. Condominium associations may not prevent unit owners from displaying, in a respectful manner, one portable, removable United States flag. On Armed Forces Day, Memorial Day, Flag Day, Independence Day, and Veterans Day, condominium associations may not prevent owners from displaying, in a respectful manner, portable, removable official flags, not larger than 4.5 feet by 6 feet that represent the United States Army, Navy, Air Force, Marine Corps, or Coast Guard.[39] Additionally, condominium associations may not prevent unit owners from attaching a religious object not to exceed 3 inches wide, 6 inches high, and 1.5 inches deep on the owner's door frame or mantel.[40]

7-4   MANDATORY MEMBERSHIPS

In addition to aesthetic controls, community associations preserve property values through their connection with country clubs that maintain grounds and facilities in a manner that benefits the surrounding community. Indeed, many Florida community associations, whether homeowners' associations or condominium associations, are developed as part of country club communities. The country club is typically a separate corporate entity that owns and operates property and amenities for the use of its members.[41]

The country club can have a positive impact on the property value and marketability of residences in a number of ways. Owners benefit from the availability of nearby recreational facilities and

---

[39] Fla. Stat. § 718.113(4) (2016).

[40] Fla. Stat. § 718.113(6) (2016).

[41] Amenities may include golf courses, tennis courts, fitness facilities, swimming pools, spas, meeting rooms, and dining facilities. Country clubs often offer varying levels of membership, such as social memberships, dining memberships, sports memberships, and golf memberships, some of which confer an equity interest in the club. Each level of membership varies in price depending on access to club amenities.

the neighborhood security country clubs offer via their control of roads and access points in the community. Country clubs also maintain grounds and landscaping, beautifying the community's streetscapes.

Since maintenance of grounds and facilities requires a steady flow of membership dues, many country club communities are developed with the expectation that the residents of the surrounding communities will become members. Ideally, the country club and the surrounding community associations enter into a mutually beneficial relationship. The membership dues of the residents from the surrounding community help sustain the country club, which in turn maintains its grounds and facilities, preserving and increasing the value and marketability of the residents' homes. To ensure this mutually beneficial relationship, the governing documents of country club-affiliated community associations often contain covenants that run with the land requiring prospective owners to obtain a membership in the country club incident to purchase of a residence. This covenant is as enforceable as any other.

In other country club communities, membership in the club is entirely voluntary, meaning that prospective purchasers have no obligation to bear the cost of club membership and the country club has no guarantee that new owners will join. This can lead to conflicts, however, if club members feel that non-members are benefiting from the presence of the club without having to pay for it, which may come to a head if declining club memberships lead to financial trouble for the club.

To address this problem, many associations in country club communities have passed mandatory club membership amendments, an issue over which there has been a great deal of litigation. While non-club members allege that their pool of prospective purchasers is negatively impacted by mandatory membership, community associations assert their right to amend their documents as they see fit, and country clubs fight for their equitable interest in a guaranteed flow of new members. The courts typically apply a reasonableness test to mandatory membership amendments, examining whether they destroy the scheme of development and constitute an unreasonable restraint on alienation.

7-5   SCHEME OF DEVELOPMENT

Mandatory membership amendments are often imposed prior to turnover pursuant to the developer's reservation of the right to modify the restrictive covenants. In ruling on the enforceability of developer-imposed amendments, courts read a reasonableness requirement into the reservation of power, which "undercuts the grantor's unfettered control and provides the mutual burden and benefit to both grantor and grantees necessary to sustain the covenants."[42] This allows the subdivision to "substantially retain the character and restrictions contemplated by the grantor and each grantee at the conveyance."[43]

When a developer subdivides a tract of land and imposes restrictions on the separate parcels, all parcel owners may enforce the restrictions against all other parcel owners on the theory that there is a "mutuality of covenant and consideration," or on the theory that the restrictions constitute "mutual negative equitable easements,"[44] which are enforceable as contractual rights.[45] However, without limits on the developer's power to modify restrictions, "which supplied the mutual benefit or consideration necessary to allow enforcement," the character of the community could be entirely changed with no consideration or benefit to the owners.[46]

To avoid this, the courts apply a scheme-of-development reasonableness test to the developer's power to amend the documents, to ensure that it is exercised in a reasonable manner that does not destroy the general scheme of development.[47] This test is intended to protect the character and restrictions contemplated by the developer and each owner at the time of conveyance. Any amendment that changes the scheme of a particular development in its entirety requires approval of 100 percent of the owners.

The scheme-of-development test was applied in a case involving a subdivision with restrictive covenants ceding significant control over property to individual homeowners. Applying the test,

---

[42] *Nelle v. Loch Haven Homeowners' Ass'n*, 413 So. 2d 28, 29 (Fla. 1982).
[43] *Nelle v. Loch Haven Homeowners' Ass'n*, 413 So. 2d 28, 29 (Fla. 1982).
[44] *Hagan v. Sabal Palms*, 186 So. 2d 302, 307 (Fla. 2d Dist. Ct. App. 1966).
[45] *Dade Cty. v. Matheson*, 605 So. 2d 469, 474 (Fla. 3d Dist. Ct. App. 1992).
[46] *Nelle v. Loch Haven Homeowners' Ass'n*, 413 So. 2d 28, 29 (Fla. 1982).
[47] *Flamingo Ranch Estates v. Sunshine Ranches Homeowners*, 303 So. 2d 665, 666 (Fla. 4th Dist. Ct. App. 1974).

the court invalidated the creation of a mandatory homeowner's association, with broad powers of enforcement, assessment, maintenance, and rule enactment.[48] The court reasoned that since the homeowners' individual control over property "is lost when mandatorily transferred to a homeowner's association," this represented an impermissible fundamental change in the scheme of development.[49]

This case can be distinguished, however, from cases that do not involve owners with the type of individual control over their property that exists in communities lacking governing associations with broad powers of enforcement, maintenance, and rule enactment. Indeed, people who buy into community associations are on notice that their property is subject to the association's authority to enforce restrictions, levy assessments, perform maintenance on owners' property, and record and enforce liens against owners' property.

This case can also be distinguished from cases involving amendments adopted by non-developer owners following turnover. When examining the validity of homeowner imposed amendments, there is no need to balance the interests of the owners against the developer's "unfettered control." Proponents may argue that non-developer proposed amendments should be analyzed under the Florida formulation of California's *Lamden* test,[50] under which

---

[48.] *Holiday Pines Prop. Owners Ass'n v. Wetherington*, 596 So. 2d 84 (Fla. 4th Dist. Ct. App. 1992) (developer created a subdivision in 1978 with protective covenants and use restrictions, but no homeowners' association to govern property use; in 1983, the developer and some of the residents enacted robust mechanisms to enforce property use restrictions, specifically through (1) the creation of an architectural review board to approve parcel improvement plans and specifications, and (2) a homeowner's association with the power to make and amend regulations governing property use; some of the lot owners did not approve these amendments; in 1987, the developer instituted amendments that (a) made homeowners' association membership and its accompanying fees mandatory, (b) granted the association attorney's fees for covenant restriction enforcement matters, (c) permitted the association to perform maintenance on owner's property, and (d) allowed the creation and enforcement of liens against the owner's property for failure to meet monetary obligations to the association; applying the scheme-of-development reasonableness test, the court held that the developer's 1987 amendments were an unreasonable exercise of power to modify restrictions that destroyed the general plan of development, since these amendments made mandatory the previously voluntary membership in the homeowners' association, depriving homeowners of individual control over their property).

[49.] *Holiday Pines Prop. Owners Ass'n v. Wetherington*, 596 So. 2d 84, 87 (Fla. 4th Dist. Ct. App. 1992).

[50.] *Hollywood Towers Condo. Ass'n v. Hampton*, 40 So. 3d 787 (Fla. 4th Dist. Ct. App. 2010) (trial court granted a permanent injunction requiring an owner to allow the association access to her unit to perform repair work, despite testimony from the owner's

courts defer to a duly constituted community association board that (1) exercises discretion within its authority, as set forth in the relevant statutes and the association's governing documents, and (2) acts "upon reasonable investigation, in good faith and with regard for the best interests of the community association and its members."[51] Under this test, courts defer to decisions that are (a) within the scope of the association's authority, and (b) "reasonable," meaning that the association litigation has not "acted arbitrarily, capriciously, or in bad faith."[52]

For example, the Supreme Court of Florida upheld an amendment, adopted by owners in compliance with the declaration, which reduced the permissible period of condominium leasing from a period in excess of one year to a period of no more than nine months in a twelve-month period.[53] Ultimately, however, the Florida Legislature addressed this issue by adopting a rule that amendments prohibiting owners from renting their units, setting minimum or maximum rental terms, or limiting the number of times a unit can be rented during a period, are only effective against consenting owners and owners who acquire title after the effective date of the amendment.[54]

The analysis employed by most Florida courts suggests that member-adopted mandatory membership amendments, as opposed to developer-adopted amendments, should not be put

---

expert that exterior work was sufficient; on appeal, the court held (1) that the business judgment rule applies not only to immunize directors and officers from personal liability, but also to immunize the association itself, (2) that courts defer to associations' decisions that are reasonable and within the scope of the association's authority, and (3) decisions are "reasonable" as long as the association has not "acted arbitrarily, capriciously, or in bad faith"; the appeal court remanded to the trial court to apply the *Lamden* test to determine whether the association acted appropriately in demanding access to the owner's unit); *see* Chapter 4, § 4-3:5.

[51.] *Lamden v. La Jolla Shores Clubdominium Homeowners Ass'n*, 21 Cal. 4th 249, 980 P.2d 940, 942 (1999); *see* Chapter 4, § 4-3:5.

[52.] *Hollywood Towers Condo. Ass'n v. Hampton*, 40 So. 3d 787 (Fla. 4th Dist. Ct. App. 2010); *see* Chapter 4, § 4-3:5.

[53.] *Woodside Vill. Condo. Ass'n v. Jahren*, 806 So. 2d 452, 461 (Fla. 2002) (when plaintiffs purchased their condominium, the declaration provided that units could be leased without prior board approval for a period in excess of one year; the Supreme Court held that the amendment to the declaration reducing the lease period to no more than nine months in a twelve-month period was entirely valid based on the fact that owners were "on notice that the unique form of ownership they acquired when they purchased their units in the [condominium] was subject to change through the amendment process, and that they would be bound by properly adopted amendments"); *see* Chapter 2, § 2-8.

[54.] Fla. Stat. § 718.110(13) (2016).

to a scheme-of-development test. In short, if the amendment is (1) properly adopted,[55] and (2) not arbitrary, capricious, or in bad faith,[56] it should be enforceable.[57] However, the public policy reflected in these decisions has not been adopted universally. Specifically, the scheme of development test was applied to owner-adopted amendments to governing documents in at least one Florida court.[58] Under this test, a "reasonable" amendment is one that is "not arbitrary, capricious, or in bad faith," meaning that it does not destroy the general plan of development.[59] Subsequent to this decision, the Florida Legislature adopted Section 720.3075, specifically stating that the scheme of development test applies to pre-turnover amendments made by the developer.[60]

7-6 TRANSFER RESTRICTIONS

Mandatory membership provisions and other covenants restricting property transfer represent "unreasonable restraints on alienation" when they contain impermissible limitations on property transfer rights. Generally, after an absolute conveyance in fee simple, the grantor may not enforce conditions or provisions that (1) prohibit the grantee from conveying the property without the grantor's consent, or (2) require the grantee to sell only to a particular person or persons.[61] Such provisions are "repugnant

---

[55.] *Woodside Vill. Condo. Ass'n v. Jahren*, 806 So. 2d 452 (Fla. 2002).

[56.] See *Hollywood Towers Condo. Ass'n v. Hampton*, 40 So. 3d 787 (Fla. 4th Dist. Ct. App. 2010).

[57.] See *Woodside Vill. Condo. Ass'n v. Jahren*, 806 So. 2d 452 (Fla. 2002); *Hollywood Towers Condo. Ass'n v. Hampton*, 40 So. 3d 787 (Fla. 4th Dist. Ct. App. 2010).

[58.] *Klinow v. Island Court at Boca W. Prop. Owners' Ass'n*, 64 So. 3d 177 (Fla. 4th Dist. Ct. App. 2011).

[59.] *Klinow v. Island Court at Boca W. Prop. Owners' Ass'n*, 64 So. 3d 177, 180 (Fla. 4th Dist. Ct. App. 2011) (owners challenged an amendment to the original governing documents passed by two-thirds approval of the voting members, which allowed the homeowners' associations to replace privately owned driveway and walkway materials; since the amendment benefited the association and the owners equally, resulting in a more aesthetically pleasing community "without fundamentally changing any homeowner's personal property or community plans," the court held that "no radical change of plan would occur as to make the changes unreasonable" and permitted the amendment); *see* Chapter 4, § 4-3:5.

[60.] Fla. Stat. § 720.3075 (2016).

[61.] *Davis v. Geyer*, 151 Fla. 362, 370, 9 So. 2d 727, 730 (1942) (holding that an agreement executed in conjunction with property conveyed by warranty deed that prohibited the grantee's subsequent sale of the property without grantor approval was void since it

and void."[62] To determine the validity of transfer restrictions, courts assess the "duration, type of alienation precluded, or the size of the class precluded from taking."[63]

A restrictive covenant in a community association's declaration is conceptually different, however, than an ordinary grantor's arbitrary and absolute right to approve a grantee's subsequent purchaser. The primary difference is the public policies at stake. While rules against unreasonable restraints on alienation further the public policy in favor of economic and commercial development, community associations have a competing interest in self-determination and the right to protect community welfare and property values.

As a result, Florida courts recognize the right of community associations to impose certain restrictions, such as screening prospective purchasers and tenants with criminal background checks to keep the community free of threats to the residents' health and safety. Communities may also completely curtail an owner's right to lease by imposing minimum lease durations and restrictions on the number of times an owner can lease in a given period in order to discourage a transient environment in which short term occupants have little investment in preserving the community's quality and character.

To balance competing public policies, Florida courts apply a reasonableness test to community association's restraints on alienation. For example, the court deemed "reasonable" a condominium association restriction that prohibited leasing units "to others as a regular practice for business, speculative, investment or other similar purposes," but that allowed the board under special circumstances, and to avoid undue hardship, to approve leases of at least four consecutive months but no more than 12 consecutive months.[64]

As a restraint on alienation, the court analyzed the restriction in terms of duration, type of alienation precluded, and the size of the precluded class, taking into account the need for greater limitations

---

represented a condition annexed to the grant or devise of land which prohibited the grantee or devisee from alienating that land, which is unenforceable under Florida law).

[62] *Davis v. Geyer*, 151 Fla. 362, 370, 9 So. 2d 727, 730 (1942).

[63] *Camino Gardens Ass'n v. McKim*, 612 So. 2d 636, 639 (Fla. 4th Dist. Ct. App. 1993).

[64] *Seagate Condo. Ass'n v. Duffy*, 330 So. 2d 484, 486 (Fla. 4th Dist. Ct. App. 1976).

upon individual owners' in the context of condominium living.[65] In light of the difficulties associated with living in a tourism community in South Florida and the objective of inhibiting transiency to foster a residential atmosphere, the leasing restrictions were deemed entirely reasonable. The court held that attaining the community's goals outweighed "the social value" of retaining an individual unit owner's "absolutely unqualified right to dispose of his property in any way and for such duration or purpose as he alone so desires."[66]

The court also noted that the leasing restriction was neither an unlimited nor an unreasonable restraint on alienation, since it prohibited only a specific form of alienation (leasing), made exceptions for hardship cases, and could be terminated at any time by a vote of the condominium unit owners.[67] Following this ruling, section 718.110(13) was adopted, which provides that amendments prohibiting owners from renting their units, setting minimum or maximum rental terms, or limiting the number of times a unit can be rented during a period, are only effective against owners who consent to the amendment and owners who acquire title after the effective date of the amendment.[68]

7-6:1   Association Approval of Transfers

Both Chapter 720 and the Condominium Act recognize associations' power to approve leases or other transfers.[69] Under the Condominium Act, associations whose declarations or bylaws authorize lease approval may withhold such approval based on unit

---

[65] *Seagate Condo. Ass'n v. Duffy*, 330 So. 2d 484, 486 (Fla. 4th Dist. Ct. App. 1976) (citing *Hidden Harbour Estates v. Norman*, 309 So. 2d 180, 181-82 (Fla. 4th Dist. Ct. App. 1975)) ("inherent in the condominium concept is the principle that to promote the health, happiness, and peace of mind of the majority of the unit owners since they are living in such close proximity and using facilities in common, each unit owner must give up a certain degree of freedom of choice which he might otherwise enjoy").

[66] *Seagate Condo. Ass'n v. Duffy*, 330 So. 2d 484, 486 (Fla. 4th Dist. Ct. App. 1976).

[67] *Seagate Condo. Ass'n v. Duffy*, 330 So. 2d 484, 486 (Fla. 4th Dist. Ct. App. 1976).

[68] Fla. Stat. § 718.110(13) (2016).

[69] Fla. Stat. § 720.303(5)(C)(2) (2016) (in this subsection's discussion of the association's obligation to maintain official records and make them available to members for inspection and photocopying, it alludes to the association's power to approve transfers, stating that the association may not allow access to "[i]nformation obtained by an association in connection with the *approval of the lease, sale, or other transfer* of a parcel") (*emphasis added*); Fla. Stat. § 718.116(4) (2016).

owners' delinquency in assessment payments.[70] The Condominium Act also sets forth certain regulations regarding covenants on leasing and transfer. As stated above, the Condominium Act does not allow the association to impose a restriction prohibiting rentals, and restrictions on lease terms, against owners who do not consent, unless the owner purchased the unit after the effective date of the restrictions.[71]

In addition, the association may not make any charge in connection with a lease, mortgage, or transfer unless the association is required to approve the transfer and the fee is provided for in the governing documents. Any such fee may not exceed $100 per applicant. A husband and wife are considered one applicant, as is a parent and child. The association may not charge for approval of a lease renewal. If permitted by the declaration or bylaws, the association may require the tenant to place a security deposit into an escrow account maintained by the association in an amount not to exceed one month's rent. Disputes regarding this deposit are governed by the Florida Residential Landlord and Tenant Act.[72]

7-6:2   Rights of First Refusal

7-6:2.1   Prohibition Against Forced Sales

Many condominium declarations provide a right of first refusal to the association entitling it to purchase property at the same price and on the same terms and conditions contained in good faith offers to third parties.

In Florida, rights of first refusal are enforceable as long as they do not constitute an unreasonable restraint of alienation. As with any other declaration provision, the express language of the right of first refusal provision (1) controls, (2) is strictly construed, and (3) will be strictly enforced.

The right of first refusal generally presumes a voluntary sale by an owner who manifests a willingness to accept an offer from a third party. The right of first refusal does not empower the association to compel unwilling owners to sell.

---

70. Fla. Stat. § 718.116(4) (2016).
71. Fla. Stat. § 718.110(13) (2016).
72. Fla. Stat. § 718.112(2)(i) (2016).

For example, where a condominium owner conveyed his unit without conforming to declaration provisions entitling the association to pre-transfer notification, approval, and right of first refusal, the association could not *force* the owner to convey the unit to the association, since the declaration's unambiguous language permitted the owner to *refuse* and *withdraw and/or reject* the offer.[73] In such cases, the court cannot order owners to sell to the association. It can only strictly enforce the declaration by recognizing the association's right to purchase along with the owners' option to withdraw the offer to sell.

7-6:2.2 Right of First Refusal Does Not Violate the Rule Against Perpetuities

Property owners have unsuccessfully challenged condominium associations' right of first refusal on the grounds that it violates the rule against perpetuities. In fact, the Florida Supreme Court explicitly held that the right of first refusal is not subject to either the statutory or common law rules against perpetuities.[74] While both the statutory and common law rule against perpetuities prohibit remote vesting of a property interest,[75] the Court determined that

---

[73] *Edlund v. Seagull Townhomes Condo. Ass'n*, 928 So. 2d 405, 406-07 (Fla. 3d Dist. Ct. App. 2006) (owner violated the condominium declaration by quitclaiming interest in his unit to his parents, without notifying the association, receiving association approval, or permitting the association to exercise its right of first refusal; the association filed suit and the parents re-conveyed the property to their son, after which the association acknowledged the first transfer and amended the complaint to allege that the re-conveyance was a nullity because it was not approved, in addition to seeking specific performance of its right of first refusal to purchase the unit; summary judgment was entered in the association's favor on the grounds that the initial transfer was approved by the association, making the parents the owners, and that the parents' re-transfer was "null and void" because it had no association approval, entitling the association to specific performance according to its right of first refusal to purchase the condominium for fair market value; the appeals court disagreed and held that the association could not force the parents to convey the unit to the association because the declaration's unambiguous language permitted the owners to withdraw and/or reject the offer).

[74] *Old Port Cove Holdings v. Old Port Cove Condo. Ass'n One*, 986 So. 2d 1279, 1287 (Fla. 2008) (in a dispute between a condominium association and owners who were successors-in-interest to a developer who executed an agreement with the association granting it a right of first refusal in a parcel of property, the developer's successors sued to quiet title and for a declaratory judgment that the association's right of first refusal was invalid as violative of the common law rule against perpetuities; the Court held that rights of first refusal are not subject to either the statutory rule or the common law rule against perpetuities).

[75] *See Adams v. Vidal*, 60 So. 2d 545, 549 (Fla. 1952) (defining the common law rule against perpetuities as a prohibition against property interests that vest "later than twenty-one years after some life in being at the creation of the interest"); *Iglehart v. Phillips*, 383 So. 2d 610, 614 (Fla. 1980) (explaining that the common law rule against perpetuities'

---

the right of first refusal does not create a property interest at all.[76] Unlike an option, which is "a unilateral contract which gives the option holder the right to purchase under the terms and conditions of the option agreement,"[77] a right of first refusal only entitles the holder to elect to purchase property at a fixed price or at the same price and on the same terms as those contained in a good faith third party offer *if* the owner indicates a willingness to accept the offer. While an option contract can force an unwilling owner to sell, a right of first refusal requires a manifest intent on the part of the owner to *accept* an offer from a third party.

A right of first refusal may ripen into an option if the owner decides to sell. In Florida, courts have consistently held that an option contract only creates an interest in property when "an optionee exercises the right to purchase in accordance with the terms of his option."[78] Since an option in and of itself does not create an interest in property, a right of first refusal, which may or may not ripen into an option, certainly does not create an interest in property. As the right of first refusal creates no property interest whatsoever, it doesn't violate the rule against perpetuities' prohibition against remote vesting of property interests.[79]

7-7   ENFORCEMENT METHODS

7-7:1   Fines and Suspensions

Associations have a number of tools available to enforce its governing documents and reasonable rules. If simple notifications

---

purpose is to prevent "remote vesting of an estate or interest therein" that may serve as "a restraint on the right to create future interests"); Fla. Stat. § 689.225(2) (2012) (adopting the common law rule against perpetuities as follows: "A nonvested property interest in real or personal property is invalid unless: 1. When the interest is created, it is certain to vest or terminate no later than 21 years after the death of an individual then alive; or 2. The interest either vests or terminates within 90 years after its creation."); Fla. Stat. § 689.225(7) (2012) (providing that this statute is "the sole expression of any rule against perpetuities or remoteness in vesting in this state" and that "[n]o common-law rule against perpetuities or remoteness in vesting shall exist with respect to any interest or power regardless of whether such interest or power is governed by this section").

[76.] *Old Port Cove Holdings v. Old Port Cove Condo. Ass'n One*, 986 So. 2d 1279, 1287 (Fla. 2008).

[77.] *S. Inv. Corp. v. Norton*, 57 So. 2d 1, 2 (Fla. 1952).

[78.] *Gautier v. Lapof*, 91 So. 2d 324, 326 (Fla. 1956).

[79.] *Old Port Cove Holdings v. Old Port Cove Condo. Ass'n One*, 986 So. 2d 1279, 1287 (Fla. 2008).

don't remedy violations, the association can levy reasonable fines against owners, tenants, guests, or invitees of up to $100 for each violation. For continuing violations, the association can levy up to $100 per day with a single notice and an opportunity for a hearing. The fine may not exceed $1,000 in the aggregate unless some other amount is set forth in the governing documents. If the recipient of the fine refuses to pay, the association may sue to recover the fine. The prevailing party in this type of litigation is entitled to recover reasonable attorney's fees.[80] In addition to fines, a community association may also suspend the rights of owners, tenants, guests, or invitees to use the common areas and facilities.[81]

Chapter 720 provides that a fine of less than $1,000 may not become a lien against a parcel.[82] The Condominium Act provides that a fine may not become a lien against a unit at all,[83] even when a condominium association's governing documents permit it.[84] For example, an association argued that it was within its rights to foreclose a lien on an owner's unit for failure to pay a fine because its governing documents defined fines as "common expense[s] ... leviable by the Committee ... and collectible in the same manner as any other common expense."[85]

While the trial court agreed and ordered the owner's unit to be sold at public sale, the appeals court held that the condominium documents' language was inconsistent with the Condominium Act

---

[80] Fla. Stat. § 720.305(2) (2016); Fla. Stat. § 718.303(3) (2016).

[81] Fla. Stat. § 720305(2)(a)(3) (2016); Fla. Stat. § 718.303(3)(a)(4) (2016).

[82] Fla. Stat. § 720.305(2) (2016).

[83] Fla. Stat. § 718.303(3) (2016).

[84] *Elbadramany v. Oceans Seven Condo. Ass'n.*, 461 So. 2d 1001, 1002-1003 (Fla. 5th Dist. Ct. App. 1984).

[85] *Elbadramany v. Oceans Seven Condo. Ass'n.*, 461 So. 2d 1001, 1002-1003 (Fla. 5th Dist. Ct. App. 1984) (owner received several violation letters and a $5-per-day fine for breaking the association's parking rules; after nine and a half months, the trial court ordered a public sale of the owner's unit based on the association's foreclosure on its lien against the owner's unit for failure to pay the $930 fine; the appeals court held that despite the fact that the condominium documents permitted the association to impose a lien for fines, which the association defined as "common expenses," the fine was only applicable to select individuals and therefore could not be defined as an assessment collectible from all owners in proportion to their ownership interests in common elements; since the fine was not a common expense under the Condominium Act, despite language in the condominium documents to the contrary, the court held that the lien could not serve as a basis for a foreclosure judgment).

and therefore unenforceable.[86] Specifically, under the Condominium Act assessments are collected from *all* unit owners in proportion to their ownership interests in the common elements. Since fines cannot be collected from *all* unit owners in proportion to their ownership interest, they are by definition not common expenses upon which liens may be foreclosed. Therefore, permitting fines to be classified as such would be completely inconsistent with the Condominium Act. Accordingly, the lien could not serve as a basis for a foreclosure judgment.[87]

To impose a fine or suspension, the association must provide 14 days' notice and an opportunity for a hearing. Continuing violations only require a single notice and an opportunity for a hearing. Chapter 720 provides that the hearing must take place before a committee of at least three members appointed by the board, who are not themselves board members or employees of the association, or their spouses, parents, children, or siblings.[88] The Condominium Act provides that the hearing must take place before a committee of unit owners who are neither board members nor persons residing in a board member's home.[89] To uphold the fine or suspension, the committee must approve the sanction by majority vote. Otherwise, it may not be imposed.[90] Chapter 720 provides that if the committee approves the fine or suspension, and the association imposes it, the association must provide written notice by mail or hand delivery to the owner and, if applicable, the tenant or invitee.[91]

If the association is unsuccessful in its efforts to coerce compliance, both Chapter 720 and the Condominium Act provide a statutory cause of action to enforce an association's restrictive covenants. Specifically, the association or any of its members may sue to enforce the community's governing documents and rules. Liability may be imposed against the association, members of the association, board members, tenants, guests, and invitees. The

---

[86.] *Elbadramany v. Oceans Seven Condo. Ass'n.*, 461 So. 2d 1001, 1002-1003 (Fla. 5th Dist. Ct. App. 1984).

[87.] *Elbadramany v. Oceans Seven Condo. Ass'n.*, 461 So. 2d 1001, 1002-1003 (Fla. 5th Dist. Ct. App. 1984).

[88.] Fla. Stat. § 720.305(2) (2016).

[89.] Fla. Stat. § 718.303(3) (2016).

[90.] Fla. Stat. § 720.305(2) (2016); Fla. Stat. § 718.303(3) (2016).

[91.] Fla. Stat. § 720.305(2) (2016).

prevailing party in litigation over enforcement of the governing documents is entitled to recover reasonable attorney's fees.[92]

7-7:2 Mandatory Mediation and Arbitration

Certain types of covenant enforcement disputes are subject to presuit mediation requirements. Chapter 720 requires presuit mediation as a precondition to filing suit for disputes between an association and a parcel owner regarding use of or changes to the parcel or the common areas and other covenant enforcement disputes. Presuit mediation is also required for disputes regarding amendments to association documents, meetings of the board and committees appointed by the board, membership meetings, and access to the official records.[93] For any disagreement under the Condominium Act "that involves use of a unit or the appurtenances thereto, including use of the common elements," disputing parties must submit a petition for arbitration to the Division of Florida Condominiums, Timeshares, and Mobile Homes in the Department of Business and Professional Regulation as a precondition to filing suit.[94] This includes disputes over the following: the authority of the board to require any owner to take any action, or not to take any action, involving the owner's unit or the appurtenances thereto; the authority of the board to alter or add to a common area or element; the failure of the association to properly conduct elections; the failure of the association to give adequate notice of meetings or other actions; the failure of the association to properly conduct meetings; or the failure of the association to allow inspection of books and records.[95]

The presuit requirements set forth in Chapter 720 and the Condominium Act filter out association-owner disagreements involving common disputes that are typically factually simple. Most covenant enforcement disputes can be resolved by mediators or arbitrators without extensive discovery, expert testimony, and extensive attorney's fees associated with litigation.

[92.] Fla. Stat. § 720.305(1) (2016); Fla. Stat. § 718.303(1) (2016).
[93.] Fla. Stat. § 720.311(2) (2016).
[94.] Fla. Admin. Code R. 61B-45.013 (2016).
[95.] Fla. Stat. § 718.1255(1) (2016).

7-7:3   Statute of Limitations

The statutory period of limitations for community association actions for breach of governing documents is five years. Petitions for mediation or arbitration discussed above toll the applicable statute of limitations.[96] When parties sue for specific performance under the contractual terms of a declaration of condominium, there are two potential terms for the statute of limitations. While there is a one-year statute of limitations for specific performance of a contract under section 95.11(5)(a),[97] there is a five-year statute of limitations for the enforcement of the rights and obligations in a condominium declaration under section 95.11(2)(b).[98]

When confronted with this conflict, the court opined that reasonable arguments can be made on the applicability of either statute of limitations.[99] Under such circumstances, when there is doubt as to the applicability of a statute of limitations, Florida courts recognize that the issue is generally resolved in favor of the claimant.[100] Using this analysis, the court resolved the matter in favor of the claimant, holding that the five year limitations period for actions founded on a contract applied in the case at hand.[101]

7-8   ESTOPPEL

The community association has an obligation to enforce its covenants uniformly and in a non-discriminatory manner. This is critical to the owners' confidence in their board of directors and management personnel. Uniform enforcement also allows the owners to feel that property governance conforms to their expectations at purchase. When the board of directors or management fails to

---

[96] Fla. Stat. § 720.311(1) (2016); Fla. Stat. § 718.1255(4)(i) (2016).

[97] Fla. Stat. § 95.11(5)(a) (2016).

[98] Fla. Stat. § 95.11(2)(b) (2016).

[99] *Sheoah Highlands v. Daugherty*, 837 So. 2d 579, 582 (Fla. 5th Dist. Ct. App. 2003) (in a suit against the association and the board of directors, a condominium owner attempted to enforce declaration restrictions regarding screened enclosures on the common property, which it alleged the association permitted some unit owners to violate; the association raised a statute of limitations defense arguing that the owner's suit was for specific performance of the declaration and was therefore barred by the one-year statute of limitations for specific performance of a contract under section 95.11(5)(a); the owner argued that enforcement of the rights and obligations set forth in the declaration is a legal or equitable action on a contract within the scope section 95.11(2)(b), which proscribes a five-year statute of limitations).

[100] *J.B. v. Sacred Heart Hosp. of Pensacola*, 635 So. 2d 945, 947 (Fla. 1994).

[101] *Sheoah Highlands v. Daugherty*, 837 So. 2d 579, 582 (Fla. 5th Dist. Ct. App. 2003).

enforce the covenants, when enforcement is inconsistent, or when personal biases are a factor in enforcement decisions, the association risks losing its authority, legally and psychologically.

Specifically, inconsistent governing document enforcement leaves an association vulnerable to affirmative defenses based on estoppel.[102] The Florida Supreme Court defines estoppel as "the preclusion of a person from asserting a fact by previous conduct inconsistent therewith, on his own part, or the part of those under whom he claims."[103] A community association will be estopped from enforcing its restrictions if it (1) makes a representation to an owner as to some material fact, which representation is contrary to the enforcement of the restrictions; (2) the owner relies on the association's representation; and (3) the owner changes his or her position to his or her detriment, because of the reliance on the association's representation.[104] For example, the court held that an owner established each element of estoppel in a case in which the community association affirmatively indicated approval of the owner's installation of shutters at an open board meeting, on which the owner relied to begin shutter installation, after which the association changed its position without making any effort to alert the owner.[105] Under these circumstances, the association was

---

[102] *Quality Shell Homes & Supply v. Roley*, 186 So. 2d 837, 840 (Fla. 1st Dist. Ct. App. 1966) ("Estoppel rests on the principles of equity, justice, and morality.").

[103] *Coogler v. Rogers*, 25 Fla. 853, 873, 7 So. 391, 394 (1889).

[104] *Quality Shell Homes & Supply v. Roley*, 186 So. 2d 837, 841 (Fla. 1st Dist. Ct. App. 1966) (providing the elements of estoppel: (1) a representation by the party estopped to the party claiming the estoppel as to some material fact, which representation is contrary to the condition of affairs later asserted by the estopped party; (2) a reliance upon this representation by the party claiming the estoppel; and (3) a change in the position of the party claiming the estoppel to his detriment, caused by the representation and his reliance thereon).

[105] *Fifty-Six Sixty Collins Ave. Condo. v. Dawson*, 354 So. 2d 432, 434 (Fla. 3d Dist. Ct. App. 1978) (the association sued to prevent a condominium unit owner from using the shutters on her condominium's balcony, claiming that the owner did not obtain the required consent to install them; the owner argued that the association was estopped from denying approval because she justifiably relied on the association's representations when she executed shutter installation contract; specifically, the owner relied on (a) the board's affirmative vote approving shutter installation in the condominium four months prior to execution of her shutter contract, (b) her conversation with the property manager expressing her intention to construct a balcony enclosure on the terrace of the condominium unit, (c) the lack of protest on the part of the association once installation began, and (d) the association's progress inquiries to the installer; based on the fact that the association affirmatively indicated approval of the shutters at an open board meeting and made no effort to alert the owner of its change in position after becoming aware that she began installation, the

estopped from arguing that the owner did not obtain the required consent to install her shutters.[106]

Principals of estoppel only apply in this context, however, if there is some affirmative act on the part of the association and the association's failure to enforce its rules leads the owner to act in reliance. As an equitable doctrine, estoppel "is applied only where to refuse its application would be virtually to sanction the perpetration of a fraud."[107] In addition, the principle of estoppel generally has no application to transactions that are unlawful or contrary to public policy.[108] Since violating a community association's governing documents is both unlawful and a violation of public policy, the act allegedly supporting estoppel must be compelling enough to clearly establish that the equities favor the violating party.

It is not enough for an owner to simply establish that the association failed to take an affirmative act to prevent the violation.[109] This was illustrated in a case in which owners continued to renovate condominium property, despite (1) being informed prior to purchase that the property was not part of their unit, and (2) the consistent protests of the association.[110] The court held that "no estoppel by silence can arise unless the party asserting the estoppel claim is ignorant of the truth."[111] Since the owners were well aware of their

---

court held that the association was estopped from arguing that the owner did not obtain the required consent to install her shutters).

[106] *Fifty-Six Sixty Collins Ave. Condo. v. Dawson*, 354 So. 2d 432 (Fla. 3d Dist. Ct. App. 1978).

[107] *Brickell Bay Club Condo. Ass'n v. Hernstadt*, 512 So. 2d 994, 996 (Fla. 3d Dist. Ct. App. 1987).

[108] *Brickell Bay Club Condo. Ass'n v. Hernstadt*, 512 So. 2d 994, 996 (Fla. 3d Dist. Ct. App. 1987).

[109] *Brickell Bay Club Condo. Ass'n v. Hernstadt*, 512 So. 2d 994, 996 (Fla. 3d Dist. Ct. App. 1987).

[110] *Brickell Bay Club Condo. Ass'n v. Hernstadt*, 512 So. 2d 994, 996 (Fla. 3d Dist. Ct. App. 1987) (owners converted a structure located on the condominium roof, adjacent to their unit, into a bathroom and bedroom, after being informed prior to purchase that the structure was not part of their unit; not only did the owners not obtain the association's approval as required by the declaration, the association's engineers specifically disapproved the owners' plan; after the renovations began, the association's attorney advised the owners they were trespassing; when the renovations were completed nine months later, the association demanded that the owners discontinue use of the bathroom and bedroom unless 75 percent of the owners gave consent; at trial, the court disagreed with the owners' argument that the association's failure to take affirmative steps to prevent the renovations justified application of waiver and estoppel principles).

[111] *Brickell Bay Club Condo. Ass'n v. Hernstadt*, 512 So. 2d 994, 996 (Fla. 3d Dist. Ct. App. 1987).

obligations before and during renovations, waiver and estoppel would not prevent the association from enforcing its restrictions.[112]

The court came to a similar conclusion in a case in which a condominium association filed a complaint to enjoin a unit owner who built a patio on the common elements. The court rejected the argument of the owner, who never received the requisite association permission, that the association's failure to object operated as estoppel or as a waiver of the association's enforcement of the governing documents.[113] The court held that statements by the board that it could not grant or deny permission did not amount to assent, and that management's seemingly favorable attitude toward the construction plan did not justify the owner's reliance.[114] As such, the owner failed to establish the elements of estoppel.[115]

To help avoid estoppel and waiver arguments, community associations can include anti-waiver provisions in their declarations. For instance, the court found the following anti-waiver provision to be entirely enforceable: "failure by the Association to enforce any restriction shall in no event be deemed a waiver of the right to do so thereafter."[116] In this case, the owner's estoppel argument failed, in part, because of the valid anti-waiver provision.[117]

7-8:1   Selective Enforcement

A court will not enforce covenants that have been unequally, arbitrarily, unreasonably, or selectively enforced.[118] An owner may raise selective enforcement, an affirmative defense rooted in

---

[112.] *Brickell Bay Club Condo. Ass'n v. Hernstadt*, 512 So. 2d 994, 996 (Fla. 3d Dist. Ct. App. 1987).

[113.] *Fountains of Palm Beach Condo., Inc. No. 5 v. Farkas*, 355 So. 2d 163, 164 (Fla. 4th Dist. Ct. App. 1978).

[114.] *Fountains of Palm Beach Condo., Inc. No. 5 v. Farkas*, 355 So. 2d 163, 164 (Fla. 4th Dist. Ct. App. 1978).

[115.] *Fountains of Palm Beach Condo., Inc. No. 5 v. Farkas*, 355 So. 2d 163, 164 (Fla. 4th Dist. Ct. App. 1978).

[116.] *Emerald Estates Cmty. Ass'n v. Gorodetzer*, 819 So. 2d 190, 194 (Fla. 4th Dist. Ct. App. 2002).

[117.] *Emerald Estates Cmty. Ass'n v. Gorodetzer*, 819 So. 2d 190, 194 (Fla. 4th Dist. Ct. App. 2002) (owner who installed radio antennae without the association's approval argued that the association was estopped from denying approval in part because they already had antennae on their property and the developer's representative told him installation would not be a problem).

[118.] *Kenyon v. Polo Park Homeowners Ass'n*, 907 So. 2d 1226, 1228 (Fla. 2d Dist. Ct. App. 2005).

estoppel, to prevent the association from enforcing its restrictions when it has failed to enforce them consistently and uniformly.[119] For instance, selective enforcement was used to prevent a condominium from forcing an owner to comply with the declaration's anti-pet rules.[120] In this case, the association had a spotty history of enforcing the condominium declaration's clear prohibition against pets, explicitly permitting certain residents to keep dogs and cats and ignoring residents who flouted the rule. By allowing residents to keep animals in their units, the association lost its authority to enforce its pet restriction against the owner in this case.[121]

An association's failure to enforce its restrictions will not always estop the association under a theory of selective enforcement. This is particularly true when the association's failure to enforce occurred during the period of developer control and the association can show a consistent effort to enforce the restrictions since turnover. For instance, an association was granted injunctive relief to force owners to restore their terraces to their original condition in compliance with the declaration, despite the fact that the developer gave permission to the owners to violate the declaration prohibition against altering the building's exterior.[122] Beginning at turnover, however, the association had consistently taken action to prevent further violations. As such, the court found that the association consistently enforced "the mutual agreement entered into by all the unit owners," and that the developer's failure

---

[119.] *White Egret Condo. v. Franklin*, 379 So. 2d 346, 352 (Fla. 1979).

[120.] *Prisco v. Forest Villas Condo. Apartments*, 847 So. 2d 1012, 1015 (Fla. 4th Dist. Ct. App. 2003).

[121.] *Prisco v. Forest Villas Condo. Apartments*, 847 So. 2d 1012, 1015 (Fla. 4th Dist. Ct. App. 2003) (the association sued an owner to enjoin her from keeping a dog in violation of the declaration's pet restriction; the owner raised selective enforcement as an affirmative defense, based on the association's lack of action to enforce the pet restriction against other owners who kept cats and dogs; the association responded by stating that soon after the owner alerted it to the other pet violations it began enforcement against those owners as well; the owner's affidavits demonstrated a lack of enforcement and included testimony from a resident that she kept cats for years after being assured that her cats would be grandfathered in and the board would not enforce the restriction against her, and that she saw cats in the windows and on the balconies of many units; another resident's affidavit stated he had always lived with his dog in the condominium and entered into an agreed judgment with the association after it unsuccessfully attempted to enforce its pet restriction against him; he also stated that he saw cats in the windows and on the balconies; the court held that through its selective and arbitrary enforcement of its pet restriction, the association lost its authority to enforce the rule against the owner in this case).

[122.] *Ladner v. Plaza Del Prado Condo. Ass'n*, 423 So. 2d 927, 930 (Fla. 3d Dist. Ct. App. 1982).

to enforce the rules was not selective and arbitrary conduct by the association.[123]

Similarly, an association was permitted to enforce an under-16 age restriction in the association's declaration when the developer failed to enforce it in a uniform manner. Based on the owners' attempts to enforce the age restriction after turnover, through letter writing and litigation, the court did "not find competent evidence to support a finding that the association did anything other than attempt to enforce the restriction whenever it found a violation."[124] As such, the court found the association was entitled to an injunction preventing violation of the age restriction.[125]

[123.] *Ladner v. Plaza Del Prado Condo. Ass'n*, 423 So. 2d 927, 930 (Fla. 3d Dist. Ct. App. 1982).

[124.] *Estates of Fort Lauderdale Prop. Owners' Ass'n v. Kalet*, 492 So. 2d 1340, 1342 (Fla. 4th 1986).

[125.] *Estates of Fort Lauderdale Prop. Owners' Ass'n v. Kalet*, 492 So. 2d 1340, 1342 (Fla. 4th 1986).

Chapter 8

Alternative Dispute Resolution

8-1 INTRODUCTION TO ALTERNATIVE DISPUTE RESOLUTION

For certain community association disputes, the Florida Legislature requires alternative dispute resolution processes, such as mediation and arbitration, as a precondition to filing suit. As discussed in both Chapter 720 and the Condominium Act, the purpose of alternative dispute resolution is to reduce court dockets and trials and offer a more efficient and cost-effective alternative to litigation.[1] The Condominium Act also recognizes alternative dispute resolution's role in rectifying unit owners' perceived financial disadvantage in condominium association litigation.[2]

Depending on the nature of the dispute, as discussed in detail below, the association or the owner initiating the dispute must file a petition for binding arbitration, nonbinding arbitration, or presuit mediation. Filing tolls the applicable statute of limitations.[3]

8-2 HOMEOWNERS' ASSOCIATION DISPUTES

Under Chapter 720, presuit mediation is a precondition in suits between homeowners' associations and owners regarding parcel and common area use and alterations, as well as other covenant enforcement disputes. Presuit mediation is also required for

---

[1] Fla. Stat. § 720.311(1) (2016); Fla. Stat. § 718.1255(3)(b) (2016).

[2] Fla. Stat. § 718.1255(3)(a) (2016) ("Specifically, a condominium association, with its statutory assessment authority, is often more able to bear the costs and expenses of litigation than the unit owner who must rely on his or her own financial resources to satisfy the costs of litigation against the association.").

[3] Fla. Stat. § 720.311(1) (2016); Fla. Stat. § 718.1255(4)(i) (2016).

disputes regarding association documents amendments, board and committee meetings, membership meetings, and access to the official records. This does not apply to election meetings disputes, which are subject to binding arbitration. Presuit mediation is also not required for disputes regarding collection of assessments, fines, or other financial obligations, including attorney's fees and costs, or any action to enforce a prior mediation settlement agreement between the parties.[4]

Homeowners' association board of director election and recall disputes are subject to binding arbitration in accordance with the provisions of the Condominium Act and the rules adopted by the Division of Florida Condominiums, Timeshares, and Mobile Homes in the Department of Business and Professional Regulation (Division). Neither election nor recall disputes are eligible for presuit mediation.[5]

The aggrieved party must serve the responding party with a written demand to participate in presuit mediation in substantially the form set forth in section 720.311(2)(a).[6] Service of the presuit mediation demand must be by certified mail, return receipt requested, with a copy sent by first-class mail to the responding party's address as it last appears in the association's official records. The responding party has 20 days from the date the demand was mailed to serve a written response. The response must be by certified mail, return receipt requested, with a copy sent by first-class mail to the address on the demand.[7]

Presuit mediation must be conducted in accordance with Rule 1.720 of the Florida Rules of Civil Procedure. Unless stipulated by the parties in writing, each party must appear at mediation either in person or through a party representative with full authority to settle without further consultation. For any insured party, an insurance carrier representative must appear who is not the carrier's outside counsel and "who has full authority to settle in an amount up to the amount of the plaintiff's last demand

---

4. Fla. Stat. § 720.311(2) (2016).
5. Fla. Stat. § 720.311(1) (2016).
6. Fla. Stat. § 720.311(2)(a) (2016).
7. Fla. Stat. § 720.311(2)(b) (2016).

or policy limits, whichever is less, without further consultation."[8] Presuit mediation communications are confidential to the same extent as communications at court-ordered mediation.[9]

A party to presuit mediation has a privilege to refuse to testify and to prevent others from testifying regarding mediation communications, unless the communications fall within section 44.405's limited exceptions.[10] An arbitrator or judge may not consider any information or evidence arising from the mediation proceeding, except (1) in determining whether to impose sanctions for failure to attend mediation or (2) in a mediated settlement agreement enforcement procedure.[11]

Non-parties may not attend the presuit mediation without the consent of all parties. Both parties may attend with counsel, and the association may appoint a corporate representative. If mediation is attended by a quorum of the board, the mediation is not considered a board meeting requiring notice to the membership.[12] The mediation must be conducted by a circuit civil mediator certified pursuant to the Florida Supreme Court's requirements.[13]

If emergency relief is required, motions for temporary injunctive relief may be filed with the court without complying with presuit mediation requirements. After the emergency is resolved, the court may either refer the parties to a court-administered mediation program or require presuit mediation pursuant to Chapter 720.[14]

The parties must share mediation costs equally, including the mediator's fee, unless the parties agree otherwise, and the mediator may require advance payment. Failure to respond to a demand or response, to agree upon a mediator, to pay fees and costs within the time required by the mediator, or to appear for a scheduled mediation without mediator approval, constitutes a failure or refusal to participate in the mediation process. This operates as an impasse by such party and the other party can proceed in court and

---

8. Fla. R. Civ. P. Rule 1.720(b) (2016).

9. Fla. Stat. § 720.311(2) (2016); see Fla. Stat. § 44.405 (2016).

10. Fla. Stat. § 44.405(2) (2016).

11. Fla. Stat. § 720.311(2)(a) (2016).

12. Fla. Stat. § 720.311(2)(a) (2016).

13. Fla. Stat. § 720.311(2)(d) (2016).

14. Fla. Stat. § 720.311(2)(a) (2016).

seek the costs and fees associated with mediation. Additionally, those who fail or refuse to participate in the entire mediation process may not recover attorney's fees and costs in subsequent dispute-related litigation. An "impasse" occurs if the mediation cannot be conducted within 90 days of mailing of the mediation participation offer, unless both parties agree to an extension.[15]

If presuit mediation does not resolve all issues, the parties may file the unresolved dispute in court or agree to enter into binding or nonbinding arbitration pursuant to Condominium Act procedures and Division rules. The arbitration may be conducted by a Florida Department of Business and Professional Regulation arbitrator or by a private department-certified arbitrator. If all parties do not agree to arbitration, any party may file the dispute in court. A final order resulting from nonbinding arbitration is final and enforceable if a complaint for trial de novo is not filed in court within 30 days after entry of the order. All presuit mediation costs and attorney's fees are recoverable by the prevailing party of any subsequent arbitration, litigation, or settlement agreement enforcement action.[16]

8-3   CONDOMINIUM ASSOCIATION DISPUTES

Condominium association claimants must petition the Division for requisite section 718.1255 nonbinding arbitration[17] to filter out "factually simple" association-owner disagreements related to keys, pets, proxies, renters, election violations, and offensive exterior decoration or maintenance of a unit, which can be arbitrated "without extensive discovery, expert testimony or sophisticated legal assistance."[18]

Since presuit arbitration is a condition precedent to filing suit, the appropriate remedy for failure to petition the Division is dismissal of the suit, not a stay.[19] A party who raises their opponent's failure to arbitrate after litigation has waived the defense, since it is impossible to advance the statute's goals of improving judicial economy and reducing litigation costs *after* litigation has already occurred.[20]

---

15. Fla. Stat. § 720.311(2)(b) (2016).
16. Fla. Stat. § 720.311(2)(c) (2016).
17. Fla. Stat. § 718.1255(4)(a) (2016).
18. *Carlandia v. Obernauer*, 695 So. 2d 408, 410 (Fla. 4th Dist. Ct. App. 1997).
19. *Neate v. Cypress Club Condo.*, 718 So. 2d 390, 392 (Fla. 4th Dist. Ct. App. 1998).
20. *Sterling Condo. Ass'n v. Herrera*, 690 So. 2d 703, 704 (Fla. 3d Dist. Ct. App. 1997).

Mandatory nonbinding arbitration applies to any "dispute" between two or more parties regarding a disagreement over the following: the board's authority to require any owner to take or refrain from any action involving the owner's unit or the appurtenances thereto; the board's authority to alter or add to a common area or element; the association's failure to properly conduct elections; the association's failure to give adequate notice of meetings or other actions; the association's failure to properly conduct meetings; or the association's failure to allow inspection of books and records.[21]

The Division defines "dispute" as any "disagreement that involves use of a unit or the appurtenances thereto, including use of the common elements."[22] This definition excludes disagreements over the association's alleged failure to properly enforce the condominium documents, unless the controversy otherwise constitutes a "dispute" as defined by the Condominium Act and the Division's rules.[23]

In interpreting the section 718.1255 non-binding arbitration requirement, the Division adopted a rule that this precondition only applies to residential units. Since appellate courts give great deference to an administrative agency's interpretation of its statutes,[24] Florida courts enforce this Division rule.[25]

The only disputes eligible for arbitration are those between owners and the association or the board of directors. Tenants and other unit owners with an interest in the proceeding may also be named as respondents, but controversies between or among unit owners, or between or among unit owners and tenants, are not eligible for arbitration except where the association is a party and the dispute is otherwise eligible for arbitration.[26]

[21.] Fla. Stat. § 718.1255(1) (2016).

[22.] Fla. Admin. Code R. 61B-45.013 (2016).

[23.] Fla. Admin. Code R. 61B-45.013 (2016).

[24.] *Brenner v. Dep't of Banking & Fin.*, 892 So. 2d 1129, 1130 (Fla. 3d Dist. Ct. App. 2004).

[25.] *United Grand Condo. Owners v. Grand Condo. Ass'n*, 929 So. 2d 24, 25 (Fla. 3d Dist. Ct. App. 2006) (upholding the Division's rule that only disputes involving residential associations and residential units are bound by the section 718.1255 pre-litigation arbitration requirement; holding that a dispute between condominium owners and a mixed-use condominium association containing residential units, retail units, commercial units, and a parking unit was not subject to the section 718.1255 pre-litigation arbitration requirement).

[26.] Fla. Admin. Code R. 61B-45.013 (2016).

Nonbinding arbitration is not required for any disagreement that primarily involves title to a unit or common element;[27] warranty interpretation or enforcement; levying and collection of fees or assessments; tenant eviction or removal; alleged breaches of fiduciary duty by directors; or claims for damages based on the association's alleged failure to maintain the condominium property.[28] Disputes that are moot, abstract, hypothetical, or otherwise lack the requirements of a case or controversy may not be arbitrated. Disputes regarding an association's alleged failure to properly repair, replace, or maintain the common elements, common areas, or association property are also not arbitrable, unless the petition alleges that property use is directly affected.[29]

Upon filing, the Division reviews the petition to determine whether the dispute complies with all pertinent prerequisites.[30] The petition must include proof that the petitioner gave the respondents (1) advance written notice of the dispute's nature; (2) a demand for relief and a reasonable opportunity to comply; and (3) notice of the intention to petition for arbitration or other legal action if the parties fail to resolve the dispute. If the petitioner doesn't allege or prove compliance with these prerequisites, the petition must be dismissed without prejudice.[31]

In emergency cases that are not amenable to arbitration, a party may move to stay the arbitration in the form of a verified petition with allegations supporting a temporary injunction. In response to an appropriate motion and supporting papers, the Division

---

[27.] Fla. Stat. § 718.1255(1)(b); *see Habitat II Condo. v. Kerr*, 948 So. 2d 809, 812 (Fla. 4th Dist. Ct. App. 2007) (holding that the presuit arbitration requirement did not apply to a dispute over unit ownership transfer provisions in a condominium association's governing documents, because the dispute required determination as to title, which exempted it from mandatory arbitration under the section 718.1255 "title" exception; specifically, an owner sold her unit without regard to the condominium association's right of first refusal, which entitled the association or its designee to buy or lease the unit on the terms contained in the outside offer; the association sought damages and an injunction to force transfer of the property, or in the alternative void the transfer and force an offer of the property on the same terms; the court dismissed the buyer's motion to dismiss, which alleged the association's failure to comply with the section 718.1255 arbitration requirement, based on the section 718.1255 "title" exception).

[28.] Fla. Stat. § 718.1255(1) (2016).

[29.] Fla. Admin. Code R. 61B-45.013 (2016).

[30.] Fla. Stat. § 718.1255(4)(c) (2016).

[31.] Fla. Stat. § 718.1255(4)(b) (2016).

may abate the arbitration pending a court hearing on a motion for temporary injunction.[32]

If the Division is satisfied that a dispute exists and that the petition substantially meets the prerequisites discussed above, it serves the petition on all respondents,[33] after which any party may request arbitrator-referred mediation. If the Division determines that all parties agree to mediation, the dispute must be referred to mediation. Even without agreement, the arbitrator may refer a dispute to mediation at any time.[34]

Prior to mediation, the parties must select a mutually acceptable mediator from an arbitrator-supplied list of Division-certified volunteer and paid mediators. If the parties are unable to agree on a mediator, the arbitrator will appoint a certified mediator. If any party fails to attend a duly noticed mediation conference without arbitrator or mediator permission, the arbitrator will impose sanctions, including the striking of pleadings, the entry of an order of dismissal or default, and costs and attorneys' fees incurred by the other parties. Barring agreement by the parties or an arbitrator order to the contrary, "appearance" at mediation is in-person, either by the party or a representative with full settlement authority without further consultation. An association may comply by having present one or more representatives with full authority to negotiate a settlement and recommend that the board ratify the settlement within five days from the mediation date. Unless there is agreement to the contrary, the parties share equally in mediation costs.[35]

As required under Chapter 720, presuit mediation must conform to Rule 1.720 of the Florida Rules of Civil Procedure. Unless stipulated in writing by the parties, each party must appear at mediation either in person or through a party representative having full authority to settle without further consultation. In addition, insured parties must be accompanied by an insurance carrier representative who is not the carrier's outside counsel and who has full settlement authority for "an amount up to the

---

amount of the plaintiff's last demand or policy limits, whichever is less, without further consultation."[36] Mediation communications are confidential to the same extent as court-ordered mediation communications.[37] A party to condominium association dispute mediation has a privilege to refuse to testify and to prevent any other person from testifying regarding mediation communications, unless the communications fall within section 44.405's limited exceptions.[38]

Without the consent of all parties, non-parties to the dispute are not allowed to attend the mediation. Each party may appear with counsel and corporate representatives.[39] If the mediation is successful and the parties reach an agreement, the settlement may be enforced through the county or circuit court, as applicable, and any costs and fees incurred in settlement enforcement must be awarded to the prevailing party in any enforcement action.[40] If the mediator declares an impasse, the arbitration proceeding terminates, unless all parties agree in writing to continue arbitration. The arbitrator may not consider any evidence relating to the unsuccessful mediation, except in a proceeding to impose sanctions for failure to appear at mediation. If the parties do not agree to continue arbitration, the arbitrator enters a dismissal order after which either party may file suit.[41]

The prevailing party is entitled to the costs of the arbitration and reasonable attorney's fees in an amount determined by the arbitrator, including costs for arbitration proceedings and for preparing for and attending any scheduled mediation.[42] In any subsequent litigation, the prevailing party is also entitled to recover any costs and attorneys' fees incurred in connection with arbitration and mediation.[43] Regardless of who prevails at arbitration, if a trial de novo is instituted after arbitration, the party who prevails in the trial de novo by obtaining a judgment more favorable than the

---

[36.] Fla. R. Civ. P. Rule 1.720(b) (2015).
[37.] Fla. Stat. § 718.1255(4)(h) (2016); *see* Fla. Stat. § 44.405 (2016).
[38.] Fla. Stat. § 44.405(2) (2016).
[39.] Fla. Stat. § 718.1255(4)(h) (2016).
[40.] Fla. Stat. § 718.1255(4)(m) (2016).
[41.] Fla. Stat. § 718.1255(4)(h) (2016).
[42.] Fla. Stat. § 718.1255(4)(k) (2016).
[43.] Fla. Stat. § 718.1255(4)(h) (2016).

arbitration decision is entitled to attorney's fees for the arbitration and the subsequent litigation.[44]

8-3:1 Arbitration Procedures

Mandatory nonbinding arbitration is conducted in accordance with the Division rules set forth in Florida Administrative Code Rule 61B-45.[45] A party to arbitration has the right, at their own expense, to representation by a Florida attorney or a non-attorney who can "demonstrate ... familiarity with and understanding of the arbitration rules of procedure, and with any relevant portions of" the Condominium Act and the Division rules.[46] A non-attorney representative must complete the Division's Qualified Representative Application form. The arbitrator determines whether the prospective representative is authorized and qualified to appear in the arbitration proceedings and capable of representing the party's rights and interests. Non-attorney representatives are bound by the Division's code of conduct, which requires that they exercise due diligence in filing and arguing any motion or pleading, advise the client to observe and to obey the law, and refrain from engaging in conduct involving dishonesty, fraud, deceit or misrepresentation, among other standards.[47]

Upon receipt of the petition, the Division first determines whether it has jurisdiction over the controversy. If the Division determines that the dispute is not subject to nonbinding arbitration, the petition is dismissed. A dismissal for lack of jurisdiction is not an adjudication on the merits and the petitioner need not comply with the 30-day deadline for filing for a trial de novo, which only applies to claims subject to arbitration.[48]

---

[44] *Huff v. Vill. of Stuart Ass'n*, 741 So. 2d 1217, 1219 (Fla. 4th Dist. Ct. App. 1999); *see* Fla. Stat. § 718.1255(4)(l) (2012) ("The party who files a complaint for a trial de novo shall be assessed the other party's arbitration costs, court costs, and other reasonable costs, including attorney's fees, investigation expenses, and expenses for expert or other testimony or evidence incurred after the arbitration hearing if the judgment upon the trial de novo is not more favorable than the arbitration decision. If the judgment is more favorable, the party who filed a complaint for trial de novo shall be awarded reasonable court costs and attorneys fees.").

[45] Fla. Stat. § 718.1255(4)(i) (2016).

[46] Fla. Admin. Code R. 61B-45.004 (2016).

[47] Fla. Admin. Code R. 61B-45.004 (2016).

[48] *National Ventures v. Water Glades 300 Condo.*, 847 So. 2d 1070, 1073 (Fla. 4th Dist. Ct. App. 2003).

Parties may file motions for emergency relief or temporary injunction. In response, the arbitrators hold an evidentiary hearing as soon as possible after the motion and supporting arbitration petition are filed and served on the opposing party. The moving party must post a bond before the temporary injunction is entered. The bond must be deemed sufficient by the arbitrator, upon taking testimony, to pay the costs and damages sustained by a potentially wrongfully enjoined adverse party.[49]

While a case is pending and within 15 days of entry of a final order, no party may communicate verbally or in writing with an arbitrator in the absence of any other party regarding the merits of the case.[50] An application to the arbitrator for any relief must be made by written motion, served on all parties, unless made during a hearing. The arbitrator will conduct proceedings and make orders deemed necessary to dispose of issues raised by motion. The non-moving parties may, within seven days of service of a written motion, file a written response in opposition.[51] The arbitrator may conduct any proceeding, including motion hearings, by telephone conference. Any time after a petition has been filed, the arbitrator may direct the parties to confer to clarify and simplify issues, discuss the possibility of settlement, examine exhibits, exchange names and addresses of witnesses, resolve procedural matters, and enter into prehearing stipulations.[52]

The arbitrator will issue subpoenas in response to requests for witness attendance and document production. Any party on whose behalf a subpoena is issued may apply to the court for orders compelling attendance and production.[53] Witnesses are entitled to fees and mileage for their attendance.[54]

While the arbitrator may discretionarily permit discovery in accordance with the Florida Rules of Civil Procedure,[55] it is to be used sparingly and only for information and documents

---

[49] Fla. Admin. Code R. 61B-45.011 (2016).
[50] Fla. Admin. Code R. 61B-45.007 (2016).
[51] Fla. Admin. Code R. 61B-45.011 (2016).
[52] Fla. Admin. Code R. 61B-45.036 (2016).
[53] Fla. Stat. § 718.1255(4)(j) (2016).
[54] Fla. Stat. § 92.142 (2016).
[55] Fla. Stat. § 718.1255(4)(j) (2016).

"necessary for the proper disposition of the petition."[56] A motion to conduct discovery must describe with specificity the necessary method with which the party intends to seek requested discovery. In addition to obtaining discovery in accordance with the Florida Rules of Civil Procedure, unit owners can rely on their subsection 718.111(12) right to access official records.[57] This section requires the association to make its official records available within five working days after receipt of a written request by a unit owner.[58]

The arbitrator may issue appropriate orders to effectuate discovery and prevent delay. Enforcement of an order directing discovery must be petitioned for in the circuit court of the judicial circuit in which the non-compliant party resides.[59] A party may be subject to sanctions for violations of the Division's procedural rules or violations of reasonable nonfinal orders issued by an arbitrator which are not under judicial review.[60] Sanctions include dismissal of the petition or individual claims or imposition of fees and costs where the violation is deemed willful, intentional, or a result of neglect. Dismissal pursuant to this rule is not considered a decision on the merits. A respondent's failure to comply with an arbitrator's lawful order or with Division rules will result in striking the answer or individual defenses or imposition of costs and attorney's fees as appropriate.[61]

Summary disposition and simplified arbitration procedures are available for cases with no disputed issues of material fact. A final order denying relief to the petitioner may be entered any time after the filing of the petition and answer if the arbitrator finds no disputed issues of material fact and no preliminary basis for relief. If the petition warrants relief and there are no meritorious defenses, the arbitrator may enter a summary final order awarding relief. Without disputed issues of material fact, there are no formal evidentiary hearings and the arbitrator need only consider the pleadings and evidence filed by the parties.[62]

---

56. Fla. Admin. Code R. 61B-45.024 (2016).
57. Fla. Admin. Code R. 61B-45.024 (2016).
58. Fla. Stat. § 718.111(12)(b) (2016).
59. Fla. Admin. Code R. 61B-45.024 (2016).
60. Fla. Stat. § 718.1255(4)(j) (2016).
61. Fla. Admin. Code R. 61B-45.036 (2016).
62. Fla. Admin. Code R. 61B-45.030 (2016).

Formal hearings are open to the public. Each party may present evidence, cross-examine opposing witnesses, enter objections, and rebut their opponent's evidence. Oral testimony is given under oath, which the arbitrator is authorized to administer. Since arbitrations are less formal than court proceedings, the formal rules of evidence do not generally apply. "[T]he kind of evidence on which reasonable, prudent persons rely in the conduct of their affairs" is admissible,[63] while irrelevant and unduly repetitious evidence inadmissible. Hearsay evidence is admissible "to supplement or explain other evidence," but is not sufficient "in itself to support a finding, unless the hearsay evidence would be admissible over objection in a civil action." The rules of privilege apply to the same extent as civil actions.[64]

After the final hearing, the parties may submit proposed findings of fact, conclusions of law, and proposed orders, or legal briefs or memoranda on the issues, within a time designated by the arbitrator. The arbitrator's order is entered within 45 days after the hearing, receipt by the arbitrator of the hearing transcript, or receipt of any post-hearing memoranda. The order may include prohibitory injunctive relief, monetary damages, declaratory relief, or any other relief deemed just and equitable.[65]

An arbitration decision is presented in writing and is final if the parties initially agreed to binding arbitration. For nonbinding arbitration, the decision becomes final unless a party files a complaint for a trial de novo in a court of competent jurisdiction in which the condominium is located within 30 days.[66] The 30-day requirement is a jurisdictional precondition to bringing suit under section 718.1255.[67] The deadline is calculated from the date of mailing of the final order. A final or nonfinal order is effective upon its issuance unless a stay has been issued. A party who appeals by filing for a trial de novo may seek a stay of the order within 30 days of issuance by filing a motion to stay with the arbitrator.[68]

---

[63] Fla. Admin. Code R. 61B-45.039 (2016).

[64] Fla. Admin. Code R. 61B-45.039 (2016).

[65] Fla. Admin. Code R. 61B-45.043 (2016).

[66] Fla. Stat. § 718.1255(4) (2016).

[67] *Cypress Bend Condo. I Ass'n v. Dexner*, 705 So. 2d 681, 682 (Fla. 4th Dist. Ct. App. 1998).

[68] Fla. Admin. Code R. 61B-45.043 (2016).

A party may move for a rehearing within 15 days of entry of the final order. The motion must state the legal or factual issues that the arbitrator "overlooked or misapprehended."[69] The moving party may not simply repeat arguments on the merits of the final order. The non-moving party may respond within 10 days of service of the motion. The arbitrator is limited to modifying the final order only on a showing that the arbitrator clearly erred on the law or the facts. A timely motion for rehearing suspends the operation of the final order, the deadline for filing for trial de novo, a motion for entitlement to fees and costs, or a petition for enforcement.[70]

A party to arbitration may enforce an arbitration award by filing a petition in a court of competent jurisdiction in which the condominium is located. The petition may not be granted until after the 30 days for filing a complaint for trial de novo has expired. A party who succeeds in his or her enforcement petition is entitled to reasonable attorney's fees and costs incurred in enforcing the arbitration award.[71]

If judicial proceedings are initiated, the final decision of the arbitrator is admissible evidence in the trial de novo.[72] On review of the arbitration proceeding, the party filing the complaint for trial de novo has the initial burden of persuasion. Barring reversal of the arbitrator by the circuit court, the arbitrator's decision remains valid. The party who prevails in the arbitration need not file a claim to establish its rights in the arbitrator's order.[73]

A party must notice their intent to seek fees and costs in writing prior to rendition of the final order. The prevailing party must file its motion for fees and costs no later than 45 days after rendition of the final order. If a complaint for trial de novo is timely filed, however, the motion for fees and costs must be filed within 45 days of the conclusion of that appeal and any subsequent appeal. Failure to plead or timely file for fees and costs precludes the prevailing party from recovering fees and costs.

[69.] Fla. Admin. Code R. 61B-45.044(1) (2016).

[70.] Fla. Admin. Code R. 61B-45.044 (2016).

[71.] Fla. Stat. § 718.1255(4)(m) (2016).

[72.] Fla. Stat. § 718.1255(4) (2016).

[73.] *Kahn v. Villas at Eagles Point Condo. Ass'n*, 693 So. 2d 1029, 1030 (Fla. 2d Dist. Ct. App. 1997).

The motion must state the basis for the petition, the amount of attorney's fees and costs, and the hourly rate. The moving party must submit an affidavit by the attorney who performed the work that states the number of years the attorney has been practicing law. The affidavit must indicate each activity for which compensation is sought, and state the time spent on each activity. If the case involves multiple issues which are separate and distinct, the affidavit must identify the issue for which each activity was performed. If the moving party seeks costs, they must attach receipts or other documents providing evidence thereof. The arbitrator need not conduct any hearing or consider expert advice or testimony to determine a reasonable hourly fee and a reasonable total award. A timely filed complaint for trial de novo will stay any proceeding for fees and costs. The stay remains in effect until the conclusion of the appeal.[74]

[74.] Fla. Admin. Code R. 61B-45.048 (2016).

Chapter 9

Collection Practices

9-1   INTRODUCTION

Assessments are often a community association's only source of income. Without regular payment of assessments, community associations may experience financial distress and be forced to downgrade amenities, close recreational facilities, lay off staff, and reduce security. While this has a negative impact on quality of life, happiness, safety, and property values, it is the only option for communities suffering economically. In communities with high foreclosure rates, associations struggle to maintain regular assessment income, as defaulting owners increase the burden on their paying neighbors.

To protect the financial viability of community associations, the Florida Legislature has set forth strict procedural guidelines for establishing and levying assessments, collecting unpaid assessments, and imposing penalties on owners who fail to pay. The process of establishing and levying assessments is meant to be as transparent as possible. Assessments are typically established at annual budget meetings that are open to the membership. This protects owners by ensuring that elected board members establish reasonable assessments in accordance with Florida statutes and the association's governing documents. In addition, this places the membership on notice of their financial obligation to the association. This is critical, as an owner's failure to pay may result in a lien against his or her unit.

Both the Condominium Act and the Cooperative Act define "assessment" as "a share of the funds which are required for the payment of common expenses, which from time to time is assessed against the unit owner."[1] The Homeowners' Associations Act defines "assessment" as sums paid by parcel owners to the association that are "authorized in the governing documents, which if not paid by the owner of a parcel, can result in a lien against the parcel."[2]

An owner's obligation to pay assessments is "conditional solely on whether the unit owner holds title" and whether the assessment conforms with the governing documents and Florida statutes.[3] There is no statutory basis, and no argument based in case law, to suggest that an owner may withhold payment of assessments because he or she dislikes the actions of the board of directors, or believes they have been negligent in the operation of the community. This is true even if the expense is due to an unauthorized act of the board of directors.[4]

Furthermore, owners may not refuse to pay valid assessments as a self-help remedy "to cure unauthorized acts by officers or directors of an association," even if the assessments are made necessary by the board members' breach of their fiduciary duty.[5] For instance, a homeowner may not forego payment of assessments because of the association's failure to maintain the common elements, as an owner's duty to pay assessments is conditioned solely on his or her acquisition of title.[6] So long as an expense is "properly incurred by the association," the owners may be assessed, and they must pay their share.[7] While an owner may not forgo payment of assessments because of the association's negligence in the operation of the community, the assessment itself must be valid. If an owner specifically denies that the association properly levied the assessment, the association bears the burden of proving the validity of the assessment.[8]

---

[1] Fla. Stat. § 718.103(1) (2016); Fla. Stat. § 719.103(1) (2016).

[2] Fla. Stat. § 720.301(1) (2016).

[3] *Ocean Trail Unit Owners Ass'n v. Mead*, 650 So. 2d 4, 7 (Fla. 1994).

[4] *Ocean Trail Unit Owners Ass'n v. Mead*, 650 So. 2d 4, 7 (Fla. 1994).

[5] *Coral Way Condo. Invs. v. 21/22 Condo. Ass'n*, 66 So. 3d 1038, 1041 (Fla. 3d Dist. Ct. App. 2011).

[6] *Abbey Park Homeowners Ass'n v. Bowen*, 508 So. 2d 554, 555 (Fla. 4th Dist. Ct. App. 1987) (holding as a matter of law that an association's failure to maintain the common elements does not justify an owner's refusal to pay assessments because the "duty to pay [assessments is] conditioned solely on ... acquisition of title as stated in the declaration").

[7] Fla. Stat. § 718.103 (2016); Fla. Stat. § 719.103 (2016).

[8] *Berg v. Bridle Path Homeowners Ass'n*, 809 So. 2d 32, 34 (Fla. 4th Dist. Ct. App. 2002) ("[A] homeowners association is obligated to show that it has properly levied the assessment

9-2   ASSESSMENT LIABILITY

9-2:1   Homeowners' Associations

For any homeowners' association created after October 1, 1995, the governing documents must specify members' proportional shares of common expenses and all assessments must be within a member's proportional share.[9] Share size may vary by ownership classes, which are based on service levels or other relevant factors.[10]

Regardless of how title to property has been acquired, an owner "is liable for all assessments that come due while he or she is the parcel owner."[11] The owner may not avoid assessments because they are not using the common areas, or by abandoning their parcel.[12] In addition, a unit owner is "jointly and severally liable with the previous parcel owner for all unpaid assessments that came due up to the time of transfer of title."[13]

Delinquent assessments bear interest at the rate set forth in the governing documents. If the governing documents are silent, interest accrues at the rate of 18 percent per year.[14] If provided for in the governing documents, the association may charge a late fee "not to exceed the greater of $25 or 5 percent of the amount of each installment that is paid past the due date."[15] Payments accepted by the association are applied first to interest, then to any late fee, then to any costs and reasonable attorney's fees incurred in collection, and then to the delinquent assessment.[16]

9-2:2   Condominium Associations

As is true for homeowners' associations, condominium associations pay for common expenses by collecting assessments

---

in accordance with the community's declaration of restrictive covenants and by-laws when the defendant challenges the lack of compliance specifically and with particularity.") (*internal citations omitted*).

[9]   Fla. Stat. § 720.308(1) (2016).
[10] Fla. Stat. § 720.308(1)(a) (2016).
[11] Fla. Stat. § 720.3085(2)(a) (2016).
[12] Fla. Stat. § 720.3085(2)(a) (2016).
[13] Fla. Stat. § 720.3085(2)(b) (2016).
[14] Fla. Stat. § 720.3085(3) (2016).
[15] Fla. Stat. § 720.3085(3)(a) (2016).
[16] Fla. Stat. § 720.3085(3)(b) (2016).

against units in the proportions or percentages provided in the declaration. For residential or mixed-use condominiums created after January 1, 1996, each unit's share of the condominium's common expenses shall be the same as the unit's "appurtenant ownership interest in the common elements."[17] Common expenses are defined by statute to include expenses incurred in the

> operation, maintenance, repair, replacement, or protection of the common elements and association property ... and any other expense ... designated as [a] common expense by this chapter, the declaration, the documents creating the association, or the bylaws.[18]

Chapter 718 lists additional expenses, "reasonably related to [unit owners'] general benefit ... even if such expenses do not attach to the common elements or property of the condominium,"[19] that may be paid with assessments against units. These include transportation services, insurance for directors and officers, road maintenance and operation expenses, in-house communications, and security services. Such services must either be (1) contemplated in the condominium documents or by-laws, or (2) continuously provided by the condominium association from the date the developer turned over control to the unit owners.[20] A condominium association may even assess unit owners to pay judgments, attorney fees, and costs incurred in connection with a lawsuit brought by unit owners against the association.[21]

[17.] Fla. Stat. § 718.115(2) (2016).

[18.] Fla. Stat. § 718.115(1)(a) (2016).

[19.] Fla. Stat. § 718.115(1)(a) (2016).

[20.] *Scudder v. Greenbrier C. Condo. Ass'n*, 663 So. 2d 1362, 1365 (Fla. 4th Dist. Ct. App. 1995); Fla. Stat. § 718.115(1)(a) (2016).

[21.] *Ocean Trail Unit Owners Ass'n v. Mead*, 650 So. 2d 4, 6-7 (Fla. 1994) (holding that a condominium association could enforce a special assessment to pay judgments, attorney's fees, and legal costs related to a successful owner-initiated lawsuit in which the association's purchase of real property was invalidated as an unauthorized act; the Supreme Court of Florida concluded that the association's board of directors reasonably believed that the assessment was necessary to pay the judgments and protect the association's common properties from execution and levy, and the judgments were therefore a common expense for which the association had authority to impose an assessment; the Court reasoned, "If assessments cannot be enforced to pay judgments which have been entered against the association and which can be executed against the association property, the condominium could be destroyed, to the detriment of all the owners.").

The condominium association's bylaws must provide the manner of collecting assessments, which shall be levied at least quarterly so that the association has funds available to pay for "all of the anticipated current operating expenses and for all of the unpaid operating expenses previously incurred."[22] The condominium association may accelerate assessments of delinquent owners to include amounts due for the remainder of the budget year in which a claim of lien is filed for the unpaid assessments.[23]

As is the case with homeowners' associations, regardless of how title to a condominium unit has been acquired, the unit owner "is liable for all assessments which come due while he or she is the unit owner."[24] In addition, there is joint and several liability with previous owners "for all unpaid assessments that came due up to the time of transfer of title."[25] A unit owner may not be excused from assessments "unless all other unit owners are likewise proportionately excluded from payment."[26] In addition, assessment liability cannot be avoided by waiving "the use or enjoyment of any common element or by abandonment of the unit for which the assessments are made."[27] Similarly, an association may not reject necessary repairs, since this is a violation of its statutory duty under section 718.116 to maintain the condominium's common elements.[28]

Delinquent assessments bear interest at the rate set forth in the declaration. If the declaration is silent, interest accrues at the rate of 18 percent per year. If provided for in the governing documents, the association may charge a late fee not to exceed "the greater of $25 or 5 percent of each delinquent installment for which

---

22. Fla. Stat. § 718.112(1)(g) (2016).
23. Fla. Stat. § 718.112(2)(g) (2016).
24. Fla. Stat. § 718.116(1)(a) (2016).
25. Fla. Stat. § 718.116(1)(a) (2016).
26. Fla. Stat. § 718.116(9)(a) (2016).
27. Fla. Stat. § 718.116(2) (2016).
28. *In re Colony Beach & Tennis Club Ass'n*, 456 B.R. 545, 562 (M.D. Fla. 2011) (the association board of a condominium complex and resort hotel voted to reject a $10.6 million "emergency assessment" for repair and improvement of common elements, which the court held violated section 718.116's provision that "liability for assessments may not be avoided by waiver of the use or enjoyment of any common element or by abandonment of the unit for which the assessments are made"; the court reasoned that a majority of the members effectively attempted to avoid liability for assessments by waiving en masse the "enjoyment of ... common elements," which eventually deteriorated beyond use, by which they "violated en masse [s]ection 718.116(2)"); *see* Fla. Stat. § 718.116(2) (2016).

the payment is late."[29] Payments received by the association are applied first to interest, then to any late fee, then to any costs and reasonable attorney's fees incurred in collection, and then to the delinquent assessment.[30] Within 15 days after receiving a written request from a unit owner or a unit mortgagee, the association must provide a certificate signed by an officer or agent stating all monetary obligations owed to the association by the unit owner with respect to the condominium parcel.[31]

9-3 STATUTORY PROTECTION AGAINST UNFAIR AND ABUSIVE ASSESSMENT COLLECTION PRACTICES

Community association members may benefit from protection against unfair and abusive assessment collection under both the Fair Debt Collection Practices Act[32] (FDCPA) and the Florida Consumer Collection Practices Act[33] (FCCPA). The purpose of the FDCPA is to "eliminate abusive debt collection practices" in order to protect consumers, while ensuring that collectors, who refrain from such practices, "are not competitively disadvantaged."[34] In order to prevail on an FDCPA claim, a plaintiff must prove that:

> (1) the plaintiff has been the object of collection activity arising from a consumer debt, (2) the defendant is a debt collector as defined by the FDCPA, and (3) the defendant has engaged in an act or omission prohibited by the FDCPA.[35]

The FCCPA similarly protects Florida consumers, and is expressly meant to be "in addition to the requirements and regulations of the federal act."[36]

There is disagreement among Florida courts as to whether the FDCPA and the FCCPA apply to the collection of community

---

[29.] Fla. Stat. § 718.116(3) (2016).

[30.] Fla. Stat. § 718.116(3) (2016).

[31.] Fla. Stat. § 718.116(8) (2016).

[32.] 15 U.S.C. § 1692 et seq.

[33.] Fla. Stat. § 559.55 et seq.

[34.] 15 U.S.C. § 1692(e) (2017).

[35.] *Kaplan v. Assetcare*, 88 F. Supp. 2d 1355, 1360-61 (S.D. Fla. 2000) (*quoting Sibley v. Firstcollect*, 913 F. Supp. 469, 470 (M.D. La. 1995)).

[36.] Fla. Stat. § 559.552 (2016).

association maintenance assessments. Specifically, courts differ as to whether community association assessments are "debts" as defined by the FDCPA and the FCCPA. According to the Fifth District Court of Appeal, "assessments are not consumer 'debts' within the purview of [the FDCPA],"[37] under which "debt" is defined as

> any obligation ... of a consumer to pay money arising out of a transaction in which the money, property, insurance, or services which are the subject of the transaction are primarily for personal, family, or household purposes.[38]

The court relied on a series of decisions holding that the FDCPA and the FCCPA's definition of "debt" does "not embrace assessments of property owners for the mutual maintenance of the commonly held areas of the community."[39] Specifically, a case[40] was cited in which the court contrasted "debt," defined as a transaction involving the "offer or extension of credit"[41] arising "at a minimum" from the "rendition of a service or purchase of property or other item of value,"[42] with condominium assessments, which (1) "arise by contract with the purchase of real estate," (2) "are assessed on a regular basis," and (3) "like rent, do not reflect deferred payments on a prior debt."[43] The court also relied on precedent that a subdivision's assessment to maintain a private road is not a debt since it is not an obligation "incurred to receive consumer goods or services."[44]

The United States District Court for the Middle District of Florida took an opposing view, specifically holding that the

---

[37.] *Bryan v. Clayton*, 698 So. 2d 1236, 1237 (Fla. 5th Dist. Ct. App. 1997).

[38.] 15 U.S.C. § 1692(a)(5) (2017).

[39.] *Bryan v. Clayton*, 698 So. 2d 1236, 1237 (Fla. 5th Dist. Ct. App. 1997).

[40.] *Azar v. Hayter*, 874 F. Supp. 1314, 1318 (N.D. Fla. 1995) *aff'd*, 66 F.3d 342 (11th Cir. 1995).

[41.] *Azar v. Hayter*, 874 F. Supp. 1314, 1318 (N.D. Fla. 1995) *aff'd*, 66 F.3d 342 (11th Cir. 1995) (citing *Zimmerman v. HBO*, 834 F.2d 1163, 1168 (3d Cir. 1987)).

[42.] *Azar v. Hayter*, 874 F. Supp. 1314, 1318 (N.D. Fla. 1995) *aff'd*, 66 F.3d 342 (11th Cir. 1995) (citing *Staub v. Harris*, 626 F.2d 275, 278 (3d Cir. 1980)).

[43.] *Azar v. Hayter*, 874 F. Supp. 1314, 1318 (N.D. Fla. 1995) *aff'd*, 66 F.3d 342 (11th Cir. 1995) (concluding that assessments reflect "no evidence of a pro tanto exchange").

[44.] *Nance v. Petty, Livingston Dawson, & Devening*, 881 F. Supp. 223, 225 (W.D. Va. 1994).

FDCPA applies to the collection of maintenance assessments.[45] The court reasoned that the assessments at issue met the definition of "debt" pursuant to the FDCPA because they (1) were for personal or family purposes, and (2) were obligations arising out of a transaction for the purchase of an interest in the community. Therefore, the court found that maintenance assessments are "debts" subject to the protection of the FDCPA.[46]

When the FDCPA and the FCCPA apply, owners benefit from broad protection against prohibited assessment collection practices. Under the FDCPA, no debt collector may "harass, oppress, or abuse" a debtor.[47] Such violations may occur, for example, through threats of violence or engaging in criminal activity that injures the debtor physically or emotionally or otherwise injures the debtor's property.[48] Even the use of profanity in communicating with a debtor may constitute a violation.[49] It is also unlawful for a debt collector to publish a debtor's identity to persons other than those authorized under the FDCPA, such as consumer reporting agencies.[50] Other acts constituting violations include placing excessive telephone calls to a debtor, causing a telephone to ring continuously, and failing to properly disclose a debt collector's identity during a call.[51]

Further, debt collectors may not make "false, deceptive, or misleading" statements during collection efforts.[52] This includes (1) false statements about the debt's amount or legal status or about the debt collector's alleged affiliation with a governmental entity or consumer reporting agency, or (2) utilizing a false business name.[53] A debt collector is also prohibited from stating that a debtor will be arrested or incarcerated, or have his or her property or wages seized or garnished, without such action being lawful and actually

---

[45] *Fuller v. Becker & Poliakoff*, 192 F. Supp. 2d 1361, 1368 (M.D. Fla. 2002).
[46] *Fuller v. Becker & Poliakoff*, 192 F. Supp. 2d 1361, 1368 (M.D. Fla. 2002).
[47] 15 U.S.C. § 1692d (2017).
[48] 15 U.S.C. § 1692(d)(1) (2017).
[49] 15 U.S.C. § 1692(d)(2) (2017).
[50] 15 U.S.C. § 1692(d)(3) (2017).
[51] *See* 15 U.S.C. § 1692(d)(5), (6) (2017).
[52] 15 U.S.C. § 1692(e) (2017).
[53] 15 U.S.C. § 1692(e)(1), (2), (14), (16) (2017).

intended.[54] In addition, a collector may not knowingly state or threaten to convey false information to other persons, or fail to properly disclose that the debt is disputed.[55]

Misrepresentations may also include falsely stating that the communication is from an attorney or is a legal document.[56] Other prohibited misrepresentations include failing to initially disclose to a debtor, in written or oral communication, that the purpose of the communication is to collect a debt.[57] In addition, debt collectors may not use "unfair or unconscionable" collection methods,[58] such as attempting to collect amounts that are not permitted contractually or under the law[59] or prematurely depositing, or threatening to prematurely deposit, postdated checks.[60]

The FCCPA provides similar protection to consumers[61] and specifies that, in construing its provisions, "due consideration and great weight shall be given to the [FDCPA] interpretations of the Federal Trade Commission and the federal courts."[62] The FCCPA prohibits threats or use of "force or violence" in any debt collection, as well as harassing or abusive behavior,[63] and profane and abusive language in communicating with debtors.[64] It is also forbidden to call debtors between 9:00 p.m. and 8:00 a.m.[65]

The debt collector may not communicate with a debtor's employer prior to obtaining final judgment without the debtor's authorization, disclose information about a debtor to a third person without an actual business need for the information, or reveal the existence of a debt to others while failing to disclose that the debt is disputed.[66] In addition, the FCCPA prohibits the

---

[54.] 15 U.S.C. § 1692(e)(4) (2017).
[55.] 15 U.S.C. § 1692(e)(8) (2017).
[56.] 15 U.S.C. § 1692(e)(3), (13), (15) (2017).
[57.] 15 U.S.C. § 1692(e)(11) (2017).
[58.] 15 U.S.C. § 1692(f) (2017).
[59.] 15 U.S.C. § 1692(f)(1) (2017).
[60.] 15 U.S.C. § 1692(f)(4) (2017).
[61.] Fla. Stat. § 559.551 (2016).
[62.] *Oppenheim v. I.C. Sys., Inc.*, 627 F.3d 833, 839 (11th Cir. 2010) (citing Fla. Stat. § 559.77(5)).
[63.] Fla. Stat. § 559.72 (2016).
[64.] Fla. Stat. § 559.72(8) (2016).
[65.] Fla. Stat. § 559.72(17) (2016).
[66.] *See* Fla. Stat. § 559.72(4), (6) (2016).

publication of "deadbeat lists" as a tactic to coerce consumers to pay the debt.[67]

Under the FCCPA, debt collectors also must not provide any false impression that their communication is authorized by the government or by an attorney.[68] It is also unlawful to directly contact a debtor with knowledge that counsel has been retained in order to refute the debt.[69] Further, debt collection agents must properly identify themselves or their respective companies upon request by debtors.[70]

9-4   LIEN RIGHTS

9-4:1   Homeowners' Associations

A homeowners' association has a lien on each parcel to secure the payment of assessments if authorized by its governing documents.[71] The lien is effective from and relates back to the recording of the original declaration. As to first mortgages of record, the lien is effective from the recording of the claim of lien in the public records of the county in which the parcel is located.[72] Even if the homeowners' association's declaration of covenants gives clear notice that its lien relates back to the declaration filing, the claim of lien must be recorded before it may take priority over a competing mortgage.[73]

The claim of lien must describe the parcel and state the name of the owner, the name and address of the homeowners' association, the assessments due, and the due date. The claim of lien secures all unpaid assessments that are due and that may accrue subsequent to the recording of the claim of lien and before entry of a certificate of title. The claim of lien also secures interest, late charges, and reasonable collection costs and attorney's fees incurred by the association.[74]

[67.] Fla. Stat. § 559.72(14) (2016).
[68.] Fla. Stat. § 559.72(10), (12) (2016).
[69.] Fla. Stat. § 559.72(18) (2016).
[70.] Fla. Stat. § 559.72(15) (2016).
[71.] Fla. Stat. § 720.3085(1) (2016).
[72.] Fla. Stat. § 720.3085(1) (2016).
[73.] *In re Jimenez*, 472 B.R. 106, 111 (Bankr. M.D. Fla. 2012).
[74.] Fla. Stat. § 720.3085(1)(a) (2016).

Homeowners' associations must provide 45 days' notice of intent to lien or a demand for past due assessments before the lien may be filed against a parcel. The written notice or demand must provide the owner with 45 days to make full payment, which may include payment of attorney's fees and costs associated with the preparation and delivery of the written demand. The notice or demand must be sent (1) by registered or certified mail, return receipt requested, (2) by first-class United States mail to the owner at his or her last address as reflected in the association's records if the address is within the United States, and (3) to the owner at the parcel address if the owner's address as reflected in the association's records is not the parcel address. If outside the United States, it is sufficient to send the notice or demand to that address and to the parcel address by first-class United States mail.[75]

By recording a notice of contest of lien in conformance with the proper statutory form,[76] a unit owner may require the association to enforce a recorded claim of lien. After notice of contest of lien has been recorded, the circuit court clerk must mail a copy of the notice to the association by certified mail, return receipt requested, at the address shown in the claim of lien. After service, the association has 90 days in which to file an action to enforce the lien. If the action is not filed within the 90-day period, the lien is void. However, the 90-day period shall be extended for any length of time during which the association is prevented from filing its action because of a stay resulting from a bankruptcy petition filing.[77]

The association may foreclose on its lien in the same manner a real property mortgage is foreclosed. The association may also bring an action to recover a monetary judgment for the unpaid assessments without waiving any claim of lien. The association is entitled to recover the reasonable attorney's fees it incurred in an action to foreclose a lien or an action to recover a money judgment for unpaid assessments.[78] If the parcel owner remains in possession of the parcel following the entry of the foreclosure judgment, the

---

[75] Fla. Stat. § 720.3085(4) (2016).
[76] Fla. Stat. § 720.3085(1)(b) (2016).
[77] Fla. Stat. § 720.3085(1)(b) (2016).
[78] Fla. Stat. § 720.3085(1)(c) (2016).

court may require the owner to pay a reasonable rent. If the parcel is leased during the foreclosure action, the association may collect rent via the appointment of a receiver, whose expenses must be paid by the losing party in the foreclosure action.[79] The homeowners' association may purchase the parcel at the foreclosure sale and hold, lease, mortgage, or convey the parcel.[80]

If the parcel is not subject to a mortgage foreclosure or a notice of tax certificate sale, and the parcel owner is not a debtor in bankruptcy proceedings, the parcel owner may serve and file a qualifying offer in conformance with the specified statutory form.[81] A qualifying offer is a written offer to pay all amounts secured by the lien and accruing during the pendency of the offer. The owner may serve and file one qualifying offer any time after service of the summons and 30 days before the trial of or the trial docket for the lien foreclosure action.[82] The parcel owner must deliver a copy of the qualifying offer to the association's attorney by hand delivery, obtaining a written receipt, or by certified mail, return receipt requested.[83] This stays the foreclosure action for up to 60 days following the date of service of the qualifying offer and no sooner than 30 days before the date of trial, arbitration, or the beginning of the trial docket, whichever occurs first. The purpose of the stay is to permit the parcel owner to pay all amounts secured by the lien plus any amounts accruing during the pendency of the offer.[84]

If the parcel owner makes a qualifying offer, the association may not add the cost of any legal fees incurred during the stay other than costs incurred (1) in defense of a mortgage foreclosure action concerning the parcel, (2) in a bankruptcy proceeding in which the parcel owner is a debtor, or (3) in response to filings by a party other than the association in the association's lien foreclosure action.[85] If the parcel owner breaches the qualifying offer, the stay shall be vacated and the association may proceed in its action to obtain a

---

[79] Fla. Stat. § 720.3085(1)(e) (2016).
[80] Fla. Stat. § 720.3085(1)(f) (2016).
[81] Fla. Stat. § 720.3085(6)(c) (2016).
[82] Fla. Stat. § 720.3085(6) (2016).
[83] Fla. Stat. § 720.3085(6)(a) (2016).
[84] Fla. Stat. § 720.3085(6)(b) (2016).
[85] Fla. Stat. § 720.3085(6)(c) (2016).

foreclosure judgment for the amount in the qualifying offer and any amounts accruing after the date of the qualifying offer.[86]

9-4:2 Condominium Associations

While a homeowners' association's liens to secure assessment payments require authorization in its governing documents, a condominium association's lien rights are statutory.[87] The lien is effective from the recording of the original declaration of condominium, or, for a phase condominium, the last to occur of the recording of the original declaration or amendment thereto creating the parcel. As to first mortgages of record, the lien is effective from the recording of the claim of lien in the public records of the county in which the condominium parcel is located.[88]

The claim of lien must describe the condominium parcel, and state the name of the record owner, the name and address of the association, the amount due, and the due dates. The Condominium Act requires an officer or authorized agent of the association to execute and acknowledge the claim of lien. The lien is not effective one year after the recording of the claim of lien unless an action to enforce the lien is commenced, or unless litigation is prohibited by an automatic stay resulting from a bankruptcy petition.[89]

Condominium associations must provide 30 days' notice of intent to lien. Delivery to the owner must be (1) by registered or certified mail, return receipt requested, (2) by first-class United States mail to the owner at his or her last address as reflected in the association's records if the address is within the United States, and (3) directly to the unit if the owner's address as reflected in the association's records is not the unit address. If outside the United States, the condominium association may send the notice to that address and to the unit address by first-class United States mail.[90] The claim of lien secures all unpaid assessments, as well as interest and all reasonable collection costs and attorney's fees that are due

---

[86]. Fla. Stat. § 720.3085(7) (2016).
[87]. Fla. Stat. § 718.116(5)(a) (2016) ("[the] association has a lien on each condominium parcel to secure the payment of assessments").
[88]. Fla. Stat. § 718.116(5)(a) (2016).
[89]. Fla. Stat. § 718.116(5)(b) (2016).
[90]. Fla. Stat. § 718.121(4) (2016).

and that may accrue after the claim of lien is recorded and through the entry of a final judgment.[91]

By recording a notice of contest of lien in conformance with the proper statutory form,[92] a unit owner may require the association to enforce a recorded claim of lien. After notice of contest of lien has been recorded, the circuit court clerk must mail a copy of the notice to the association by certified mail, return receipt requested, at the address shown in the claim of lien. After service of the notice of contest of lien, the association has 90 days in which to file an action to enforce the lien. If the action is not filed within the 90-day period, the lien is void. However, the 90-day period is extended for any length of time during which the association is prevented from filing its action because of a bankruptcy stay.[93]

The association may bring an action to foreclose its lien in the same manner a mortgage of real property is foreclosed. The association may also bring an action to recover a monetary judgment for the unpaid assessments without waiving any claim of lien. The association is entitled to recover reasonable attorney's fees incurred in such actions.[94]

The court may not enter a foreclosure judgment in favor of a condominium association until at least 30 days after the association gives written notice to the unit owner of its intention to foreclose. The condominium association may not recover its fees if this notice is not given at least 30 days before the foreclosure action is filed, and if the unpaid assessments, including those coming due after the claim of lien is recorded, are paid before the entry of a final judgment of foreclosure. This notice requirement is satisfied if the unit owner records a notice of contest of lien. The notice requirement does not apply if an action to foreclose a mortgage on the unit is pending before any court, provided that "the rights of the association would be affected by such foreclosure" and "actual, constructive, or substitute service of process has been made on the unit owner."[95]

---

91. Fla. Stat. § 718.116(5)(b) (2016).
92. Fla. Stat. § 718.116(5)(c) (2016).
93. Fla. Stat. § 718.116(5)(c) (2016).
94. Fla. Stat. § 718.116(6)(a) (2016).
95. Fla. Stat. § 718.116(6)(b) (2016).

Following entry of the foreclosure judgment, if the owner remains in possession of the unit, the court may require the owner to pay a reasonable rent. The association is entitled to the appointment of a receiver to collect the rent, whose expenses shall be paid by the losing party in the foreclosure action.[96] The condominium association may purchase the condominium parcel at the foreclosure sale and hold, lease, mortgage, or convey it.[97]

9-5 PENALTIES

Both homeowners' associations and condominium associations have similar statutory rights to impose penalties on owners who are delinquent in their financial obligations to the association. Both types of associations may deprive delinquent owners of rights such as the right to use the common property and the right to vote, but may not take away certain fundamental property rights, such as the right of access.

If an owner is more than 90 days delinquent in payment of a financial obligation to either a homeowners' association or a condominium association, the association may suspend the rights of the member, or the member's tenant, guest, or invitee, to use the common property and facilities until the monetary obligation is paid in full. There are no statutory preconditions for notice and hearing.[98] A homeowners' association may not, however, prevent the use of portions of common areas that provide access or utility services to the owner's parcel, nor may it inhibit an owner's or tenant's vehicular and pedestrian access to the parcel or their ability to park.[99] Similarly, a condominium association is not allowed to suspend use of limited common elements that service the owner's unit, common elements needed to access the unit, utility services provided to the unit, parking spaces, or elevators.[100]

[96.] Fla. Stat. § 718.116(6)(c) (2016).

[97.] Fla. Stat. § 718.116(6)(d) (2016). At the time of the drafting of this update in May 2017, the Florida Legislature is considering Senate Bill 1682, which could go into effect on July 1, 2017, that would have the effect of amending Fla. Stat. § 718.3025 to prevent management companies and board members from purchasing a unit at a foreclosure sale resulting from the association's foreclosure of the association's lien for unpaid assessments or take a deed in lieu of foreclosure.

[98.] Fla. Stat. § 720.305(3) (2016); Fla. Stat. § 718.303(4) (2016).

[99.] Fla. Stat. § 720.305(3) (2016).

[100.] Fla. Stat. § 718.303(3) (2016).

As noted, a homeowners' association or a condominium association may also suspend the voting rights of owners that are more than 90 days delinquent, until full payment of all obligations currently due or overdue. A suspended owner's voting interest does not count toward the total number of voting interests needed for any purpose, including, but not limited to, the number of voting interests necessary for a quorum, the number of voting interests necessary to conduct an election, or the number of votes required by statute or by the governing documents to approve an action.[101] Suspension of both the right of common property use and the right to vote requires only approval at a properly noticed board meeting, and notification by mail or hand delivery to the owner and, if applicable, the owner's occupant.[102]

In addition to the foregoing, if the governing documents require lease approval, a condominium association may withhold approval based on a unit owner's assessment payment delinquency.[103]

If a tenant occupies the parcel or condominium unit and the owner is delinquent in any monetary obligation to the association, the association may demand subsequent rental payments from the tenant. The tenant's liability to the association, however, may not exceed the amount that the tenant owes its landlord.[104] The association may demand that the tenant continue to pay rent to the association until the delinquent monetary obligation is paid in full, or until the tenant discontinues tenancy.[105] Rent payments to the association immunize the tenant from any property owner rent claims for all amounts timely paid to the association.[106] If the tenant refuses to pay the association, the association may sue for

---

[101.] Fla. Stat. § 720.305(4) (2016); Fla. Stat. § 718.303(5) (2016). At the time of the drafting of this update in May 2017, the Florida Legislature is considering Senate Bill 1682, which could go into effect on July 1, 2017, that would amend Fla. Stat. § 718.303(5) to provide that voting rights may only be suspended when the delinquency is more than $1,000. Proof of the obligation would have to be provided to the unit owner or member 30 days before the suspension takes effect.

[102.] Fla. Stat. § 720.305(5) (2016); Fla. Stat. § 718.303(6) (2016).

[103.] Fla. Stat. § 718.116(4) (2016).

[104.] Fla. Stat. § 720.3085(8) (2016); Fla. Stat. § 718.116(11)(c) (2016).

[105.] Fla. Stat. § 720.3085(8)(a) (2016); Fla. Stat. § 718.116(11)(a) (2016).

[106.] Fla. Stat. § 720.3085(8)(a)(1) (2016); Fla. Stat. § 718.116(11)(a)(1) (2016).

eviction under the Florida Residential Landlord and Tenant Act[107] as if the association were a landlord.[108]

9-6 ASSESSMENT GUARANTEES

9-6:1 Homeowners' Associations

While the developer controls the homeowners' association, it may excuse itself from assessments on its parcels for any periods set forth in the declaration during which the developer agrees to pay operating expenses that exceed the association's income, including assessments from members.[109] "Developer guarantees" may also cap parcel owner assessments at a fixed dollar amount. During the guarantee period, the developer is similarly excused from assessments for its parcels. In exchange, the developer obligates itself to pay any operating expenses that exceed assessment-generated funds at the guaranteed level and any other revenue collected by the association.[110]

If not set forth in the declaration or the purchase contracts, developer guarantees require approval by a majority of non-developer voting interests.[111] The guarantee period is finite, with a beginning and end date or event.[112] While the guarantee may contemplate an extension, the end date must be the same for all members.[113] During the guarantee period, member assessments shall not exceed the maximum obligation based on (a) the member's proportionate share of expenses and (b) the total adopted budget as described in the governing documents.[114] If during this period the association's income, including members' assessments at the guaranteed level, is insufficient to provide timely payment of all assessments, the guarantor must advance sufficient cash to pay the assessments when payment is due.[115]

[107.] Fla. Stat. § 83.001 et seq. (2016).
[108.] Fla. Stat. § 720.3085(8)(d) (2016); Fla. Stat. § 718.116(11)(d) (2016).
[109.] Fla. Stat. § 720.308(1)(b) (2016).
[110.] Fla. Stat. § 720.308(2) (2016).
[111.] Fla. Stat. § 720.308(2)(a) (2016).
[112.] Fla. Stat. § 720.308(2)(b) (2016).
[113.] Fla. Stat. § 720.308(2)(b) (2016).
[114.] Fla. Stat. § 720.308(3) (2016).
[115.] Fla. Stat. § 720.308(4)(a) (2016).

9-6:2   Condominium Associations

If authorized by the declaration, a condominium developer may excuse itself from paying assessments for its units for a period after declaration recording. During this period, the developer must pay common expenses that exceed the assessments levied on other unit owners in the same condominium. The guarantee period must not extend past "the first day of the fourth calendar month following the month" in which the first purchase contract for a unit in that condominium closes.[116]

The developer may also excuse itself from assessments against its unsold units for the period during which it guarantees unit owners in the same condominium (1) an assessment cap and (2) coverage of any common expenses that exceed the guaranteed amount. The rationale for guarantee provisions is that developers should be excused from paying assessments on their unsold units during the initial sales phase when these units are "not consuming services of the association."[117] The guarantee may be set forth in the purchase contract, declaration, prospectus, or a written agreement between the developer and a majority of the unit owners other than the developer. The developer may extend the guarantee for one or more periods as set forth in such document.[118]

Only regular periodic assessments for common expenses as provided for in the declaration and prospectus and disclosed in the estimated operating budget shall be used for payment of common expenses during the period in which the developer is excused from payment of assessments. Funds that are "receivable from unit purchasers or unit owners and payable to the association," such as "capital contributions or startup funds collected from unit purchasers at closing," may not be used for payment of common expenses during this period.[119]

[116.] Fla. Stat. § 718.116(9)(a)(1) (2016).

[117.] *Tara Manatee v. Fairway Gardens at Tara Condo. Ass'n*, 870 So. 2d 32, 33 (Fla. 2d Dist. Ct. App. 2003).

[118.] Fla. Stat. § 718.116(9)(a)(2) (2016).

[119.] Fla. Stat. § 718.116(9)(b) (2016).

9-7   LIABILITY FOR ASSESSMENTS FOLLOWING FORECLOSURE SALE

The liability of successful bidders at bank foreclosure sales for pre-foreclosure assessments which accrued to the previous owner is a controversial, open issue in Florida. For both homeowners' and condominium associations, an owner is liable for all assessments that come due while he or she is the parcel owner regardless of how his or her title to property has been acquired, "including by purchase at a foreclosure sale or by deed in lieu of foreclosure."[120] In addition, both homeowners' and condominium association owners are jointly and severally liable "with the previous owner for all unpaid assessments that came due up to the time of transfer of title."[121]

Nevertheless, upon acquisition of a condominium via a foreclosure sale, successful bidders assert that foreclosure judgments foreclose, and thus bar any claim for unpaid assessments which accrued with the prior owner. Such successful bidders argue that the legislature did not intend to include owners who take title at a foreclosure sale or by deed in lieu of foreclosure among those who are jointly and severally liable with the previous owner for all unpaid assessments until the time of transfer of title.

The issue in cases concerning joint and several liability for prior assessments often hinges on the interpretation and application of sections 720.3085 and 718.116. Community associations argue that the plain language of both statutes suggests no exception for successful bidders at foreclosure sales with respect to joint and several liability for past due assessments. In addition, both Chapter 720 and the Condominium Act specifically impose liability on first mortgagees who acquire title by foreclosure or by deed in lieu of foreclosure for the unpaid assessments that became due before the mortgagee's acquisition of title.[122] Community associations argue that exempting successful bidders at foreclosure sales from these statutes' provisions would lead to an absurd outcome: first mortgagees *would be* liable for prior assessments, while successful bidders would have *no*

---

120. Fla. Stat. § 720.3085(2)(a) (2016); Fla. Stat. § 718.116(1)(a) (2016).
121. Fla. Stat. § 720.3085(2)(b) (2016); Fla. Stat. § 718.116(1)(a) (2016).
122. Fla. Stat. § 720.3085(2)(c) (2016); Fla. Stat. § 718.116(1)(b) (2016).

liability when purchasing the same property at that same first mortgagee's foreclosure sale.

Since it seems unlikely that the legislature sought to advance such a public policy, successful bidders at foreclosure sales may attempt to avail themselves of the "safe harbor" provisions of Chapter 720 and the Condominium Act, which limit the liability of first mortgagees for unpaid assessments that became due before the mortgagee's acquisition of title. Specifically, first mortgagee liability is limited to the lesser of (1) the parcel's unpaid common expenses and regular periodic or special assessments that accrued or came due during the 12 months immediately preceding the acquisition of title and for which payment in full has not been received by the association, or (2) 1 percent of the original mortgage debt.[123] Recent precedent, however, suggests that "safe harbor" provisions are only available to first mortgagees or a subsequent holder of the first mortgage.[124]

Finally, when declarations contain language which either limits, or eviscerates, the liability of first mortgagees where they acquire title via foreclosure sale, successful bidders at foreclosure can argue that the association's governing documents supersede any need to interpret Florida statutes. Since such provisions are often ambiguously worded and do not narrowly circumscribe such limitations of liability to first mortgagees, successful bidders can argue that their liability for prior assessments should similarly be limited given that they also acquire the property via foreclosure sale.

There is inconsistency among Florida courts when statutory rights conflict with the rights provided by a community association's declaration. One position views statutory provisions as default rules around which associations are free to contract, subject to certain limitations. For instance, the Court held that the retroactive application of a statute governing voting in mixed use condominiums was unconstitutional as a violation of the Florida Constitution's prohibition against any "law impairing the obligation of contracts," since the condominium declaration lacked

---

[123.] Fla. Stat. § 720.3085(2)(c) (2016); Fla. Stat. § 718.116(1)(b) (2016).
[124.] *Bay Holdings v. 2000 Island Blvd. Condo. Ass'n*, 895 So. 2d 1197 (Fla. 3d Dist. Ct. App. 2005).

specific language indicating that it was subject to future statutory amendments.[125]

The competing position views Florida statutes as laws around which parties may *not* contract. The rationale for this position is that state statutes represent legislative declarations of public policy, which govern throughout the entire state.[126] Since the legislature saw fit to delineate specific rules that bind community associations, permitting contradictory declaration language to supersede such rules would permit private parties to violate clearly communicated public policy.

9-8   SLANDER OF TITLE

In the context of community association litigation, slander of title claims often arise in response to an association's efforts to foreclose on a claim of lien filed against a member's property. Through a claim for slander of title, the association member alleges that the association made a defamatory statement that has a negative impact on the owner's property interest. A plaintiff sets forth a claim for slander of title by establishing the malicious publication of a falsehood concerning title that impairs the marketability of property.[127] While malice is an element, a plaintiff's initial burden of demonstrating malice is exceedingly light, since it is presumed upon a showing that the defendant communicated untrue statements to a third person which disparage the plaintiff's title, causing actual or special damage.[128] The association may rebut the presumption of malice by showing that it believed in good faith that the statements in the claim of lien were accurate, creating a privilege that shifts the burden to the plaintiff to prove "actual malice."[129]

Once the plaintiff has established that the defendant communicated to a third party a false and malicious statement disparaging the plaintiff's title, the plaintiff must prove that the

---

[125.] *Cohn v. Grand Condo. Ass'n*, 62 So. 3d 1120, 1121 (Fla. 2011); *see* Chapter 2, § 2-7:2, n.60 (discussing the facts of *Cohn*); Fla. Stat. § 718.404; Fla. Const. art. I, § 10.

[126.] *City of Miami v. Benson*, 63 So. 2d 916, 921 (Fla. 1953).

[127.] *Miceli v. Gilmac Developers*, 467 So. 2d 404, 406 (Fla. 2d Dist. Ct. App. 1985).

[128.] *Continental Dev. Corp. of Florida v. Duval Title & Abstract*, 356 So. 2d 925, 927 (Fla. 2d Dist. Ct. App. 1978).

[129.] *Residential Cmtys. of Am. v. Escondido Cmty. Ass'n*, 645 So. 2d 149 (Fla. 5th Dist. Ct. App. 1994).

falsehood played a material and substantial part in inducing others not to deal with the plaintiff.[130] Additionally, the plaintiff must demonstrate actual pecuniary loss. The last two elements are typically established through proof that the alleged improper liens prevented the plaintiff from selling or leasing its property.

Typically, attorney fees incurred while prosecuting or defending a claim are not recoverable in the absence of a statute or contractual agreement authorizing their recovery. In discussing the cause of action of slander of title, however, the Florida Supreme Court has stated that attorney's fees are considered part of recoverable damages.[131]

[130.] *McAllister v. Breakers Seville Ass'n, Inc.*, 981 So. 2d 566 (Fla. 4th Dist. Ct. App. 2008).

[131.] *Price v. Tyler*, 890 So. 2d 246, 249 (Fla. 2004); *see also S & T Builders v. Globe Props.*, 909 So. 2d 375, 376 (Fla. 4th Dist. Ct. App. 2005), *aff'd*, 944 So. 2d 302 (Fla. 2006).

Chapter 10

Fair Housing Litigation

10-1   INTRODUCTION

Community associations, through the board of directors, have a great deal of control over who receives housing and the conditions and privileges associated therewith. Whether they are aware of it or not, community members are entrusted with significant power through their ability to select directors who establish rules and regulations and manage and operate the amenities provided to residents. In many cases, directors also decide who can live in the community through their power to approve or deny prospective residents.

The board has a thankless job and constantly faces tough decisions on the use and management of others' property, which are often met with protest and resistance. This is especially true for decisions related to property use and enjoyment, violations of covenants and restrictions, transfer or lease of property, and allocation of the community's resources.

While the statutes and the association's governing documents provide procedural guidance, they do not define what is best for any given community, and they do not instruct the board on how best to effectuate the majority's views for property management. Since the board's vision for promoting the health, safety and prosperity of their communities is shaped by its members' personalities, education, and past experiences, it may be vastly different from that of other community members. Unfortunately, board members' personal opinions, experience, and political perspectives, biases, and prejudices also impact housing decisions and may result in discriminatory practices.

While we have enjoyed the benefit of almost 150 years of fair housing laws since Congress enacted the Civil Rights Act of 1866, discrimination in housing is still a very real and prevalent social ill. Clearly, if the board's actions are based on personal bias against a resident, or discriminatory animus against the class of protected persons to which the resident or prospective resident belongs, those actions violate state or federal law. The board is prohibited by state law from selective enforcement of the community association's covenants and restrictions and the board is prohibited by both state and federal law from enforcing those restrictions in a way that discriminates on the basis of race, color, national origin, sex, handicap, familial status, or religion. Even if the board members harbor no ill-will toward any particular protected class and have no intent to discriminate, they cannot take any action that has a discriminatory effect on members of a protected group. In addition, the board is bound by law to make reasonable accommodations for handicapped persons so that they have the same opportunity to enjoy the community, regardless of their disability.

While federal and state law prohibits housing discrimination, it does not impose a code of civility. Nor does it guarantee fairness, or prevent difficult, harsh decisions in the community's best interests, or foolish, capricious decisions at the whims of the board of directors. Even if the board's motivations are non-discriminatory, its responsibility in enforcing the community association's governing documents and managing and restricting other's property use makes it natural for residents and prospective residents to assume that they are being targeted unfairly. When the board impinges upon property use or stands in the way of prospective residents and their dream homes, individuals often see no legitimacy in its decisions and perceive that they are being victimized. In certain cases, individuals' sincere belief that they are being targeted because of animus toward their protected class may be based in reality.

Whether the alleged housing discrimination is bona fide or altogether false is all too often a decision that is ultimately decided by the court. Claims of housing discrimination are somewhat unique, however, in that both the claimant and the housing provider may take advantage of alternative means of dispute resolution imposed as a mandatory prerequisite to filing suit. Both state and federal governments have adopted anti-housing discrimination policies and legislation which mandates a neutral investigation of the housing claim and pre-suit mediation administered either by the United States Department of Housing and Urban Development (HUD) or a certified state agency such as the Florida Commission on Human Relations (FCHR).

10-2   ADMINISTRATIVE PROCESS

10-2:1   Exhaustion of Administrative Remedies

Section 760.34 establishes administrative remedies for violations of the Florida Fair Housing Act (Florida FHA) and provides the right to file a complaint with the FCHR to those who claim injury from a "discriminatory housing practice" and those who believe that they "will be injured by a discriminatory housing practice."[1] At least one appellate court interpreting the Florida FHA has adopted the approach in Florida Civil Rights Act cases[2] requiring that complaints "be filed either with the Commission or its federal counterpart by anyone who wishes to pursue either a lawsuit or an administrative proceeding under this act."[3]

10-2:2   The United States Department of Housing and Urban Development

HUD was established in 1965 when Lyndon B. Johnson signed the Department of Housing and Urban Development Act. HUD is a cabinet-level department in the executive branch of the federal government whose mission is

> to create strong, sustainable, inclusive communities and quality affordable homes for all. HUD is working to strengthen the housing market to bolster the economy and protect consumers; meet the need for quality affordable rental homes; utilize

---

[1] Fla. Stat. § 760.34 (2016).

[2] *Belletete v. Halford*, 886 So. 2d 308, 310 (Fla. 4th Dist. Ct. App. 2004); *contra Milsap v. Cornerstone Residential Mgmt., Inc.*, 05-60033-CIV-JOHNSON, 2010 WL 427436, at *4 (S.D. Fla. 2010) (describing Belletete as an "anomoly," and opining that "the Florida Supreme Court would not require exhaustion of administrative remedies as a prerequisite to filing a claim under the FFHA in court").

[3] *Ross v. Jim Adams Ford*, 871 So. 2d 312, 315 (Fla. 2d Dist. Ct. App. 2004).

> housing as a platform for improving quality of life;
> [and] build inclusive and sustainable communities
> free from discrimination....[4]

Complaints of alleged housing discrimination can be filed directly with HUD using a HUD Form 903 Online Complaint.[5] However, whenever a complaint alleges a discriminatory housing practice within the jurisdiction of a state agency, HUD will refer the complaint to the certified agency.[6] In Florida, HUD will refer the complaint to the FCHR.

10-2:3   The Florida Commission on Human Relations

In 1969, the Florida Legislature created the FCHR, which is charged both with promoting and encouraging "fair treatment and equal opportunity for all persons regardless of race, color, religion, sex, national origin, age, handicap, or marital status" and eliminating discrimination between "religious, racial, and ethnic groups and their members."[7] The FCHR is funded by tax dollars. However, the FCHR boasts a significant return on the taxpayer's investment by resolving cases early at the administrative level, which relieves crowded court dockets and helps avoid litigation costs. The FCHR estimates that they saved approximately $15 million in avoided litigation costs for fiscal year 2015–2016, amounting to a 238 percent return on the state's investment.[8]

In fiscal year 2015–2016, 182 housing cases were received by the FCHR, which found reasonable cause to believe discrimination actually occurred in only 20 of them.[9] This number clearly reflects the FCHR's role in filtering out frivolous cases. While the fair housing complainant is not prohibited from filing suit upon the FCHR's dismissal of their claim, a finding of no reasonable cause

---

[4] U.S. Department of Housing and Urban Development, http://portal.hud.gov/hudportal/HUD?src=/about/mission (last visited May 16, 2017).

[5] HUD Form 903 Online Complaint is available at https://portal.hud.gov/FHEO903/Form903/Form903Start.action (last visited May 16, 2017).

[6] 42 U.S.C. § 3610(f) (2017).

[7] Fla. Stat. § 760.05 (2016).

[8] *See* Florida Commission on Human Relations Annual Report 2015-2016, available at http://fchr.state.fl.us/fchr/content/download/10795/60254/file/FCHR_annual%20report2017.pdf (last visited May 16, 2017).

[9] *See* Florida Commission on Human Relations Annual Report 2015-2016, available at http://fchr.state.fl.us/fchr/content/download/10795/60254/file/FCHR_annual%20report2017.pdf (last visited May 16, 2017).

to believe discrimination occurred gives many complainants pause to reflect on their claim, discouraging them from litigation. Not only does this help prevent meritless court cases, it helps preserve the public opinion of fair housing enforcement itself, which may otherwise suffer as a result of baseless claims.

Under the Florida Administrative Code, the FCHR is required to encourage parties to settle.[10] To this end, it provides a free mediator for confidential mediation so that the parties can fashion their own relief. This can save a great deal of time and money and potentially frees each party from litigation's inherent uncertainty.

10-2:4 Administrative Procedures

Statutory provisions govern the FCHR's procedures for investigating and conciliating fair housing complaints and enforcing the FHA. The Office of Housing Investigations investigates complaints. The Executive Director of the FCHR may also designate investigators from any public agency, state, local or federal, that is charged with the administration of fair housing laws.[11]

The administrative process begins with a written and verified complaint filed at the FCHR's office by any person who claims to have been injured, or believes they will be injured, by a discriminatory housing practice.[12] The complaint must be filed within one year of the alleged discrimination,[13] unless the alleged discriminatory housing practice is of a continuing nature, in which case the complaint may be filed within one year of the date on which the discrimination ceased.

The complaint must contain a clear and concise statement of the facts and must disclose any proceedings involving the alleged discrimination that have been commenced before any other agency which are known to the complainant.[14] The answer is due within 20 days of the complaint's filing notice date, and may be amended any time before the FCHR's Notice of Determination is completed.

---

[10] Fla. Admin. Code R. 60Y-7.004 (2016).
[11] Fla. Admin. Code R. 60Y-7.004(1)(a) (2016).
[12] Fla. Admin. Code R. 60Y-7.001 (2016).
[13] Fla. Stat. § 760.34(2) (2016).
[14] Fla. Admin. Code R. 60Y-7.001 (2016).

The investigation commences within 30 days of receipt of the complaint. The investigator may request a statement of particulars from the complainant, and may request from any person interviews, written interrogatories, production of documents, entry upon land for inspection and other purposes, and a written statement or affidavit.[15] The complainant's failure to cooperate with the investigation can result in dismissal of the complaint. Both the FCHR and the respondent may issue subpoenas to compel document production or personal appearances reasonably necessary for the investigation. During the investigation, the information obtained by the FCHR is only accessible to the complainant, the respondent or their authorized representative, and witnesses, when deemed necessary for disposition of the proceeding.[16]

The FCHR is specifically obligated to encourage settlement on mutually agreeable terms, which is reduced to writing in a conciliation agreement.[17] The average settlement payment in an FCHR-mediated conciliation agreement for fiscal year 2015-2016 was $10,578.[18] A conciliation agreement acts as a dismissal of the complaint and is made public unless the complainant and the respondent agree otherwise and the FCHR determines that "disclosure is not required to further the purposes of the Florida Fair Housing Act."[19] Prior to filing the conciliation agreement, the parties may bring the agreement before a Panel of Commissioners, who may adopt the conciliation agreement as a consent order.[20]

The investigation period is meant to last 100 days,[21] after which the FCHR should issue a determination of "cause" or "no cause" and a Final Investigative Report. This is a public document that may be admissible in court proceedings as probative on the issue of discrimination. Federal courts have stated that due to investigators'

[15.] Fla. Stat. § 760.32 (2016).

[16.] Fla. Admin. Code R. 60Y-7.004 (2016).

[17.] Fla. Admin. Code R. 60Y-7.004 (2016).

[18.] *See* Florida Commission on Human Relations Annual Report 2015-2016, available at http://fchr.state.fl.us/fchr/content/download/10795/60254/file/FCHR_annual%20 report2017.pdf (last visited May 16, 2017).

[19.] Fla. Stat. § 760.36 (2016).

[20.] Fla. Admin. Code R. 60Y-7.005 (2016).

[21.] Fla. Stat. § 760.34 (2016).

training and experience such determinations are "highly probative" and excluding them would be "wasteful and unnecessary."[22]

10-2:4.1 Admissibility of Determinations

Admission of cause and no cause determinations into evidence raises two primary issues: (1) the hearsay nature of the determination, and (2) the determination's probative value versus its prejudicial effect.[23] Federal policy dictates that trustworthy public records or statements setting out factual findings from a legally authorized investigation should not be excluded from evidence in civil cases if "the opponent does not show that the source of information or other circumstances indicate a lack of trustworthiness."[24] A similar Florida policy mandates the admissibility of records and reports "setting forth the activities of [an] office or agency, or matters observed pursuant to duty imposed by law as to matters which there was a duty to report," unless "the sources of information or other circumstances show their lack of trustworthiness."[25]

The Cause or No Cause Determination may be excluded, however, when the report's probative value is "substantially outweighed by a danger of" unfair prejudice.[26] Ultimately, the determination's admissibility is within the court's discretion.[27] In deciding whether and what parts of determinations and reports should be admitted, the court should consider whether the report contains legal conclusions in addition to its factual content, whether the report raises questions of trustworthiness, and whether it may result in unfair prejudice.[28]

---

[22] *Smith v. Universal Servs.*, 454 F.2d 154, 157 (5th Cir. 1972).

[23] *Byrd v. BT Foods*, 26 So. 3d 600, 605 (Fla. 4th Dist. Ct. App. 2009).

[24] Fed. R. Evid. 803(8) (2017).

[25] Fla. R. Evid. 90.803(8) (2016).

[26] Fed. R. Evid. 403 (2017); Fla. R. Evid. 90.403 (2016).

[27] *Balletti v. Sun-Sentinel*, 909 F. Supp. 1539, 1545 n.5 (S.D. Fla. 1995) (citing *Barfield v. Orange Cty.*, 911 F.2d 644, 650 (11th Cir. 1990) (explaining that while "EEOC reports and findings, as well as [state agency] findings ... are admissible and probative on the issue of" discrimination and/or retaliation, there may be circumstances in which the probative value of a determination "is outweighed by the danger of creating unfair prejudice in the minds of a jury"); *Barfield v. Orange Cty.*, 911 F.2d 644, 650 (11th Cir. 1990) (in an employment discrimination case, the court considered an FCHR No Cause Determination and Investigatory Report concluding that the employer had neither retaliated against the employee nor discriminated against or harassed her because of her gender).

[28] *Barfield v. Orange Cty.*, 911 F.2d 644, 650 (11th Cir. 1990).

There is an important distinction between the public records exception under Federal Rule of Evidence 803(8) and Florida Rule of Evidence 90.803(8),[29] which is "narrower than the federal rule"[30] in that it does not include a hearsay exception for "factual findings from a legally authorized investigation."[31] While agency determinations are "ordinarily admissible,"[32] Florida courts guard against unfair prejudice caused by disclosure of reports, which may make it impossible for juries with knowledge of a government agency's determination to objectively weigh evidence regarding discrimination.[33] Unlike judges, juries may not be aware of "the limits and vagaries of administrative determinations" and might not give appropriate weight to them.[34] Ultimately, admissibility is decided by the trial judge, who should be wary of the conclusory nature of determinations whose probative value may be negligible compared to their "substantial prejudicial effect" on juries.[35]

10-2:4.2 Post-Determination Proceedings

Regardless of the issuance of the Notice of Determination, if the FCHR does not obtain voluntary compliance with the FHA within 180 days after a complaint is filed, the complainant

---

[29.] Fed. R. Evid. 803(8) (2017) ("(8) Public Records. A record or statement of a public office if: (A) it sets out: (i) the office's activities; (ii) a matter observed while under a legal duty to report, but not including, in a criminal case, a matter observed by law-enforcement personnel; or (iii) in a civil case or against the government in a criminal case, factual findings from a legally authorized investigation; and (B) neither the source of information nor other circumstances indicate a lack of trustworthiness."); Fla. Stat. § 90.803(8) (2016) ("(8) PUBLIC RECORDS AND REPORTS.—Records, reports, statements reduced to writing, or data compilations, in any form, of public offices or agencies, setting forth the activities of the office or agency, or matters observed pursuant to duty imposed by law as to matters which there was a duty to report, excluding in criminal cases matters observed by a police officer or other law enforcement personnel, unless the sources of information or other circumstances show their lack of trustworthiness. The criminal case exclusion shall not apply to an affidavit otherwise admissible under s. 316.1934 or s. 327.354.")

[30.] Byrd v. BT Foods, 26 So. 3d 600, 605-606 (Fla. 4th Dist. Ct. App. 2009) (on appeal from a jury verdict that the employer did not discriminate against an employee with HIV, the appeal court held that the trial court abused its discretion in admitting into evidence the No Cause Determination issued by the Broward County Civil Rights Division because the determination's conclusory nature left it with "little probative value when compared to the substantial prejudicial effect it may have had on the jury's ultimate assessment").

[31.] Fed. R. Evid. 803(8) (2017).

[32.] Goldsmith v. Bagby Elevator, 513 F.3d 1261, 1288 (11th Cir. 2008).

[33.] Byrd v. BT Foods, 26 So. 3d 600, 605 (Fla. 4th Dist. Ct. App. 2009)).

[34.] Byrd v. BT Foods, 26 So. 3d 600, 606 (Fla. 4th Dist. Ct. App. 2009) (quoting Barfield v. Orange Cty., 911 F.2d 644, 651 (11th Cir. 1990)).

[35.] Byrd v. BT Foods, 26 So. 3d 600, 606 (Fla. 4th Dist. Ct. App. 2009).

may commence a civil action or petition for an administrative determination.[36] Whenever this action comes to trial, the FCHR is to cease all activity on the case.[37]

A "Notice of Determination (No Cause)" operates as a dismissal, after which the complainant has 30 days to request an administrative hearing by filing a Petition for Relief from a Discriminatory Housing Practice.[38] The FCHR also gives the complainant notice of their right to file a civil action in federal or state court within two years of the alleged discriminatory act.

If the Executive Director issues a "Notice of Determination (Cause)," the notice provides the complainant with several options: the complainant (1) may file a Petition for Relief from a Discriminatory Housing Practice within 30 days of service, (2) may request that the Attorney General bring a court action in the state's name on the complainant's behalf, (3) may request that the FCHR petition for an administrative hearing in the state's name on their behalf, or (4) may initiate a civil action no later than two years after the occurrence of the alleged discriminatory act. The two-year period excludes the time from filing of the fair housing complaint with the FCHR through the end of the administrative proceedings.[39]

In the event of a cause finding, the Executive Director may file on the FCHR's behalf a Petition for Relief from a Discriminatory Housing Practice,[40] which typically results in a hearing before a Division of Administrative Hearings Administrative Law Judge.[41] The judge must entertain arguments on all issues and allow the parties the opportunity to present witness testimony and other evidence, conduct cross-examination, submit rebuttal evidence, submit proposed findings of facts and law, and to be represented by counsel.[42] At such hearings, hearsay evidence is admissible to supplement or explain other evidence, "but it shall not be sufficient

---

[36] Fla. Stat. § 760.34(4) (2016).
[37] Fla. Stat. § 760.34(6) (2016).
[38] Fla. Admin. Code R. 60Y-7.004 (2016).
[39] 42 U.S.C. § 3613(a)(1)(B) (2017).
[40] Fla. Admin. Code R. 60Y-8.001 (2016).
[41] Fla. Admin. Code R. 60Y-4.016 (2016).
[42] Fla. Stat. § 120.57 (2016).

in itself to support a finding unless it would be admissible over objection in civil actions."[43]

Following the hearing, the judge must allow the parties to submit proposed recommended orders, after which the judge submits a recommended order to the FCHR. Following the filing of exceptions, briefs, and oral arguments, if any, the FCHR considers the record and issues a written decision,[44] either dismissing the petition or, in the event the FCHR determines that a discriminatory housing practice has occurred, issuing an order prohibiting the practice and providing relief such as damages and reasonable attorney's fees and costs.[45]

Appeals from the FCHR's decision must be made in accordance with section 120.68, which requires appellants to pursue judicial review within 30 days of the written decision by filing a Florida Rules of Appellate Division compliant notice of appeal or petition for review either in the First District, the district where a party resides, or as otherwise provided by law.[46]

10-3   CLAIM ANALYSIS

In Florida, fair housing litigation typically includes three distinct types of claims. Claims often arise from alleged discrimination in the sale or rental of housing in violation of section 760.23 which states,

> It is unlawful to refuse to sell or rent ... or otherwise
> to make unavailable or deny a dwelling to any
> person because of race, color, national origin, sex,
> handicap, familial status, or religion.[47]

Examples include a condominium board refusing to approve an owner's lease to a family based on an unenforceable rule prohibiting children in the building.

Claims also arise from violations of subsection 760.23(2), which prohibits discrimination in the

> conditions, or privileges of sale or rental of a
> dwelling, or in the provision of services or facilities

[43.] Fla. Stat. § 120.57 (2016).
[44.] Fla. Stat. § 120.57 (2016).
[45.] Fla. Admin. Code R. 60Y-8.001 (2016).
[46.] Fla. Stat. § 120.68 (2016).
[47.] Fla. Stat. § 760.23(1) (2016).

in connection therewith, because of race, color, national origin, sex, handicap, familial status, or religion.[48]

For example, a property manager is prohibited from selectively enforcing the community's parking rules against a family based on bias against their national origin.

In addition, Florida fair housing litigation often includes claims arising from a housing provider's alleged refusal to accommodate handicapped persons. Discrimination includes any

refusal to make reasonable accommodations in rules, policies, practices, or services, when such accommodations may be necessary to afford [a handicapped] person equal opportunity to use and enjoy a dwelling.[49]

For example, a condominium board is prohibited from refusing to give an exception to its no-pet rule to disabled persons needing service animals.

While each of these types of claims implicates both the Federal and Florida FHAs, Florida courts have held that the state and federal acts are "substantively identical."[50] Similarly, federal court discussions of the Federal Fair Housing Act (Federal FHA) are persuasive to Florida courts and their construction of the Florida FHA.[51] Accordingly, the Federal and Florida FHAs are discussed in conjunction below.

10-3:1 Standing to Bring a Claim

Standing is easy to establish under the FHA, which provides a cause of action to any person who claims to have been injured by a discriminatory housing practice or who believes they will be injured by an imminent discriminatory housing practice. The

---

[48.] Fla. Stat. § 760.23(2) (2016).

[49.] Fla. Stat. § 760.23(9)(b) (2016).

[50.] *Loren v. Sasser*, 309 F.3d 1296, 1300 n.9 (11th Cir. 2002).

[51.] *Dornbach v. Holley*, 854 So. 2d 211, 213 (Fla. 2d Dist. Ct. App. 2002) ("[i]n considering the application of the Florida Fair Housing Act ... the application of the FHAA by the federal courts ... [is] instructive and persuasive").

plaintiff need not belong to a protected class and does not have to show they were the target of the discriminatory housing practice.

The FHA describes any person with such claims as an "aggrieved person," which the act defines broadly. Standing under the Act is as expansive as the Constitution's minimum case or controversy requirements.[52] That is to say, the plaintiff need only show they personally suffered some actual or threatened injury as a result of the defendant's alleged unlawful conduct.[53] For instance, a religious group had standing to sue a homeowners' association for the right to use common areas for worship services even though the group was not even a community association member. The group's standing under the act arose from allegations that the association denied it common area use rights solely based upon the religious nature of its meetings, while it permitted non-religious groups to meet freely.[54]

10-3:2   Discrimination in Sale or Rental

Florida courts analogize FHA claims to Title VII employment discrimination claims[55] and analyze such claims in a similar manner.[56] As such, an FHA violation is established by showing either (1) the defendant was motivated by intent to discriminate against the plaintiff, or (2) "disparate impact," meaning that the defendant's otherwise neutral action had a discriminatory effect.[57]

10-3:2.1 Intentional Discrimination

Proving discriminatory intent requires the plaintiff to show that the defendant intended or was motivated to discriminate against members of a protected class.[58] Although increasingly rare, discriminatory intent can be proven by direct evidence, such

---

[52] *Savanna Club Worship Serv. v. Savanna Club Homeowners' Ass'n*, 456 F. Supp. 2d 1223, 1226-27 (S.D. Fla. 2005).

[53] *Gladstone Realtors v. Vill. of Bellwood*, 441 U.S. 91, 99 (1979).

[54] *Savanna Club Worship Serv. v. Savanna Club Homeowners' Ass'n*, 456 F. Supp. 2d 1223 (S.D. Fla. 2005).

[55] 42 U.S.C. § 2000(e), et seq.

[56] *Gamble v. City of Escondido*, 104 F.3d 300, 304 (9th Cir. 1997).

[57] *Larkin v. State of Mich. Dept. of Soc. Servs.*, 89 F.3d 285, 289 (6th Cir. 1996).

[58] *Reese v. Miami-Dade Cty.*, 242 F. Supp. 2d 1292, 1301 (S.D. Fla. 2002).

---

as a statement by the defendant that demonstrates animus toward a protected class. In more common circumstances in which there is an absence of direct evidence, the courts determine whether circumstantial evidence shows discriminatory intent by evaluating the following four factors: (1) the discriminatory or segregative effect of the allegedly discriminatory housing practice ("disparate impact"); (2) the historical background of the surrounding circumstances, including prior exclusionary behavior; (3) the sequence of events leading up to the challenged actions; and (4) whether there were any departures from standard practices.[59]

FHA claims of alleged intentional discrimination based on circumstantial evidence are subject to the *McDonnell Douglas v. Green* burden-shifting analysis,[60] under which the plaintiff has the initial burden of establishing a prima facie case. If the burden is met, the plaintiff is entitled to a rebuttable presumption that the defendant engaged in unlawful discrimination.[61] The burden then shifts to the defendant to establish a legitimate non-discriminatory reason for their action. If the defendant produces a legitimate non-discriminatory reason, then the burden returns to the plaintiff to establish that the defendant's reason is merely a pretext for discrimination.[62] A plaintiff may demonstrate that the defendant's reason is merely a pretext by demonstrating inconsistencies and contradictions in the defendant's position and by putting forth evidence that animus toward the protected class motivated the defendant's actions.[63]

10-3:2.2 Disparate Impact

Disparate impact analysis is applied to a facially neutral policy or practice to determine whether it has a segregative effect or "makes housing options significantly more restrictive for members of a protected group than for persons outside

---

[59.] *Bonasera v. City of Norcross*, 342 F. App'x 581, 585 (11th Cir. 2009) (adopting the multi-factor test set forth in *United States v. Hous. Auth. of City of Chickasaw*, 504 F. Supp. 716, 727 (S.D. Ala. 1980)).

[60.] *McDonnell Douglas v. Green*, 411 U.S. 792 (1973).

[61.] *Secretary, U.S. Dept. of Hous. & Urban Dev., on Behalf of Herron v. Blackwell*, 908 F.2d 864, 871 (11th Cir. 1990).

[62.] *Savanna Club Worship Serv. v. Savanna Club Homeowners' Ass'n*, 456 F. Supp. 2d 1223, 1231-32 (S.D. Fla. 2005).

[63.] *Secretary, U.S. Dept. of Hous. & Urban Dev., on Behalf of Herron v. Blackwell*, 908 F.2d 864, 871 (11th Cir. 1990).

that group."[64] When a facially neutral housing practice has a disparate impact on a protected group, it produces two kinds of discriminatory effects: (1) the facially neutral housing practice has an adverse impact on the particular protected group, and (2) the community is harmed generally by the perpetuation of segregation.[65]

Typically, discriminatory effect in disparate impact claims is demonstrated by statistics.[66] In analyzing these cases, courts favor proportional statistics over a simple examination of absolute numbers. For instance, in a disparate impact challenge to a zoning regulation that restricted housing project construction to an "urban renewal area" inhabited primarily by minorities, the lower court erroneously focused on absolute numbers in census figures. The court reasoned that since indigent whites made up the vast majority of all inhabitants eligible for subsidized housing, building the housing project in a minority area would have no disparate impact or discriminatory segregative effect. On appeal, the court instead examined proportional statistics and determined that the zoning regulation had a disproportionate impact on minorities. Based on these proportional statistics, the appeals court held that the regulation impeded integration by restricting construction of housing projects needed disproportionately by minorities to an area already 52 percent minority.[67]

10-3:3   Reasonable Accommodation

10-3:3.1   Elements of a Reasonable Accommodation Claim

Courts utilize a wholly different approach to reasonable accommodation claims, which arise when a housing provider refuses to make a change or exception to a rule, practice, or service that may be necessary for a disabled person to have an

---

[64.] *Bonasera v. City of Norcross*, 342 F. App'x 581, 585 (11th Cir. 2009) (citing *Housing Inv'rs v. City of Clanton, Ala.*, 68 F. Supp. 2d 1287, 1298 (M.D. Ala. 1999)).

[65.] *Metropolitan Hous. Dev. v. Vill. of Arlington Heights*, 558 F.2d 1283, 1290 (7th Cir. 1977).

[66.] *Hallmark Developers v. Fulton Cty., Ga.*, 466 F.3d 1276, 1286 (11th Cir. 2006).

[67.] *Huntington Branch, N.A.A.C.P. v. Town of Huntington*, 844 F.2d 926, 938 (2d Cir. 1988), *aff'd in part sub nom. Town of Huntington, N.Y. v. Huntington Branch, N.A.A.C.P.*, 488 U.S. 15 (1988).

equal opportunity to use and enjoy a dwelling. This includes the disabled person's use and enjoyment of public and common areas. To prevail on a reasonable accommodation claim, a plaintiff must establish that (1) he is disabled within the meaning of the Act, (2) he requested a reasonable accommodation, (3) such accommodation was necessary to afford him an equal opportunity to use and enjoy the dwelling, and (4) defendants refused to make the requested accommodation.[68]

A person is handicapped for purposes of the Act if they (a) suffer from a "physical or mental impairment which substantially limits one or more of such person's major life activities," (b) have "a record of having such an impairment," or (c) are "regarded as having such an impairment."[69] Major life activities include functions such as "caring for one's self, performing manual tasks, walking, seeing, hearing, speaking, breathing, learning, and working."[70] An individual faces a "substantial limitation" when he is

> (i) Unable to perform a major life activity that the average person in the general population can perform; or (ii) Significantly restricted as to the condition, manner or duration under which [he] can perform a particular major life activity as compared to the condition, manner, or duration under which the average person in the general population can perform that same major life activity.[71]

Sex offenders are not covered by the Act.[72] In addition, while "handicap" is not defined so broadly to include persons currently

---

[68.] *Schwarz v. City of Treasure Island*, 544 F.3d 1201, 1218 (11th Cir. 2008).

[69.] 42 U.S.C. § 3602(h) (2017).

[70.] 24 C.F.R. § 100.201(b) (2017).

[71.] *Soileau v. Guilford of Maine*, 105 F.3d 12, 15 (1st Cir. 1997).

[72.] Joint Statement of the Department of Housing and Urban Development and the Department of Justice, Reasonable Accommodations Under the Fair Housing Act 4 (May 17, 2004), available at http://www.hud.gov/offices/fheo/library/huddojstatement.pdf (last visited May 16, 2017).

using or addicted to a controlled substance,[73] the Act does protect persons recovering from substance abuse.[74]

A Plaintiff must actually request an accommodation and be refused in order to bring a reasonable accommodation claim under the Act.[75] Undue delay in responding to an accommodation request may be deemed a failure to provide a reasonable accommodation.[76] With that being said, the request need not be in writing.[77] Whether a requested accommodation is required by law is "highly fact-specific, requiring case-by-case determination."[78] No burden-shifting analysis is employed in these cases. The plaintiff bears the burden at all times of proving that a proposed accommodation is reasonable.[79]

10-3:3.2 Necessity and Reasonableness

The FHA only prohibits denial of reasonable accommodations that are *necessary* to the plaintiff's use and enjoyment of the property. To demonstrate necessity, the disabled person must show that the desired accommodation will ameliorate the disability's effects.[80] There must be a direct link between the requested accommodation and the equal opportunity to be provided. Reasonable accommodations are meant to address needs, not the personal preferences of disabled persons. It is insufficient to show that a refused accommodation is simply convenient or desired; rather, it must be necessary.[81] The Act only ensures that the handicapped person is provided an equal opportunity to use

---

[73] *United States v. Southern Mgmt.*, 955 F.2d 914, 922 (4th Cir. 1992).

[74] Joint Statement of the Department of Housing and Urban Development and the Department of Justice, Reasonable Accommodations Under the Fair Housing Act 4 (May 17, 2004), available at http://www.hud.gov/offices/fheo/library/huddojstatement.pdf (last visited May 16, 2017).

[75] *Schwarz v. City of Treasure Island*, 544 F.3d 1201, 1219 (11th Cir. 2008).

[76] *Overlook Mut. Homes v. Spencer*, 415 Fed. Appx. 617, 621 (6th Cir. 2011).

[77] Joint Statement of the Department of Housing and Urban Development and the Department of Justice, Reasonable Accommodations Under the Fair Housing Act 10 (May 17, 2004), available at http://www.hud.gov/offices/fheo/library/huddojstatement.pdf (last visited May 16, 2017).

[78] *United States v. California Mobile Home Park Mgmt.*, 29 F.3d 1413, 1418 (9th Cir. 1994).

[79] *Loren v. Sasser*, 309 F.3d 1296, 1302 (11th Cir. 2002).

[80] *Essling's Homes Plus v. City of St. Paul*, 356 F. Supp. 2d 971, 980 (D. Minn. 2004).

[81] *Bachman v. Swan Harbour Ass'n*, 653 N.W.2d 415, 429 (2002).

and enjoy a dwelling, not a better opportunity than members of the surrounding community.[82]

For instance, the court held that an accommodation in the form of a zoning regulation waiver to permit a group home to house more residents was *not* required by the Act, since it would not qualitatively ameliorate the effects of the residents' disabilities.[83] While such an accommodation may benefit the group home financially, it does not qualify as a necessity under the Act for which a reasonable accommodation must be made.[84]

Accommodations that are not reasonable may also be denied. An accommodation is not reasonable if it imposes undue financial and administrative burdens on the housing provider or if it would fundamentally alter the nature of their operations.[85] Whether the requested accommodation would impose an undue financial and administrative burden is determined on a case-by-case basis. Courts consider several factors, such as cost, the provider's financial resources, the benefits that the accommodation would provide to the disabled person, and the availability of less costly alternative accommodations that would ameliorate the effects of the disability.[86] If an alternative accommodation would effectively meet the disability-related needs and is reasonable, the provider must grant it.

[82.] *Schwarz v. City of Treasure Island,* 544 F.3d 1201, 1226 (11th Cir. 2008).

[83.] *Bryant Woods Inn v. Howard Cty., Md.,* 124 F.3d 597 (4th Cir. 1997).

[84.] *Bryant Woods Inn v. Howard Cty., Md.,* 124 F.3d 597, 605 (4th Cir. 1997) (a county planning board refused to waive parking-related zoning regulations to accommodate the expansion of a handicapped persons group home from eight to 15 residents; the board denied the variance request because (1) it proposed inadequate parking for an already congested area, (2) it did not increase the total number of housing opportunities for the disabled in the county, which had over 30 elderly and disabled assisted-living facilities, and (3) the group home was economically viable with eight residents; the court noted that (a) the parking regulation did not *prohibit* handicap group housing, (b) the zoning variance's aim was only to expand the size of a specific group home, and (c) the home introduced no evidence that it would be unviable, therapeutically or financially, to operate with only eight residents; the court therefore held that the home failed to prove necessity, since the accommodation did not ameliorate the effects of the residents' disabilities, and only financially benefited the home; the court concluded that the zoning variance would provide a financial advantage to the home not enjoyed by group homes that do not serve disabled persons, which is not required by the FHA).

[85.] *Bachman v. Swan Harbour Ass'n,* 653 N.W.2d 415, 430 (2002).

[86.] Joint Statement of the Department of Housing and Urban Development and the Department of Justice, Reasonable Accommodations Under the Fair Housing Act 7 (May 17, 2004), available at http://www.hud.gov/offices/fheo/library/huddojstatement.pdf (last visited May 14, 2017).

However, the financial burden must be significant before the court will determine that it impacts the reasonableness of the proposed accommodation. The court will not be concerned if the cost is only minor and the accommodation is financially feasible for the defendant. Furthermore, the determination of whether the accommodation is "cost-prohibitive" is made by the court, notwithstanding the defendant's claims regarding financial feasibility.[87]

10-3:4   Relief From Discriminatory Housing Practices

Both the Federal and Florida FHAs allow courts to impose actual damages and injunctions on defendants found liable for housing discrimination.[88] This may include damages for humiliation and embarrassment suffered by the plaintiff.[89] In addition, directors of community association may be personally liable if they are found to have contributed to the alleged FHA violations. The immunity from civil liability enjoyed by corporate officers under Fla. Stat. § 617.0834 cannot bar a claim under the FHA.[90] Punitive damages may also be granted when a defendant exhibits "callous indifference to the federally protected rights of the plaintiff."[91] For example, the court imposed punitive damages where the defendant's refusal to make what it deemed were unnecessary and cost-prohibitive elevator repairs forced a 59-year-old quadriplegic to either drag himself up and down filthy concrete stairs or be a prisoner in his home.[92] The court found that punitive damages were justified by the defendant's indifference to the plaintiff's plight and the fact that the defendant only complied with the FHA after unfavorable media

---

[87.] *Davis v. Lane Mgmt., LLC*, 524 F. Supp. 2d 1375, 1378 (S.D. Fla. 2007) (holding that defendant who refused to make elevator repairs it considered cost prohibitive violated the FHA because such repairs were in fact financially feasible for the defendant).

[88.] 42 U.S.C. § 3613(c) (2017); Fla. Stat. § 760.35(2) (2016).

[89.] *Secretary, U.S. Dept. of Hous. & Urban Dev., on Behalf of Herron v. Blackwell*, 908 F.2d 864, 872 (11th Cir. 1990).

[90.] *Sabal Palm Condos. of Pine Island Ridge Ass'n v. Fischer*, 12-60691-CIV, 2014 WL 988767 (S.D. Fla. 2014).

[91.] *Davis v. Lane Mgmt.*, 524 F. Supp. 2d 1375, 1377 (S.D. Fla. 2007); *see Ferrill v. Parker Grp.*, 168 F.3d 468, 476 (11th Cir.1999) (citing *Smith v. Wade*, 461 U.S. 30, 46-47 (1983)).

[92.] *Davis v. Lane Mgmt.*, 524 F. Supp. 2d 1375 (S.D. Fla. 2007).

coverage, "demonstrate[ing] a reckless and wanton disregard for the Plaintiff's rights under the law."[93]

In FCHR- or HUD-instituted administrative hearings, the judge may impose maximum civil penalties as follows:

> 1. Up to $10,000, if the respondent has not previously been found guilty of a violation. 2. Up to $25,000, if the respondent has been found guilty of one prior violation within the preceding 5 years. 3. Up to $50,000, if the respondent has been found guilty of two or more violations within the preceding 7 years.[94]

The Federal FHA makes attorney's fees available to the "prevailing party,"[95] but case law construing the act does not allow for fees to the plaintiff and the defendant on an equal basis. Prevailing defendants are only entitled to receive fees "upon a finding that the plaintiff's action was frivolous, unreasonable, or without foundation."[96] The Florida FHA is much more clear and states,

> If the court finds that a discriminatory housing practice has occurred, it shall issue an order prohibiting the practice and providing affirmative relief from the effects of the practice, including

---

[93]. *Davis v. Lane Mgmt.*, 524 F. Supp. 2d 1375, 1378 (S.D. Fla. 2007) (quadriplegic plaintiff sued management company who refused to repair the two elevators in his building, which defendant knew were plaintiff's only reasonable means of access to and from his second-story apartment; defendant took a number of untenable positions, maintaining that the repairs were unnecessary and cost-prohibitive and offering empty promises that someone would assist the plaintiff, which forced the plaintiff to dirty himself by crawling up and down stairs covered in spit, urine, and dog feces; as a result, plaintiff was mistreated by colleagues, neighbors, and management company employees, and on certain occasions was forced to sleep in public places and soil himself because it was too difficult to crawl back up to his home; in short, as a result of the defendant's refusal to repair the elevators the plaintiff was constantly humiliated in front of his family and neighbors, as was his teenage daughter; the plaintiff also physically injured himself crawling up and down the concrete stairs on a daily basis and suffered chronic pain, causing him to require physical therapy; after the plaintiff took his story to a news reporter, who broadcast the story on television, defendant completed the previously "cost-prohibitive" elevator repairs; the court found that defendant's indifference to the plaintiff's plight and the fact that they needed media coverage to comply with the FHA, "demonstrate[d] a reckless and wanton disregard for the Plaintiff's rights under the law" which justified liability for punitive damages).

[94]. 42 U.S.C. § 3612(g)(3) (2017); Fla. Stat. § 760.34(7)(b) (2016).

[95]. 42 U.S.C. § 3613(c)(2) (2017).

[96]. *Bryant Woods Inn v. Howard Cty., Md.*, 124 F.3d 597, 606 (4th Cir. 1997) (quoting *Christiansburg Garment v. Equal Emp't Opportunity Comm'n*, 434 U.S. 412, 421 (1978)).

injunctive and other equitable relief, actual and punitive damages, and reasonable attorney's fees and costs.[97]

There is no language in the Florida FHA suggesting that fees may be available to a prevailing defendant.

In fair housing cases, the United States Supreme Court has rejected the "catalyst" theory, under which plaintiffs are awarded fees as the "prevailing party" when they achieve desired results, even if such results are a voluntary change in defendant conduct.[98] While parties in the United States are typically required to bear their own attorney's fees, fees may be awarded to prevailing parties based on explicit contractual or statutory authority, such as the attorney's-fee-and-costs provisions in the Florida and Federal FHAs.[99] In statutes in which Congress authorizes attorney's fees, it employs "the legal term of art 'prevailing party,'" which it defines "as one who has been awarded some relief by a court."[100] The Court's reasoning is based in the Civil Rights Act's[101] legislative history, which indicates that Congress "intended to permit the interim award of counsel fees only when a party has prevailed on the merits of at least some of his claims."[102]

Based on Congress' legislative intent, a settlement agreement through a consent decree, even when the consent decree does not include an admission of liability by the defendant, may serve as the basis for an award of fees,[103] because it is "a court-ordered

---

[97.] Fla. Stat. § 760.35(2) (2016).

[98.] *Buckhannon Bd. & Care Home v. W. Virginia Dept. of Health & Human Res.*, 532 U.S. 598 (2001) (after failing a fire inspection due to its disabled residents' inability to fulfill the statutory "self-preservation" requirement, defined as the ability to remove oneself "from situations involving imminent danger, such as fire," plaintiff filed for declaratory and injunctive relief on the grounds that the "self-preservation" requirement violated the FHA and Americans with Disabilities Act (ADA); in response, the legislature eliminated the "self-preservation" requirement and the District Court granted defendant's motion to dismiss the case as moot; plaintiff requested attorney's fees as the "prevailing party" under the FHA and the ADA, claiming entitlement under the catalyst theory; ultimately, the U.S. Supreme Court rejected this theory as a means to obtain prevailing party fee awards in fair housing cases).

[99.] 42 U.S.C. § 3613(c)(2) (2017) ("the court, in its discretion, may allow the prevailing party, other than the United States, a reasonable attorney's fee and costs").

[100.] *Buckhannon Bd. & Care Home v. W. Virginia Dept. of Health & Human Res.*, 532 U.S. 598 (2001).

[101.] 42 U.S.C. § 1988.

[102.] *Hanrahan v. Hampton*, 446 U.S. 754, 758 (1980).

[103.] *Maher v. Gagne*, 448 U.S. 122, 129 (1980).

change in the legal relationship" between the parties.[104] Conversely, "a defendant's voluntary change in conduct," although perhaps accomplishing the plaintiff's objectives, "lacks the necessary judicial imprimatur on the change."[105] Based on this reasoning, the catalyst theory has been rejected as a means to obtain prevailing party fees in fair housing cases.[106]

10-4 COMPANION ANIMALS

Animals that provide help to the disabled include not only seeing-eye dogs or dogs for the deaf and hearing impaired, but also animals that support those with mental and emotional disabilities, such as anxiety and depression. Unfortunately, many of these individuals live in communities whose rules and regulations include pet restrictions instituted for the benefit of those with allergies, phobias, or a simple preference not to live among animals.

The management and boards of pet-restricted communities have a duty to enforce the rules and regulations and to represent the desires and inclinations of the majority of their members, many of whom may take offense to neighbors who are seemingly flaunting the rules by living with prohibited pets. This is almost inevitable in pet-restricted condominium buildings where dog owners must take their animals through common areas, elevators, and lobbies shared by all. This situation may result in a legal dispute between a disabled person in need of a service or emotional support animal and a community board over whether the association is required to provide a reasonable accommodation under the fair housing laws in the form of an exception to the community's pet rule.

[104.] *Buckhannon Bd. & Care Home v. W. Virginia Dept. of Health & Human Res.*, 532 U.S. 598, 604 (2001).

[105.] *Buckhannon Bd. & Care Home v. W. Virginia Dept. of Health & Human Res.*, 532 U.S. 598, 605 (2001); *but see Baldain v. Am. Home Mortg. Servicing*, CIV.S-09-0931LKK/GGH, 2010 WL 2606666 (E.D. Cal. June 28, 2010) (holding that Congress explicitly superseded *Buckhannon* in the narrow context of the Freedom of Information Act, 5 U.S.C. § 552(a) (4)(E)(ii) (2011)).

[106.] *Buckhannon Bd. & Care Home v. W. Virginia Dept. of Health & Human Res.*, 532 U.S. 598, 608 (2001) (noting that the catalyst theory may in fact serve as a disincentive to defendants' voluntary change in conduct; rejecting the argument that the catalyst theory is necessary to prevent defendants from unilaterally mooting an action before judgment in an effort to avoid attorney's fees, since (a) defendants *cannot* moot causes of action for damages, and (b) federal courts retain their power to determine a practice's legality barring absolute certainty the practice could not reasonably be expected to recur).

10-4:1   Emotional Support Animals for Mental and Emotional Disabilities

As public awareness about support animal treatment for mental and emotional disabilities increases, more disabled persons seek this form of treatment. Unfortunately, unscrupulous individuals who are not disabled, as defined by the FHA, may also request support animal prescriptions from doctors in attempts to skirt community pet rules. Because mental and emotional disabilities are not readily visible, those suffering from them may face more obstacles in receiving a reasonable accommodation than individuals with physical disabilities. In addition, many people remain skeptical of the very real impairments experienced by people suffering from mental and emotional disorders. Simple ignorance may lead to a hasty assumption that disabled people are malingering so that they can continue to live with their beloved pets.

This topic is becoming increasingly prevalent as evidenced by many websites that have been created to provide advice to those seeking accommodations for their animals.[107] HUD even provides a sample doctors' letter to request a reasonable accommodation for emotional support animals.[108] There has also been a great deal of litigation on this issue, stemming both from community associations rejecting reasonable accommodation requests from bona fide disabled individuals and from residents falsely claiming a legal right to skirt their community association's pet rules.

Courts, however, employ a very broad definition of "disability," and generally accept the idea that emotional support animals provide real therapy and support to disabled persons. As such, a community association may face significant liability in refusing to grant a reasonable accommodation to its pet rules. This is especially true given the fact that an accommodation to a pet rule is typically considered financially insignificant and only a minor inconvenience to the community association and other residents.

[107.] *See, e.g.*, http://www.servicedogcentral.org/content/ (last visited May 14, 2017); http://www.petsincondos.org/legal/ (last visited May 14, 2017).

[108.] U.S. Department of Housing and Urban Development, Sample Letter for Companion Animal, available at: http://www.hud.gov/offices/fheo/PIRC/DocumentsAbstracts/Disability-Law-Center-R8/Letters/DLC-Animal-Letter/Sample-letter-for-Companion-Animal.doc (last visited May 14, 2017).

10-4:2   Service Animals vs. Emotional Support Animals

The special training received by service animals, such as seeing-eye dogs, distinguishes them from emotional support animals and ordinary pets.[109] As defined by regulations adopted to enforce the Americans with Disabilities Act (ADA),

> Service animal means any dog that is individually trained to do work or perform tasks for the benefit of an individual with a disability, including a physical, sensory, psychiatric, intellectual, or other mental disability.[110]

Emotional support animals "do not need training to ameliorate the effects of a person's mental and emotional disabilities," since "by their very nature [they] may relieve depression and anxiety, and/or help reduce stress-induced pain in persons with certain medical conditions affected by stress."[111]

10-4:3   Emotional Support Animals and the Fair Housing Act

The FHA prohibits discrimination against any buyer or renter in the terms, conditions, or privileges of sale or rental of a dwelling, or in the provision of services or facilities in connection with such dwelling, because of a handicap of (A) that buyer or renter; (B) a person residing in or intending to reside in that dwelling after it is sold, rented, or made available; or (C) any person associated with that buyer or renter.[112] Discrimination includes refusal to make a reasonable accommodation in rules, policies, practices, or services when such an accommodation is necessary to allow a disabled person an equal opportunity to use and enjoy a dwelling.[113]

---

[109] *Prindable v. Ass'n of Apartment Owners of 2987 Kalakaua*, 304 F. Supp. 2d 1245, 1256 (D. Haw. 2003).

[110] 28 C.F.R. § 36.104 (2017).

[111] *Overlook Mut. Homes v. Spencer*, 666 F. Supp. 2d 850, 859 (S.D. Ohio 2009).

[112] 42 U.S.C. § 3604(f)(1) (2017).

[113] 42 U.S.C. § 3604(f) (2017); *see Schwarz v. City of Treasure Island*, 544 F. 3d 1201, 1218-19 (11th Cir. 2008) (providing the necessary elements of a reasonable accommodation claim: (1) plaintiff establishes they are disabled and handicapped under the FHA definition; (2) the housing provider knew or should have known of that fact; (3) the housing provider knew that an accommodation was necessary to afford the plaintiff an equal opportunity to use and enjoy the dwelling; (4) such an accommodation was reasonable; and (5) the housing provider refused to make the requested accommodation).

Under the FHA, persons who require emotional support animals to ameliorate disabilities may qualify for a reasonable accommodation to association pet rules, provided they have a legitimate disability and the animal is necessary to facilitate equal use and enjoyment of their dwelling.[114] A key question is whether specialized training as a service animal is required in order to qualify the animal as a reasonable accommodation. Under the ADA definition, emotional support animals only qualify as "service animals" if they have specialized training to provide relevant therapy or support to disabled persons.[115] The ADA definition therefore excludes emotional support animals without specialized training from qualifying as a reasonable accommodation under the FHA.[116]

Contrary to the ADA approach, HUD regulations[117] define reasonable accommodations under the FHA to "include emotional support animals, which need not be individually trained."[118] The HUD regulation removes the training requirement from its "reasonable accommodation" definition in order to ensure equal

---

[114] *See, e.g., Hawn v. Shoreline Towers Phase 1 Condo. Ass'n*, 347 F. App'x 464 (11th Cir. 2009); *see, e.g., Sun Harbor Homeowners' Ass'n v. Bonura*, 95 So. 3d 262 (Fla. 4th Dist. Ct. App. 2012), *reh'g denied* (Sept. 7, 2012).

[115] *Prindable v. Ass'n of Apartment Owners of 2987 Kalakaua*, 304 F. Supp. 2d 1245, 1255 (D. Haw. 2003) (resident with a medical letter stating that he suffers from HIV, anxiety, depression, and a "mental dysfunction that impairs his ability to work" requested an accommodation to his condominium's pet rule; the court ruled that this evidence created a genuine issue of material fact as to whether the resident satisfied the FHA's "handicap" definition but held that the plaintiff's emotional support animal was *not* necessary to ameliorate the disability's effects since it lacked specialized training; relying on the ADA's definition of service animals, the court held that an emotional support animal's lack of specialized training renders the animal unsuited to provide any relevant therapy or support to a disabled person).

[116] *In re Kenna Homes Co-op.*, 557 S.E.2d 787, 799-800 (2001) ("[W]e hold that the Federal Fair Housing Act ... require[s] that a service animal be individually trained and work for the benefit of a disabled person in order to be considered a reasonable accommodation of that person's disability.... [A] landlord or person similarly situated may require a disabled tenant who asserts the need to keep an alleged service animal to show that the animal is properly trained; [and] to produce in writing the formal assertion of the trainer that the animal has been so trained....").

[117] Pet Ownership for the Elderly and Persons With Disabilities, 73 Fed. Reg. 63834, 63836 (October 27, 2008) (prohibiting enforcement of any pet restriction against individuals with animals that are used to assist persons with disabilities, including animals that provide assistance that does not require training).

[118] *Overlook Mut. Homes v. Spencer*, 666 F. Supp. 2d 850, 861 (S.D. Ohio 2009); *Auburn Woods I Homeowners Ass'n v. Fair Emp't & Hous. Comm'n*, 18 Cal. Rptr. 3d 669, 682 (2004) (discussing the distinction between service animals and emotional support animals which typically have no disability-specific training).

---

treatment of disabled persons requiring animals that "do not need training to provide the needed assistance."[119] While the rule itself may apply only to HUD-assisted public housing, the rationale in support thereof is equally applicable to all types of housing regulated by the FHA.[120]

HUD released a policy notice on April 25, 2013, providing additional guidance on emotional support animals. In its policy notice, HUD adopts the broader term of "assistance animal," which is defined as follows:

> An assistance animal is not a pet. It is an animal that works, provides assistance, or performs tasks for the benefit of a person with a disability, or provides emotional support that alleviates one or more identified symptoms or effects of a person's disability.[121]

It is HUD's policy that persons with disabilities may request a reasonable accommodation for any assistance animal, including an emotional support animal, under the FHA. In determining whether a housing provider is required to grant a request for a reasonable accommodation for an assistance animal, the housing provider must consider the following:

(1)   Does the person seeking to use the and live with the animal have a disability—*i.e.*, a physical or mental impairment that substantially limits one or more major life activities?

(2)   Does the person making the request have a disability-related need for an assistance animal? In other words, does the animal work, provide assistance, perform tasks or services for the benefit of a person with a disability, or provide emotional support that alleviates one or more of

---

[119.] Pet Ownership for the Elderly and Persons With Disabilities, 73 Fed. Reg. 63834 (October 27, 2008).

[120.] *Overlook Mut. Homes v. Spencer*, 666 F. Supp. 2d 850, 860 (S.D. Ohio 2009).

[121.] U.S. Department of Housing and Urban Development April 25, 2013 Notice on Service Animals and Assistance Animals for People with Disabilities in Housing and HUD-Funded Programs, available at http://portal.hud.gov/hudportal/documents/huddoc?id=servanimals_ntcfheo2013-01.pdf (last visited May 14, 2017).

the identified symptoms or effects of a person's existing disability?[122]

When the answers to questions (1) and (2) are "yes," the housing provider must provide the requested accommodation, unless the accommodation is unreasonable such that it imposes an undue financial or administrative burden, or fundamentally alters the nature of the provider's services. Courts will likely find that accommodations to pet rules do not impose undue financial or administrative burdens, or alter the nature of the housing provider's operation.[123]

HUD emphasizes the fact that assistance animals are not pets. As such, a housing provider cannot charge a "pet deposit" or other fee related to the assistant animal. A housing provider can deny a requested accommodation if the assistance animal poses a direct threat to the health or safety of others, or may cause substantial damage to the property of others. The HUD notice evaluates the factors a housing provider can consider when evaluating whether or not an assistance animal poses such a threat. Specifically, a determination that an assistance animal poses a direct threat of harm to others or property must be based on an evaluation of that specific animal. In other words, mere speculation or fear about the type of harm or damage that may be caused based on breed, size, or weight is entirely inapplicable. Instead, the housing provider must rely on objective evidence about the specific animal's actual conduct – not on mere speculation or fear of the damage the animal may cause. As a result, the housing provider cannot rely on any common stereotypes associated with a particular breed when evaluating an assistance animal.

Given the broad definition of "disability" and HUD and the courts' support of the right of reasonable accommodation via emotional support animals, community associations with strict no-pet rules may face an uphill battle in enforcing such rules against disabled persons. With that being said, community associations

---

[122] U.S. Department of Housing and Urban Development April 25, 2013 Notice on Service Animals and Assistance Animals for People with Disabilities in Housing and HUD-Funded Programs, available at http://portal.hud.gov/hudportal/documents/huddoc?id=servanimals_ntcfheo2013-01.pdf (last visited May 14, 2017).

[123] *See e.g. Sabal Palm Condos. of Pine Island Ridge Ass'n v. Fischer*, 12-60691-CIV, 2014 WL 988767 (S.D. Fla. 2014).

have a strong, enforceable right to any information necessary to adequately process a reasonable accommodation request. Specifically, if claimants fail to provide substantive information on the nature of the disability and why the requested accommodation is reasonable, effectively preventing a meaningful review of the requested accommodation by the association, the claimant is not entitled to the accommodation at all.[124] A prima facie case requires a demonstration that the association *knew* that an accommodation was necessary to afford a resident equal use and enjoyment, and still denied the accommodation.[125]

A housing provider may not deny a requested accommodation, however, merely because he or she is uncertain as to whether the person requesting the accommodation is disabled or has a need for an assistance animal. If the disability and the disability-related need for the assistance animal is not readily apparent, the housing provider may ask the individual to provide documentation to support their disability and their need for the animal. If the disability is apparent, the housing provider may not request documents to support the existence of the disability. Similarly, if the need for the animal is apparent, the housing provider may not request documentation supporting the need for the animal. Additionally, even if the disability and the need for the animal are not apparent, the housing provider may not ask for detailed and extensive information regarding a person's physical or mental impairments.[126]

[124.] *Sun Harbor Homeowners' Ass'n v. Bonura*, 95 So. 3d 262, 270 (Fla. 4th Dist. Ct. App. 2012), *reh'g denied* (Sept. 7, 2012) (citing *Hawn v. Shoreline Towers Phase 1 Condo. Ass'n*, 347 F. App'x 464, 465 (11th Cir. 2009)).

[125.] *Sun Harbor Homeowners' Ass'n v. Bonura*, 2012 WL 2120923 (Fla. 4th Dist. Ct. App. 2012), *reh'g denied* (Sept. 7, 2012) (holding that plaintiff failed to provide sufficient medical documentation or testimony supporting the claim and that was "a qualified individual with a disability," were not sufficient to establish (1) a handicap, (2) that defendant had knowledge of the handicap, or (3) that defendant refused to provide an accommodation, since the letters did not state (a) how she was qualified under the FHA, (b) the limitations and difficulties from which she was suffering, or (c) why she was entitled to an emotional support animal; emphasizing that plaintiffs who fail to provide substantive information on a disability's nature and the reasonableness of a requested accommodation prevent the defendant from conducting a meaningful review of the requested accommodation and are therefore not entitled to accommodation).

[126.] U.S. Department of Housing and Urban Development April 25, 2013 Notice on Service Animals and Assistance Animals for People with Disabilities in Housing and HUD-Funded Programs, available at https://portal.hud.gov/hudportal/documents/huddoc?id=servanimals_ntcfheo2013-01.pdf (last visited May 14, 2017).

There is no easy solution when a board or property management is torn between a disabled person's request for a reasonable accommodation for their emotional support animal and the complaints of unit owners who may fear or dislike animals. The board of directors has a fiduciary duty and a duty imposed by state and federal law to treat such requests with absolute seriousness. Case law supports their ability to obtain information necessary to process the request, including details on the disability and the limitations suffered by the disabled person, and an explanation as to how the animal assists the disabled person in those limitations. Obtaining the necessary information to assess requests for reasonable accommodations protects the disabled person, the other owners, and the community association as a whole. Potential conflicts may be diffused by education about the FHA's obligations, which may also lead to early and efficient resolution of any claims.

10-5   HOUSING FOR OLDER PERSONS

The 1988 amendments to the Federal FHA include a prohibition against housing discrimination based on "familial status," which is defined as "one or more individuals (who have not attained the age of 18 years)" living with a parent or legal guardian. The definition also applies to anyone who is pregnant.[127] Because there is a legitimate interest in providing retirement communities for elderly people, the FHA includes an exemption to its prohibition against familial status discrimination for housing for older persons that is "intended for, and solely occupied by, persons 62 years of age or older" or "intended and operated for occupancy by persons 55 years of age or older."

Housing designated for persons 55 years of age or older must comply with the following strictly enforced standards to ensure that communities do not engage in prohibited discrimination:

> (i) at least 80 percent of the occupied units are occupied by at least one person who is 55 years of age or older; (ii) the housing facility or community publishes and adheres to policies and procedures that demonstrate the intent required under this

---

[127.] 42 U.S.C. § 3602(k) (2017); *see* Fla. Stat. § 760.29 (2016).

subparagraph; and (iii) the housing facility or community complies with rules issued by the Secretary for verification of occupancy.[128]

The Code of Federal Regulations discusses in detail the factors used in determining whether a housing facility or community publishes and adheres to policies and procedures that "demonstrate its intent to operate as housing for persons 55 years of age or older."[129] Courts are instructed to consider advertising used by the community to attract prospective residents, rules and regulations, leasing provisions, and public postings on common areas. Phrases such as "'adult living', 'adult community', or similar statements" are not consistent "with the intent that the housing facility or community intends to operate as housing for persons 55 years of age or older."[130] In point of fact, the community may allow occupancy by families with children so long as 80 percent or more of the occupied units are occupied by at least one person 55 years of age or older.

Any facility or community seeking qualification as 55-and-over housing must develop procedures for determining the occupancy of each unit, including identification of occupants who are 55 years of age or older in at least 80 percent of the units. This may be performed through surveys or other means, which must be updated at least every two years. The procedures must include review of reliable age documentation such as driver's licenses, birth certificates, passports, immigration cards, or any other official documents containing a birth date of comparable reliability.[131]

Courts require strict compliance with the foregoing regulations. For instance, a homeowners' association that does not properly verify that at least one occupant of each unit is 55 years of age or older *prior* to enforcing age restrictions is not entitled to the housing for older persons exemption.[132] In addition, where the only written

---

[128.] 42 U.S.C. § 3607(b)(2) (2017).

[129.] 24 C.F.R. § 100.306 (2017).

[130.] 24 C.F.R. § 100.306 (2017).

[131.] 24 C.F.R. § 100.307 (2017).

[132.] *Massaro v. Mainlands Section 1 & 2 Civic Ass'n, Inc.*, 3 F.3d 1472, 1478-1479 (11th Cir. 1993) (homeowners' association conducted three surveys of its residents to determine how many occupants were over 62 years of age and how many were over 55; the first two surveys required no independent verification or proof of age in the form of drivers' licenses or birth certificates and the association did not verify the ages of the residents until *after*

pre-enforcement rule is a restriction in the declaration prohibiting occupancy by children, this is insufficient to establish the housing for older persons' exemption. If such a rule were sufficient, "any policy against families would suffice for the exemption, swallowing the rule against such discrimination."[133]

Under certain circumstances, communities may qualify for an exemption to the prohibition against familial status discrimination based on preexisting age restrictions which are lower than the 55-year minimum, however, this would require adherence to applicable criteria which could otherwise qualify the community for an exemption, including age verification. Merely enforcing "restrictions to exclude children in a manner inconsistent with the Act" is not sufficient to qualify for the housing-for-older-persons exemption.[134]

The FHA's good faith defense is a built-in safety net that protects individuals from personal liability where the community or housing facility fails to comply with the regulations governing elder housing. It provides a defense against civil money damages for anyone reasonably relying, in good faith, on the application of the exemption. A person may demonstrate good faith reliance by showing

> (i) such person has no actual knowledge that the facility or community is not, or will not be, eligible for such exemption; and (ii) the facility or community has stated formally, in writing, that the facility or community complies with the requirements for such exemption.[135]

The housing-for-older-persons exemption to the prohibition against familial status discrimination is a good example of the FHA striking a delicate balance between a community association's self-determination and legislative regulation of housing. While

---

they took action to enforce age restrictions; the court held that the homeowners' association failed to prove entitlement to the housing for older persons exemption in part because it did not initiate adequate age-verification procedures prior to taking action against the homeowners).

[133] *Massaro v. Mainlands Section 1 & 2 Civic Ass'n, Inc.*, 3 F.3d 1472, 1479 (11th Cir. 1993).

[134] *Massaro v. Mainlands Section 1 & 2 Civic Ass'n*, 3 F.3d 1472, 1479 (11th Cir. 1993).

[135] 42 U.S.C. § 3607(b)(5) (2017).

property owners may be in the best position to promote health, welfare, and safety in the community, the FHA and other federal and state community association regulations are there to prevent tyranny of the majority.

10-6   CONCLUSION

State and federal regulations serve a myriad of purposes. Not least of all they force associations to consider the impact of its rules on the political subdivision, orienting communities in the larger historical and social context. Regulations also help communities combat segregation and provide equal opportunity housing for all members of society. The ostensible conflict between an owner's right to unfettered control, use, and transfer of private property and legal prohibitions against discrimination is largely illusory, since both share the same goals. Indeed, proponents of fair housing legislation recognize that there is no greater impediment to free use and transfer of property than the fetters of the legacies of prejudice and discrimination.

Chapter 11

Attorney's Fees

11-1   INTRODUCTION

Litigation between community associations and their members can be lengthy and aggressive. While real property and its use are at the heart of every community association related dispute, whether it is a covenant enforcement dispute, a collection action, a disagreement over title, or a fair housing claim emotions and principles often drive litigation. Owners fight for property rights they feel are being abused or taken away, while the board battles to maintain property values and a way of life against owners who shirk their obligations and take advantage.

Unfortunately, people overlook the expenses of litigation, which should elicit a more reasonable and amicable approach, in pursuit of the satisfaction of victory over a neighbor. Most prudent people will give pause if faced with the prospect of paying tens or even hundreds of thousands of dollars to their attorney. This factor, however, is counteracted by the very real possibility that the winner will emerge entirely unscathed, with his or her attorney's fees paid as the prevailing party.

In drafting the various community association acts, the Florida Legislature decided to include provisions requiring the payment of prevailing party attorney's fees. This often makes community association disputes more difficult to resolve. Litigants in lengthy suits may pass the point of no return, having no choice but to gamble on recouping their fees. Similarly, the prospect of winning, and the accompanying award of fees paid by the losing party, can be so tempting that the very real ramifications of losing are ignored. Until the law is changed, the prominent role of attorney's fees in community association litigation must be acknowledged.

11-2   THE "AMERICAN RULE"

For attorney's fees awards, Florida courts utilize the American Rule,[1] under which each party, including the successful one, bears the burden of his or her own attorney's fees.[2] In contrast, the English Rule authorizes the prevailing party, whether plaintiff or defendant, to recover attorney's fees from the opposing party.[3] Under two narrow exceptions to the American Rule, a prevailing party may recover attorney's fees: when permitted (1) by statute, or (2) by the litigants' contractual agreement.[4] The goal is to make the prevailing parties whole by putting them in the position they would have been had the matter been resolved without litigation[5] under the theory that "the prevailing party should not lose anything, at least financially, by virtue of having established the righteousness of his claim."[6]

A prevailing party is one who "prevails" on the significant issues and obtains the benefits sought in litigation.[7] If one party prevails on a certain aspect of the case, while another party prevails on another aspect of the case, the court applies a balancing test to determine how to allocate attorney's fees. When a party prevails on only some of the claims made in the litigation, the trial court must evaluate the relationship between the successful and unsuccessful claims and determine whether the fees incurred in investigation and prosecution of the successful claims can be separated from those incurred on the unsuccessful claims.[8]

---

[1] *Florida Patient's Comp. Fund v. Rowe*, 472 So. 2d 1145, 1147 (Fla. 1985).

[2] *Christiansburg Garment v. Equal Emp't Opportunity Comm'n*, 434 U.S. 412, 415 (1978).

[3] *Florida Patient's Comp. Fund v. Rowe*, 472 So. 2d 1145, 1147 (Fla. 1985).

[4] *Civix Sunrise v. Sunrise Rd. Maint. Ass'n*, 997 So. 2d 433, 434 (Fla. 2d Dist. Ct. App. 2008).

[5] *Clay v. Prudential Ins. Co. of Am.*, 617 So. 2d 433, 436 (Fla. 4th Dist. Ct. App. 1993).

[6] *Gordon Int'l Advert. v. Charlotte Cnty. Land & Title*, 170 So. 2d 59, 61 (Fla. 3d Dist. Ct. App. 1964).

[7] *Trytek v. Gale Indus.*, 3 So. 3d 1194, 1200 (Fla. 2009); *Moritz v. Hoyt Enters.*, 604 So. 2d 807, 810 (Fla. 1992).

[8] *Anglia Jacs & Co. v. Dubin*, 830 So. 2d 169, 172 (Fla. 4th Dist. Ct. App. 2002).

In community association litigation, a prevailing party may look to both statutory and contractual provisions as potential tools for recovering litigation fees. Chapters 718, 719, and 720, which govern the establishment and operation of condominiums, cooperatives, and homeowners' associations, respectively, provide attorney's fees for a prevailing party. As contracts among unit owners and the association, "spelling out mutual rights and obligations of the parties thereto,"[9] the governing documents for Florida community associations may also entitle a prevailing party to attorney's fees. Indeed, if a declaration contains a prevailing party fee provision, the declaration serves as a mechanism for recovering fees to the same extent as a contract that entitles a prevailing party to fees.

In the Condominium Act, the primary attorney's fees provision is section 718.303, which provides,

> Each unit owner, each tenant and other invitee, and each association is governed by, and must comply with the provisions of, this chapter, the declaration, the documents creating the association, and the association bylaws.... Actions for damages or for injunctive relief, or both, for failure to comply with these provisions may be brought by the association or by a unit owner.... The prevailing party in any such action... is entitled to recover reasonable attorney's fees.[10]

Chapter 720, governing homeowners' associations, has a similar provision, which states,

> Each member and the member's tenants, guests, and invitees, and each association, are governed by, and must comply with, this chapter, the governing documents of the community, and the rules of the association. Actions at law or in equity, or both, to redress alleged failure or refusal to comply with these provisions may be brought by the association or by any member.... The prevailing party in any

---

9. *Pepe v. Whispering Sands Condo. Ass'n*, 351 So. 2d 755, 757 (Fla. 2d Dist. Ct. App. 1977).

10. Fla. Stat. § 718.303(1) (2016).

such litigation is entitled to recover reasonable attorney's fees and costs.[11]

Chapter 719, governing cooperatives, also contains prevailing party attorney's fees provisions, one of which states,

> Each unit owner, each tenant and other invitee, and each association shall be governed by, and shall comply with the provisions of, this chapter, the cooperative documents, the documents creating the association, and the association bylaws, and the provisions thereof shall be deemed expressly incorporated into any lease of a unit. Actions for damages or for injunctive relief, or both, for failure to comply with these provisions may be brought by the association or by a unit owner.... The prevailing party in any such action ... is entitled to recover reasonable attorney's fees.[12]

In addition, in litigation between cooperative unit owners and developers over a contract or lease that includes attorney's fees provisions for prevailing developers, the court must also award reasonable attorney's fees to prevailing unit owners.[13]

11-3 PROPOSALS FOR SETTLEMENT

Section 768.79 and Florida Rule of Civil Procedure 1.442 provide a mechanism for shifting risk and recovering fees in the form of proposals for settlement or offers of judgment. If the defendant serves the plaintiff with a proposal for settlement, the defendant is entitled to recover reasonable costs and attorney's fees from the date of filing of the offer if the judgment is one of no liability or the judgment obtained by the plaintiff is at least 25 percent less than the offer. If a plaintiff files a demand for judgment that is not accepted by the defendant within 30 days, the plaintiff is entitled to fees incurred from the date of the filing of the demand if he or she recovers a judgment in an amount at least 25 percent greater than the offer.[14] The purpose of these provisions is to promote

---

11. Fla. Stat. § 720.305(1) (2016).
12. Fla. Stat. § 719.303(1) (2016).
13. Fla. Stat. § 719.111 (2016).
14. Fla. Stat. § 768.79 (2016); Fla. R. Civ. P. Rule 1.442 (2017).

early resolution of civil litigation by imposing an added financial burden on those who refuse to accept fair settlement offers.[15]

When both parties are entitled to attorney's fees due to a conflict between statutory and contractual rights, the statutory right does not cut off pre-existing contractual rights to attorney's fees.[16] For example, in a case in which the losing party argued that the prevailing party's contractual right to fees was cut off on the date that the losing party's rejected settlement offer was proposed, the court held that section 768.79, which is in derogation of the common law rule that each party pay its own fees, must be strictly construed as not extinguishing a prevailing party's contractual right to attorney's fees.[17] Thus the losing party was entitled to fees incurred after the date of its valid proposal for settlement, while the prevailing party had a contractual right to *all* of its costs and attorney's fees through trial on its breach of contract claim.[18] In community association litigation, a prevailing party's entitlement to attorney's fees based on the governing documents will not be cut off by a proposal for settlement. Rather, the courts will likely award fees to both the prevailing party and the party who filed the valid proposal for settlement.

11-4   FEES AS SANCTIONS

Section 57.105 also provides fees, albeit as a sanction against the losing party and their attorney for maintaining a frivolous claim or defense. Upon the initiative or motion of the court or either party, the court will award the prevailing party reasonable attorney's fees, including prejudgment interest, for any claim or defense that the losing party or their attorney knew or should have known "[w]as not supported by the material facts necessary to establish the claim or defense" or "[w]ould not be supported by the application of then-existing law to those material facts."[19] Such fees must be paid in equal amounts by the losing party and their attorney.[20]

---

[15] *Goode v. Udhwani*, 648 So. 2d 247, 248 (4th Dist. Ct. App. 1994).

[16] *Tierra Holdings v. Mercantile Bank*, 78 So. 3d 558, 566 (Fla. 1st Dist. Ct. App. 2011).

[17] *Tierra Holdings v. Mercantile Bank*, 78 So. 3d 558, 566 (Fla. 1st Dist. Ct. App. 2011).

[18] *Tierra Holdings v. Mercantile Bank*, 78 So. 3d 558, 566 (Fla. 1st Dist. Ct. App. 2011).

[19] Fla. Stat. § 57.105(1) (2016).

[20] Fla. Stat. § 57.105(1) (2016).

If the court finds that the non-moving party asserted a claim or defense that failed to raise a justiciable issue of law or fact, the court then enters an order granting the motion for attorney's fees, containing the requisite statutory finding of frivolousness. The court then assesses attorney's fees in equal amounts against both the non-moving party and the non-moving party's counsel.[21] Since section 57.105 states "the court shall award a reasonable attorney's fee," the statutory penalty is mandatory once the court determines that there is a complete absence of a justiciable issue raised by the losing party.[22]

Absolute verification of frivolousness is not required, due to its impracticality or impossibility, section 57.105 requires a party and his attorney to make a reasonable effort to investigate their claims and defenses before asserting them.[23] In addition, the court should not impose a penalty on a party who attempts to raise novel questions of law or who, in good faith, attempts to move the law in a different direction.[24] Case law also suggests that the court must make an express finding of bad faith to award fees against an attorney under section 57.105;[25] but the burden is on the attorney to show good faith, not on the moving party to show bad faith or absence of good faith.[26] Subsection 57.105(4)'s safe harbor protects parties who withdraw or correct claims, giving non-moving parties time to ensure that their positions are based on good law and facts.[27]

11-5 AMOUNT OF FEES

To calculate the prevailing party's fees in a Chapter 720 homeowners' association lawsuit or a condominium association suit brought under the Condominium Act, courts follow the

---

[21] *Broad & Cassel v. Newport Motel*, 636 So. 2d 590, 591 (Fla. 3d Dist. Ct. App. 1994).

[22] *Morton v. Heathcock*, 913 So. 2d 662, 668 (Fla. 3d Dist. Ct. App. 2005).

[23] *McHan v. Huggins*, 459 So. 2d 1172, 1174 (Fla. 5th Dist. Ct. App. 1984).

[24] *Builders Shoring & Scaffolding v. King*, 453 So. 2d 534 (Fla. 5th Dist. Ct. App. 1984).

[25] *Santini v. Cleveland Clinic Florida*, 65 So. 3d 22, 36 (Fla. 4th Dist. Ct. App. 2011), *reh'g denied* (July 26, 2011).

[26] *Andzulis v. Montgomery Rd. Acquisitions*, 831 So. 2d 237, 239 (Fla. 5th Dist. Ct. App. 2002).

[27] Fla. Stat. § 57.105(4) (2016) (requiring moving parties to serve a motion for sanctions on their opponent, and prohibiting them from filing or presenting the motion to the court unless, within 21 days after service of the motion, the challenged claim or defense is not withdrawn or corrected).

"lodestar" method,[28] modeled after a similar federal formula of that name. The lodestar formula provides an objective calculation method for reasonable fee awards and is applied when a statute authorizes an award of fees to a prevailing litigant.[29] In short, the number of hours reasonably expended is multiplied by a reasonable hourly rate, which produces the lodestar figure.[30] The court's first step in the lodestar process is determining the reasonable time spent by the attorney. The prevailing party should present records detailing the amount of work performed, which is limited to time properly billable to the client. Inadequate documentation may result in a reduction in the number of hours claimed, as will a claim for hours that the court finds to be excessive or unnecessary. Evidence sufficient to support a finding of the number of hours reasonably expended by an attorney need not include specific written time records, although such records are highly preferable and the lack thereof may in certain cases justify a reduction in the number of hours claimed.[31]

The court must then determine a reasonable hourly rate for the prevailing party's attorney's services. The rate should be based on an assumption that the fee will be paid irrespective of the result and should take into account all of the disciplinary rule factors discussed below, except the time and labor required, the legal questions' novelty and difficulty, the results obtained, and whether the fee is fixed or contingent.[32] The moving party carries the burden of establishing the prevailing market rate, which is simply the rate charged in the community for similar services by lawyers of reasonably comparable skill, experience, and reputation. As noted, multiplying the number of hours reasonably expended by a reasonable hourly rate produces the lodestar figure.[33]

In determining reasonable attorney fees, courts must also consider the following Florida Bar Code of Professional Responsibility

---

[28] *Florida Patient's Comp. Fund v. Rowe*, 472 So. 2d 1145 (Fla. 1985).

[29] *Lake Tippecanoe Owners Ass'n v. Hanauer*, 494 So. 2d 226, 227 (Fla. 2d Dist. Ct. App. 1986).

[30] *Florida Patient's Comp. Fund v. Rowe*, 472 So. 2d 1145, 1151 (Fla. 1985).

[31] *Glades v. Glades Country Club Apartments Ass'n*, 534 So. 2d 723 (Fla. 2d Dist. Ct. App. 1988).

[32] *Freedom Sav. & Loan Ass'n v. Biltmore Constr.*, 510 So. 2d 1141, 1142 (Fla. 2d Dist. Ct. App. 1987).

[33] *Florida Patient's Comp. Fund v. Rowe*, 472 So. 2d 1145, 1151 (Fla. 1985).

criteria governing fees for legal services: (1) the time and labor required, the novelty and difficulty of the question involved, and the skill requisite to perform the legal service properly; (2) the likelihood, if apparent to the client, that the acceptance of the particular employment will preclude other employment by the lawyer; (3) the fee customarily charged in the locality for similar legal services; (4) the amount in dispute and the results obtained; (5) the time limitations imposed by the client or by the circumstances; (6) the nature and length of the professional relationship with the client; (7) the experience, reputation, and ability of the lawyer or lawyers performing the services; and (8) whether the fee is fixed or contingent.[34]

A critical factor in determining whether to pursue fee claims is the fact that Florida courts generally do *not* award fees for time spent litigating fee amounts. Recent community association cases, however, suggest that there are narrow circumstances under which fees may be awarded for time litigating fee amounts. For instance, when broad language in an owner's purchase agreement provides fees for "any" litigation between the parties under the agreement, it is appropriate to include fees for time spent litigating the fee amount.[35] This holding may be used to support a similar award of fees for litigating the amount of fees in covenant enforcement disputes where the declaration includes broad prevailing party fees language.

11-5:1 Contingency Risk Multiplier

Once the court arrives at the lodestar figure, it may add or subtract from the fee based upon a "contingency risk" factor and the "results obtained."[36] In contingent fee cases, the lodestar figure calculated by the court is subject to enhancement by an appropriate "contingency risk" multiplier in the range of 1.5 to 3. If at the outset, "success was more likely than not ... the multiplier should be 1.5," "when the likelihood of success was approximately even at the outset, the multiplier should be 2," and "when success was

---

[34.] *Florida Patient's Comp. Fund v. Rowe*, 472 So. 2d 1145, 1150 (Fla. 1985).

[35.] *Waverly at Las Olas Condo. Ass'n v. Waverly Las Olas*, 88 So. 3d 386, 389 (Fla. 4th Dist. Ct. App. 2012).

[36.] *Florida Patient's Comp. Fund v. Rowe*, 472 So. 2d 1145, 1151 (Fla. 1985).

unlikely at the time the case was initiated, the multiplier should be in the range of 2.5 and 3."[37] In the context of community association litigation, in which litigants are entitled to reasonable attorney's fees pursuant to statutory provisions, fees should *only* be adjusted for "contingency risk" if the attorney is hired on a contingent basis.[38]

The "results obtained" may provide an independent basis for reducing the fee when the party prevails on a claim, but is unsuccessful on other unrelated claims.[39] When a party prevails on only a portion of the claims made in the litigation, the trial judge must evaluate the relationship between the successful and unsuccessful claims and determine whether the investigation and prosecution of the successful claims can be separated from the unsuccessful claims. In adjusting the fee based upon the success of the litigation, the court should indicate that it has considered the relationship between the amount of the fee awarded and the extent of success.[40]

11-6   LOSING ENTITLEMENT TO FEES

11-6:1   Failure to Plead Entitlement

Entitlement to fees, whether based on statute or contract, must be pled prior to trial and failure to plead is generally fatal.[41] An exception exists where the party against whom fees are being sought is on notice "and by its conduct acquiesces or otherwise fails to object to the failure to plead" entitlement to fees.[42] For instance, a party who acquiesces by listing fees as an issue for trial waives its objection to the eventual fee award for an opponent who failed to plead and merely requested fees at a pre-trial conference.[43]

---

[37]. *Florida Patient's Comp. Fund v. Rowe*, 472 So. 2d 1145, 1151 (Fla. 1985).

[38]. *Lake Tippecanoe Owners Ass'n v. Hanauer*, 494 So. 2d 226, 227 (Fla. 2d Dist. Ct. App. 1986) (holding that since the attorney was not hired on a contingency basis, the case did not qualify for the enhanced fee incorrectly arrived at by the trial judge, who multiplied the lodestar figure by a "success factor" of 1.5).

[39]. *Florida Patient's Comp. Fund v. Rowe*, 472 So. 2d 1145, 1151 (Fla. 1985).

[40]. *Florida Patient's Comp. Fund v. Rowe*, 472 So. 2d 1145, 1151 (Fla. 1985).

[41]. *Stockman v. Downs*, 573 So. 2d 835 (Fla. 1991).

[42]. *Stockman v. Downs*, 573 So. 2d 835, 838 (Fla. 1991).

[43]. *Brown v. Gardens by the Sea S. Condo. Ass'n*, 424 So. 2d 181, 184 (Fla. 4th Dist. Ct. App. 1983).

Similarly, the failure to plead entitlement to fees is not fatal when the issue is preserved by the parties' stipulation during trial that the question of attorney fees and costs will be heard at a hearing subsequent to the "final" hearing.[44] In addition, the correct grounds for a fees award must be stated and pleading entitlement under a statute inapplicable to the case will result in the award being denied.[45]

11-6:2   Time Limit for Motion Service

Pleading entitlement to attorney's fees is necessary, but not in and of itself sufficient, as Florida Rule of Civil Procedure 1.525 also requires motion service. Specifically "any party seeking a judgment taxing costs, attorneys' fees, or both" must serve a motion

> no later than 30 days after filing of the judgment,
> including a judgment of dismissal, or the service of
> a notice of voluntary dismissal, which judgment or
> notice concludes the action as to that party.[46]

This requirement is strictly applied as a bright-line rule and failure to serve a motion within 30 days of judgment generally constitutes a waiver.[47]

Where there is no judgment or voluntary dismissal, however, a "reasonable time" standard may apply. For instance, if a motion for fees is added more than 30 days after counts are dropped from a complaint without judgment, the reasonableness standard is applied. Under such circumstances, in which there is no notice of dismissal or judgment, less than two months is deemed a "reasonable" amount of time in which to file a motion for fees.[48]

---

[44] *Mainlands of Tamarac by Gulf Unit No. Four Ass'n v. Morris*, 388 So. 2d 226, 227 (Fla. 2d Dist. Ct. App. 1980).

[45] *Landmark at Hillsboro Condo. Ass'n v. Candelora*, 911 So. 2d 1272, 1274 (Fla. 4th Dist. Ct. App. 2005).

[46] Fla. R. Civ. P. Rule 1.525 (2017).

[47] *Wentworth v. Johnson*, 845 So. 2d 296, 299 (Fla. 5th Dist. Ct. App. 2003).

[48] *E & A Produce v. Superior Garlic*, 864 So. 2d 449, 451 (Fla. 3d Dist. Ct. App. 2003) (six weeks after the plaintiff filed an amended complaint, which dropped a count from the first complaint, the defendant moved for fees; the court rejected the plaintiff's argument that the motion for fees was untimely since it was not filed within 30 days pursuant to Rule 1.525; the court held that the rule did not apply because the plaintiff did not serve a notice of dismissal and there was no judgment on the dropped count; applying a reasonableness standard, the court held that less than two months was a reasonable amount of time in which to file the motion for fees).

A motion for fees under Rule 1.525 is also subject to Rule 1.100(b) requirements that all motions "shall be made in writing unless made during a hearing or trial, shall state with particularity the grounds therefor, and shall set forth the relief or order sought." Accordingly, to be valid, a motion for fees must state the source of entitlement and the amount requested.[49]

11-6:3   Losing Entitlement Before Suit Begins

A community association can lose attorney's fees if it initiates litigation too quickly or is unreasonable in its litigation efforts. For instance, the court awarded a homeowners' association a fraction of the fees and costs it requested because it filed suit too quickly and ignored the owner's diligent efforts to settle the matter.[50]

The considerations underlying this policy are codified in Chapter 720. Specifically, a party's failure to participate in the statutorily mandated presuit mediation process required for certain types of homeowners' association disputes precludes that party from seeking fees in litigation. Indeed, Chapter 720 requires presuit mediation as a precondition to filing suit for disputes between an association and a parcel owner regarding use of or changes to the parcel or the common areas and other covenant enforcement disputes. Presuit mediation is also required for disputes regarding amendments to the association documents, disputes regarding meetings of the board and committees appointed by the board, membership meetings, and access to the official records.[51] Parties

---

[49.] *Gulf Landings Ass'n v. Hershberger*, 845 So. 2d 344, 346 (Fla. 2d Dist. Ct. App. 2003).

[50.] *Southpointe Homeowners Ass'n v. Segarra*, 763 So. 2d 1186, 1187 (Fla. 4th Dist. Ct. App. 2000) (in response to a homeowners' association request for $4,645.50 in attorney's fees and $689.39 in costs, the court awarded only $785 for attorney's fees and $133.50 for costs; the court based its decision in the dispute, which arose from a homeowner's failure to timely pay approximately $294 in maintenance dues and was resolved via settlement with the agreement that the court would determine attorney's fees and costs, on the fact that at the fee hearing the owner testified about her efforts to determine the amount she owed so she could pay it, and the difficulties she encountered in obtaining that information from the association's attorney; in observing that the association had been "a little quick" to file suit, the trial court noted that the amount of requested fees was outrageous, amounting to 29.4 hours in paralegal and attorney time; the court awarded only three hours for attorney time and two hours for paralegal time and disallowed costs for a title search, as well as for filing the complaint, service of process, and mediation; the appellate court saw no abuse of discretion in the court's finding that the owner was sincere in her efforts to settle, and that the association was too quick to file suit, which justified the trial court's award of minimal fees and costs).

[51.] Fla. Stat. § 720.311(2) (2016).

who fail or refuse to participate in the entire presuit mediation process may not recover attorney's fees and costs in subsequent litigation relating to the dispute.[52]

The Condominium Act also provides mandatory procedures for resolving disputes before litigation is filed. For example, unit owners may approach their condominium board of directors with written requests for information regarding the operation of the community. A unit owner may send a written inquiry by certified mail to the board of directors. In response, the board must respond in writing within 30 days. The board must either give a substantive response, notify the inquirer that a legal opinion has been requested, or notify the inquirer that the board is seeking advice from the Division. If the board seeks advice from the Division, the board must provide a substantive response to the inquirer within 10 days after receipt of the Division's advice. If the board requests a legal opinion, the board must provide a written substantive response to the inquirer within 60 days after the receipt of the inquiry. If the association fails to provide a substantive response to the unit owner, the association may not recover attorney's fees and costs if it prevails in litigation arising from the subject matter of the inquiry.[53]

11-7   CONCLUSION

A prevailing party's statutory or contractual entitlement to fees may exacerbate community association disputes in several different ways. First and foremost, they permit the parties to bemoan a new category of injury and to perceive their opponents as indebted to them for attorney's fees. This creates a vicious cycle that rewards litigants' unwillingness to compromise by financially penalizing losing opponents in protracted legal battles. Community association cases become more difficult and more expensive to resolve as litigation continues and fees increase.

This calls for an approach that recognizes the underlying motivations. Emotions and fees often times drive these claims. Quick resolution requires the parties to reflect on their competing perspectives and the sense of duty or entitlement that has made

---

[52.] Fla. Stat. § 720.311(2)(b) (2016).
[53.] Fla. Stat. § 718.112(2)(a) (2016).

their differences irreconcilable. This can be difficult, as parties are hostile to what they perceive as an attack on their driving principles. Most parties, however, can be convinced to seek an amicable resolution when they understand that litigation is often self-destructive, particularly when it becomes an end in itself.

Attorneys should set the stage for early resolution by encouraging parties to engage in swift, informal evaluation of their competing claims, without resort to time-consuming and expensive formal discovery and depositions. Parties should be encouraged to participate in pre-suit alternative dispute resolution and to file early settlement proposals to quickly shift risk. If the parties cannot settle informally, early formal mediation may resolve the dispute. Unfortunately, if litigation is allowed to spin out of control, the attorney's fees incurred in the dispute can become their own perverse motivation.

Table of Cases

Abbey Park Homeowners Downey v. Jungle Den Villas v. Bowen,
   508 So. 2d 554 (Fla. 4th Dist. Ct. App. 1987)   9-1
Adams v. Vidal,
   60 So. 2d 545 (Fla. 1952)   7-6:2.2
All Seasons Resorts v. Dep't of Bus. Regulation, Div. of Land Sales,
   Condos. & Mobile Homes,
   455 So. 2d 544 (Fla. 1st Dist. Ct. App. 1984)   1-6:2
Alternative Dev. v. St. Lucie Club & Apartment Homes Condo. Ass'n,
   608 So. 2d 822 (Fla. 4th Dist. Ct. App. 1992)   3-5:2
Andzulis v. Montgomery Rd. Acquisitions,
   831 So. 2d 237 (Fla. 5th Dist. Ct. App. 2002)   11-4
Anglia Jacs & Co. v. Dubin,
   830 So. 2d 169 (Fla. 4th Dist. Ct. App. 2002)   11-2
Aquarian Found. v. Sholom House,
   448 So. 2d 1166 (Fla. 3d Dist. Ct. App. 1984)   2-2:3, 7-1
Auburn Woods I Homeowners Ass'n v. Fair
   Emp't & Hous. Comm'n,
   18 Cal. Rptr. 3d 669 (2004)   10-4:3
Azar v. Hayter,
   874 F. Supp. 1314 (N.D. Fla. 1995)
   aff'd, 66 F.3d 342 (11th Cir. 1995)   9-3
Bachman v. Swan Harbour Ass'n,
   653 N.W.2d 415 (2002)   10-3:3.2
Baldain v. Am. Home Mortg. Servicing,
   CIV.S-09-0931LKK/GGH, 2010 WL 2606666
   (E.D. Cal. June 28, 2010)   10-3:4
Balletti v. Sun-Sentinel,
   909 F. Supp. 1539 (S.D. Fla. 1995)   10-2:4.1
Baratta v. Valley Oak Homeowners' Ass'n at the Vineyards,
   891 So. 2d 1063 (Fla. 2d Dist. Ct. App. 2004)   1-2:2
Barfield v. Orange Cty.,
   911 F.2d 644 (11th Cir. 1990)   10-2:4.1
Bay Holdings v. 2000 Island Blvd. Condo. Ass'n,
   895 So. 2d 1197 (Fla. 3d Dist. Ct. App. 2005)   9-7
Beeman v. Island Breakers,
   591 So. 2d 1031 (Fla. 3d Dist. Ct. App. 1991)   3-3:1
Beeman v. Island Breakers, A Condo.,
   577 So. 2d 1341 (Fla. 3d Dist. Ct. App. 1990)   3-3:1
Belletete v. Halford,
   886 So. 2d 308 (Fla. 4th Dist. Ct. App. 2004)   10-2:1
Berg v. Bridle Path Homeowners Ass'n,
   809 So. 2d 32 (Fla. 4th Dist. Ct. App. 2002)   9-1
Berg v. Wagner,
   935 So. 2d 100 (Fla. 4th Dist. Ct. App. 2006)   4-3:1
Bishop Assocs. v. Belkin,
   521 So. 2d 158 (Fla. 1st Dist. Ct. App. 1988)   3-5:1, 3-5:2
Bonasera v. City of Norcross,
   342 F. App'x 581 (11th Cir. 2009)   10-3:2.1, 10-3:2.2
Brenner v. Dep't of Banking & Fin.,
   892 So. 2d 1129 (Fla. 3d Dist. Ct. App. 2004)   8-3
Brickell Bay Club Condo. Ass'n v. Hernstadt,
   512 So. 2d 994 (Fla. 3d Dist. Ct. App. 1987)   7-2:2, 7-8

Table of Cases

Broad & Cassel v. Newport Motel,
    636 So. 2d 590 (Fla. 3d Dist. Ct. App. 1994)   11-4
Brown v. Gardens by the Sea S. Condo. Ass'n,
    424 So. 2d 181 (Fla. 4th Dist. Ct. App. 1983)   11-6:1
Bryan v. Clayton,
    698 So. 2d 1236 (Fla. 5th Dist. Ct. App. 1997)   9-3
Bryant Woods Inn v. Howard Cty. Md.,
    124 F.3d 597 (4th Cir. 1997)   10-3:3.2, 10-3:4
Buckhannon Bd. & Care Home v. W. Virginia Dept.
    of Health & Human Res.,
    532 U.S. 598 (2001)   10-3:4
Builders Shoring & Scaffolding v. King,
    453 So. 2d 534 (Fla. 5th Dist. Ct. App. 1984)   11-4
Byrd v. BT Foods,
    26 So. 3d 600 (Fla. 4th Dist. Ct. App. 2009)   10-2:4.1
Camino Gardens Ass'n v. McKim,
    612 So. 2d 636 (Fla. 4th Dist. Ct. App. 1993)   7-6
Carlandia v. Obernauer,
    695 So. 2d 408 (Fla. 4th Dist. Ct. App. 1997)   8-3
Casa Del Mar Condo. Ass'n v. Richartz,
    641 So. 2d 470 (Fla. 3d Dist. Ct. App. 1994)   4-3
Cedar Cove Efficiency Condo. Ass'n v. Cedar Cove Props.,
    558 So. 2d 475 (Fla. 5th Dist. Ct. App. 1990)   5-5:3
Christiansburg Garment v. Equal Emp't Opportunity Comm'n,
    434 U.S. 412 (1978)   10-3:4, 11-2
Circle Villas Condo. Ass'n v. Circle Prop. Owners' Ass'n,
    957 So. 2d 1207 (Fla. 4th Dist. Ct. App. 2007)   1-2:3.2
City of Miami v. Benson,
    63 So. 2d 916 (Fla. 1953)   9-7
Civix Sunrise v. Sunrise Rd. Maint. Ass'n,
    997 So. 2d 433 (Fla. 2d Dist. Ct. App. 2008)   11-2
Clark v. Bluewater Key RV Ownership Park,
    197 So. 3d 59, 62 (Fla. 3d Dist. Ct. App. 2012)   1-2:3.1
Clay v. Prudential Ins. Co. of Am.,
    617 So. 2d 433 (Fla. 4th Dist. Ct. App. 1993)   11-2
Cohn v. Grand Condo. Ass'n,
    62 So. 3d 1120 (Fla. 2011)   2-7:2, 9-7
Comcast of Florida v. L'Ambiance Beach Condo. Ass'n,
    17 So. 3d 839 (Fla. 4th Dist. Ct. App. 2009)   3-3:4
Continental Corp. of Fla. v. Duval Title & Abstract,
    356 So. 2d 925 (Fla. 2d Dist. Ct. App. 1978)   9-8
Coogler v. Rogers,
    25 Fla. 853 So. 391 (1889)   7-8
Coral Way Condo. Investments v. 21/22 Condo. Ass'n,
    66 So. 3d 1038 (Fla. 3d Dist. Ct. App. 2011)   9-1
Costa Del Sol Ass'n v. State, Dep't of Bus. & Prof'l Regulation,
    Div. of Florida Land Sales, Condos., & Mobile Homes,
    987 So. 2d 734 (Fla. 3d Dist. Ct. App. 2008)   5-6:1
Cudjoe Gardens Prop. Owners Ass'n v. Payne,
    779 So. 2d 598 (Fla. 3d Dist. Ct. App. 2001)   2-2:1
Cypress Bend Condo. I Ass'n v. Dexner,
    705 So. 2d 681 (Fla. 4th Dist. Ct. App. 1998)   8-3:1
Dade Cty. v. Matheson,
    605 So. 2d 469 (Fla. 3d Dist. Ct. App. 1992)   2-2:1, 7-5
Davis v. Geyer,
    151 Fla. 362 So. 2d 727 (1942)   7-6
Davis v. Lane Management, LLC,
    524 F. Supp. 2d 1375 (S.D. Fla. 2007)   10-3:3.2, 10-3:4
Department of Bus. Regulation, Div. of Land Sales v. Siegel,
    479 So. 2d 112 (Fla. 1985)   1-3:3
Dornbach v. Holley,
    854 So. 2d 211 (Fla. 2d Dist. Ct. App. 2002)   10-3

Downey v. Jungle Den Villas Recreation Ass'n,
525 So. 2d 438 (Fla. 5th Dist. Ct. App. 1988)   1-3:3
E & A Produce v. Superior Garlic,
864 So. 2d 449 (Fla. 3d Dist. Ct. App. 2003)   11-6:2
Eastpointe Prop. Owners' Ass'n v. Cohen,
505 So. 2d 518 (Fla. 4th Dist. Ct. App. 1987)   2-6, 7-2
Edenfield v. Crisp,
186 So. 2d 545 (Fla. 2d Dist. Ct. App. 1966)   4-2:4
Edlund v. Seagull Townhomes Condo. Ass'n,
928 So. 2d 405 (Fla. 3d Dist. Ct. App. 2006)   7-6:2.1
Elbadramany v. Oceans Seven Condo. Ass'n.,
461 So. 2d 1001 (Fla. 5th Dist. Ct. App. 1984)   7-7:1
Emerald Estates Cmty. Ass'n v. Gorodetzer,
819 So. 2d 190 (Fla. 4th Dist. Ct. App. 2002)   7-8
Essling's Homes Plus v. City of St. Paul,
356 F. Supp. 2d 971 (D. Minn. 2004)   10-3:3.2
Estates of Fort Lauderdale Prop. Owners' Ass'n v. Kalet,
492 So. 2d 1340 (Fla. 4th 1986)   7-8:1
Farrington v. Casa Solana Condo. Ass'n,
517 So. 2d 70 (Fla. 3d Dist. Ct. App. 1987)   5-5:2
Ferrill v. Parker Grp.,
168 F.3d 468 (11th Cir.1999)   10-3:4
Fifty-Six Sixty Collins Ave. Condo. v. Dawson,
354 So. 2d 432 (Fla. 3d Dist. Ct. App. 1978)   7-8
Flamingo Ranch Estates v. Sunshine Ranches Homeowners,
303 So. 2d 665 (Fla. 4th Dist. Ct. App. 1974)   2-8, 7-5
Florida Farm, LLC v. 360 Developers,
45 So. 3d 810 (Fla. 3d Dist. Ct. App. 2010)   1-2:4, 5-5:1
Florida Patient's Comp. Fund v. Rowe,
472 So. 2d 1145 (Fla. 1985)   11-2, 11-5, 11-5:1
Fountains of Palm Beach Condo., Inc. No. 5 v. Farkas,
355 So. 2d 163 (Fla. 4th Dist. Ct. App. 1978)   7-8
Freedom Savings & Loan Ass'n v. Biltmore Constr.,
510 So. 2d 1141 (Fla. 2d Dist. Ct. App. 1987)   11-5
Fuller v. Becker & Poliakoff,
192 F. Supp. 2d 1361 (M.D. Fla. 2002)   9-3
Gamble v. City of Escondido,
104 F.3d 300 (9th Cir. 1997)   10-3:2
Garcia v. Crescent Plaza Condo. Ass'n,
813 So. 2d 975 (Fla. 2d Dist. Ct. App. 2002)   4-3:5
Gautier v. Lapof,
91 So. 2d 324 (Fla. 1956)   7-6:2.2
Glades v. Glades Country Club Apartments Ass'n,
534 So. 2d 723 (Fla. 2d Dist. Ct. App. 1988)   11-5
Gladstone Realtors v. Vill. of Bellwood,
441 U.S. 91 (1979)   10-3:1
Goldsmith v. Bagby Elevator,
513 F.3d 1261 (11th Cir. 2008)   10-2:4.1
Goode v. Udhwani,
648 So. 2d 247 (4th Dist. Ct. App. 1994)   11-3
Gordon Int'l Advert. v. Charlotte Cnty. Land & Title,
170 So. 2d 59 (Fla. 3d Dist. Ct. App. 1964)   11-2
Greenacre Props. v. Rao,
933 So. 2d 19 (Fla. 2d Dist. Ct. App. 2006)   1-2:3.3
Grider-Garcia v. State Farm Mut. Auto.,
14 So. 3d 1120 (Fla. 5th Dist. Ct. App. 2009)   11-2
Gulf Landings Ass'n v. Hershberger,
845 So. 2d 344 (Fla. 2d Dist. Ct. App. 2003)   11-6:2
Habitat II Condo. v. Kerr,
948 So. 2d 809 (Fla. 4th Dist. Ct. App. 2007)   8-3
Hagan v. Sabal Palms,
186 So. 2d 302 (Fla. 2d Dist. Ct. App. 1966)   2-2:1, 7-5

Table of Cases

Hallmark Developers v. Fulton Cty. Ga.,
466 F.3d 1276 (11th Cir. 2006) — 10-3:2.2
*Hamptons Dev. Corp. of Dade v. State, Dep't of Bus. Reg.,
Div. of Florida Land Sales, Condos. & Mobile Homes*,
519 So. 2d 661 (Fla. 3d Dist. Ct. App.1988) — 3-5:1
Hanrahan v. Hampton,
446 U.S. 754 (1980) — 10-3:4
Hawn v. Shoreline Towers Phase 1 Condo. Ass'n,
347 F. App'x 464 (11th Cir. 2009) — 10-4:3
*Heron at Destin W. Beach & Bay Resort Condo.
Ass'n v. Osprey at Destin W. Beach*,
94 So. 3d 623 (Fla. 1st Dist. Ct. App. 2012),
reh'g denied (Aug. 21, 2012) — 1-3:1, 2-2:1, 2-5, 7-2
Hidden Harbour Estates v. Basso,
393 So. 2d 637 (Fla. 4th Dist. Ct. App. 1981) — 2-2:2, 2-6, 7-1, 7-2
Hidden Harbour Estates v. Norman,
309 So. 2d 180 (Fla. 4th Dist. Ct. App. 1975) — 1-3:2, 2-6, 7-2, 7-6
Hobbs v. Weinkauf,
940 So. 2d 1151 (Fla. 2d Dist. Ct. App. 2006) — 4-3, 5-7:2
Holiday Pines Prop. Owners Ass'n v. Wetherington,
596 So. 2d 84 (Fla. 4th Dist. Ct. App. 1992) — 2-8, 7-5
Hollywood Towers Condo. Ass'n v. Hampton,
40 So. 3d 787 (Fla. 4th Dist. Ct. App. 2010) — 4-3:5, 7-5
Homeowner's Ass'n of Overlook v. Seabrooke Homeowners' Ass'n,
62 So. 3d 667 (Fla. 2d Dist. Ct. App. 2011) — 5-11:3
Housing Investors v. City of Clanton, Ala.,
68 F. Supp. 2d 1287 (M.D. Ala. 1999) — 10-3:2.2
Huff v. Vill. of Stuart Ass'n,
741 So. 2d 1217 (Fla. 4th Dist. Ct. App. 1999) — 8-3
Huntington Branch, N.A.A.C.P. v. Town of Huntington,
844 F.2d 926 (2d Cir. 1988) *aff'd in part sub nom.
Town of Huntington, N.Y. v. Huntington Branch,
N.A.A.C.P.*, 488 U.S. 15 (1988) — 10-3:2.2
Iglehart v. Phillips,
383 So. 2d 610 (Fla. 1980) — 7-6:2.2
In re Colony Beach & Tennis Club Ass'n,
456 B.R. 545 (M.D. Fla. 2011) — 4-3:5, 9-2:2
In re Jimenez,
472 B.R. 106 (Bankr. M.D. Fla. 2012) — 9-4:1
In re Kenna Homes Co-op,
557 S.E.2d 787 (2001) — 10-3:3.2, 10-4:3
In re Mona Lisa at Celebration,
472 B.R. 582 (Bankr. M.D. Fla. 2012) — 3-3:2
J. M. Montgomery Roofing Co. v. Fred Howland,
98 So. 2d 484 (Fla. 1957) — 5-5:2
J.B. v. Sacred Heart Hosp. of Pensacola,
635 So. 2d 945 (Fla. 1994) — 7-7:3
Juno By The Sea N. Condo. Ass'n v. Manfredonia,
397 So. 2d 297 (Fla. 4th Dist. Ct. App. 1980) — 5-5:3
Kahn v. Villas at Eagles Point Condo. Ass'n,
693 So. 2d 1029 (Fla. 2d Dist. Ct. App. 1997) — 8-3:1
Kaplan v. Assetcare,
88 F. Supp. 2d 1355 (S.D. Fla. 2000) — 9-3
Kenyon v. Polo Park Homeowners Ass'n,
907 So. 2d 1226 (Fla. 2d Dist. Ct. App. 2005) — 7-8:1
Key Largo Ocean Resort Co-Op v. Monroe Cty.,
5 So. 3d 31 (Fla. 3d Dist. Ct. App. 2009) — 1-4:2
Klinow v. Island Court at Boca W. Prop. Owners' Ass'n,
64 So. 3d 177 (Fla. 4th Dist. Ct. App. 2011) — 4-3:5, 7-5
Koplowitz v. Imperial Towers Condo.,
478 So. 2d 504 (Fla. 4th Dist. Ct. App. 1985) — 5-5:2
Ladner v. Plaza Del Prado Condo. Ass'n,
423 So. 2d 927 (Fla. 3d Dist. Ct. App. 1982) — 7-8:1

Lake Forest Master Cmty. Ass'n v. Orlando Lake Forest Joint Venture,
  10 So. 3d 1187 (Fla. 5th Dist. Ct. App. 2009) — 5-11:1, 6-3:1
Lake Tippecanoe Owners Ass'n v. Hanauer,
  494 So. 2d 226 (Fla. 2d Dist. Ct. App. 1986) — 11-5, 11-5:1
Lamden v. La Jolla Shores Clubdominium Homeowners Ass'n,
  21 Cal. 4th 249, 980 P.2d 940, 942 (1999) — 4-3:5, 7-5
Landmark at Hillsboro Condo. Ass'n v. Candelora,
  911 So. 2d 1272 (Fla. 4th Dist. Ct. App. 2005) — 11-6:1
Larkin v. State of Mich. Dept. of Soc. Services,
  89 F.3d 285 (6th Cir. 1996) — 10-3:2
Lehman v. Trust Co. of Am.,
  57 Fla. 473 (Fla. 1909) — 4-2:4
Loren v. Sasser,
  309 F.3d 1296 (11th Cir. 2002) — 10-3, 10-3:3.1
Maher v. Gagne,
  448 U.S. 122 (1980) — 10-3:4
Maillard v. Dowdell,
  528 So. 2d 512 (Fla. 3rd Dist. Ct. App. 1988) — 4-3:1
Mainlands of Tamarac by Gulf Unit No. Four Ass'n v. Morris,
  388 So. 2d 226 (Fla. 2d Dist. Ct. App. 1980) — 11-6:1
Massaro v. Mainlands Section 1 & 2 Civic Ass'n,
  3 F.3d 1472 (11th Cir. 1993) — 10-5
McAllister v. Breakers Seville Ass'n,
  981 So. 2d 566 (Fla. 4th Dist. Ct. App. 2008) — 1-4:1, 9-8
McDonnell Douglas v. Green,
  411 U.S. 792 (1973) — 10-3:2.1
McHan v. Huggins,
  459 So. 2d 1172 (Fla. 5th Dist. Ct. App. 1984) — 11-4
Metro-Dade Invs. v. Granada Lakes Villas Condo,
  74 So. 3d 593 (Fla. 2d Dist. Ct. App. 2011)
  review granted, 97 So. 3d 823 (Fla. 2012) — 4-2:4
Metropolitan Hous. Dev. v. Vill. of Arlington Heights,
  558 F.2d 1283 (7th Cir. 1977) — 10-3:2.2
Miceli v. Gilmac Developers,
  467 So. 2d 404 (Fla. 2d Dist. Ct. App. 1985) — 9-8
Milsap v. Cornerstone Residential Mgmt., Inc.,
  05-60033-CIV-JOHNSON, 2010 WL 427436, at *4 (S.D. Fla. 2010) — 10-2:1
Mirror Lake Co. v. Kirk Sec. Corp.,
  124 So. 719 (Fla. 1929) — 4-2:4
Moritz v. Hoyt Enters.,
  604 So. 2d 807 (Fla. 1992) — 11-2
Morton v. Heathcock,
  913 So. 2d 662 (Fla. 3d Dist. Ct. App. 2005) — 11-4
Munder v. Circle One Condo.,
  596 So. 2d 144 (Fla. 4th Dist. Ct. App. 1992) — 4-3:3
Nance v. Petty, Livingston, Dawson, & Devening,
  881 F. Supp. 223 (W.D. Va. 1994) — 9-3
National Ventures v. Water Glades 300 Condo.,
  847 So. 2d 1070 (Fla. 4th Dist. Ct. App. 2003) — 8-3:1
Neate v. Cypress Club Condo.,
  718 So. 2d 390 (Fla. 4th Dist. Ct. App. 1998) — 8-3
Nelle v. Loch Haven Homeowners' Ass'n,
  413 So. 2d 28 (Fla. 1982) — 2-8, 7-5
Neuman v. Grandview At Emerald Hills,
  861 So. 2d 494 (Fla. 4th Dist. Ct. App. 2003) — 7-2:2
Ocean Trail Unit Owners Ass'n v. Mead,
  650 So. 2d 4 (Fla. 1994) — 5-11, 9-1, 9-2:2
Old Port Cove Holdings v. Old Port Cove Condo. Ass'n One,
  986 So. 2d 1279 (Fla. 2008) — 7-6:2.2
Oppenheim v. I.C. System, Inc.,
  627 F.3d 833 (11th Cir. 2010) — 9-3
Overlook Mut. Homes v. Spencer,
  666 F. Supp. 2d 850 (S.D. Ohio 2009) — 10-4:2, 10-4:3

Table of Cases

Papazian v. Kullhanjian,
78 So. 2d 85 (Fla. 1955)   4-2:4
Pelican Island Prop. Owners Ass'n v. Murphy,
554 So. 2d 1179 (Fla.2d Dist. Ct. App. 1989)   2-2:1
Pepe v. Whispering Sands Condo. Ass'n,
351 So. 2d 755 (Fla. 2d Dist. Ct. App. 1977)   1-1:2, 2-1, 2-2:1, 7-1, 11-2
Perlow v. Goldberg,
700 So. 2d 148 (Fla. 3d Dist. Ct. App. 1997)   4-3:3
Pines of Boca Barwood Condo. Ass'n v. Cavouti,
605 So. 2d 984 (Fla. 4th Dist. Ct. App. 1992)   2-2:2, 7-1
Price v. Tyler,
890 So. 2d 246 (Fla. 2004)   9-8
Princeton Homes v. Morgan,
38 So. 3d 207 (Fla. 4th Dist. Ct. App. 2010)   3-2:2
Prindable v. Ass'n of Apartment Owners of 2987 Kalakaua,
304 F. Supp. 2d 1245 (D. Haw. 2003)   10-4:2, 10-4:3
Prisco v. Forest Villas Condo. Apartments,
847 So. 2d 1012 (Fla. 4th Dist. Ct. App. 2003)   7-8:1
Quality Shell Homes & Supply v. Roley,
186 So. 2d 837 (Fla. 1st Dist. Ct. App. 1966)   7-8
Raines v. Palm Beach Leisureville Community Ass'n,
413 So. 2d 30 (Fla. 1982)   1-3:3
Raphael v. Silverman,
22 So. 3d 837 (Fla. 4th Dist. Ct. App. 2009)   4-3:4
Reese v. Miami-Dade Cty.,
242 F. Supp. 2d 1292 (S.D. Fla. 2002)   10-3:2.1
Residential Communities of America v. Escondido Community Ass'n,
645 So. 2d 149 (Fla. 5th Dist. Ct. App. 1994)   9-8
Ross v. Jim Adams Ford,
871 So. 2d 312 (Fla. 2d Dist. Ct. App. 2004)   10-2:1
S & T Builders v. Globe Properties,
909 So. 2d 375 (Fla. 4th Dist. Ct. App. 2005)
aff'd, 944 So. 2d 302 (Fla. 2006)   9-8
S. Inv. Corp. v. Norton,
57 So. 2d 1 (Fla. 1952)   7-6:2.2
Sabal Palm Condos. of Pine Island Ridge Ass'n v. Fischer,
12-60691-CIV, 2014 WL 988767 (S.D. Fla. 2014)   10-3:4, 10-4:3
Santini v. Cleveland Clinic Florida,
65 So. 3d 22 (Fla. 4th Dist. Ct. App. 2011),
reh'g denied (July 26, 2011)   11-4
Savanna Club Worship Serv., Inc. v. Savanna
Club Homeowners' Ass'n,
456 F. Supp. 2d 1223 (S.D. Fla. 2005)   1-2:4, 5-5:1, 10-3:1, 10-3:2.1
Schmidt v. Sherrill,
442 So. 2d 963 (Fla. 4th Dist. Ct. App. 1983)   1-3:1
Schwarz v. City of Treasure Island,
544 F. 3d 1201 (11th Cir. 2008)   10-3:3.1, 10-3:3.2, 10-4:3
Scudder v. Greenbrier C. Condo. Ass'n,
663 So. 2d 1362 (Fla. 4th Dist. Ct. App. 1995)   9-2:2
Seagate Condo. Ass'n v. Duffy,
330 So. 2d 484 (Fla. 4th Dist. Ct. App. 1976)   1-3:2, 7-6
Secretary, U.S. Dept. of Hous. & Urban Dev.,
on Behalf of Herron v. Blackwell,
908 F.2d 864 (11th Cir. 1990)   10-3:2.1, 10-3:4
Sheoah Highlands v. Daugherty,
837 So. 2d 579 (Fla. 5th Dist. Ct. App. 2003)   7-7:3
Sibley v. Firstcollect,
913 F. Supp. 469 (M.D. La. 1995)   9-3
Smith v. Universal Services,
454 F.2d 154 (5th Cir. 1972)   10-2:4
Smith v. Wade,
461 U.S. 30 (1983)   10-3:4

Soileau v. Guilford of Maine,
    105 F.3d 12 (1st Cir. 1997)   10-3:3.1
Sonny Boy v. Asnani,
    879 So. 2d 25 (Fla. 5th Dist. Ct. App. 2004)   4-3:3
Southern Walls v. Stilwell Corp.,
    810 So. 2d 566 (Fla. 5th Dist. Ct. App. 2002)   1-4:1
Southpointe Homeowners Ass'n v. Segarra,
    763 So. 2d 1186 (Fla. 4th Dist. Ct. App. 2000)   11-6:3
Southtrust Bank & Right Equip. Co. of Pinellas Cty. v. Exp. Ins. Services,
    190 F. Supp. 2d 1304 (M.D. Fla. 2002)   4-3:1
Staub v. Harris,
    626 F.2d 275 (3d Cir. 1980)   9-3
Stephl v. Moore,
    94 Fla. 313, 114 So. 455 (Fla. 1927)   2-2:1
Sterling Condo. Ass'n v. Herrera,
    690 So. 2d 703 (Fla. 3d Dist. Ct. App. 1997)   8-3
Sterling Vill. Condo. v. Breitenbach,
    251 So. 2d 685 (Fla. 4th Dist. Ct. App. 1971)   1-3:2
Stockman v. Downs,
    573 So. 2d 835 (Fla. 1991)   11-6:1
Sun Harbor Homeowners' Ass'n v. Bonura,
    2012 WL 2120923 (Fla. 4th Dist. Ct. App. 2012),
    reh'g denied (Sept. 7, 2012)   10-4:3
Tara Manatee v. Fairway Gardens at Tara Condo. Ass'n,
    870 So. 2d 32 (Fla. 2d Dist. Ct. App. 2003)   9-6:2
Taylor Woodrow Homes Florida v. 4/46-A,
    850 So. 2d 536 (Fla. 5th Dist. Ct. App. 2003)   4-3:1
Tierra Holdings v. Mercantile Bank,
    78 So. 3d 558 (Fla. 1st Dist. Ct. App. 2011)   11-3
Tiffany Plaza Condo. v. Spencer,
    416 So. 2d 823 (Fla. 2d Dist. Ct. App. 1982)   5-5:2
Tranquil Harbour Dev. v. BBT,
    79 So. 3d 84 (Fla. 1st Dist. Ct. App. 2011), *reh'g denied* (Feb. 13, 2012) 1-1:3
Trytek v. Gale Indus.,
    3 So. 3d 1194 (Fla. 2009)   11-2
United Grand Condo. Owners v. Grand Condo. Ass'n,
    929 So. 2d 24 (Fla. 3d Dist. Ct. App. 2006)   8-3
United States v. California Mobile Home Park Mgmt.,
    29 F.3d 1413 (9th Cir. 1994)   10-3:3.1
United States v. Hous. Auth. of City of Chickasaw,
    504 F. Supp. 716 (S.D. Ala. 1980)   10-3:2.1
United States v. Southern Mgmt.,
    955 F.2d 914 (4th Cir. 1992)   10-3:3.1
Waverly at Las Olas Condo. Ass'n v. Waverly Las Olas,
    88 So. 3d 386 (Fla. 4th Dist. Ct. App. 2012)   11-5
Wellington Prop. Mgmt. v. Parc Corniche Condo. Ass'n,
    755 So. 2d 824 (Fla. 5th Dist. Ct. App. 2000)   2-8:2
Wentworth v. Johnson,
    845 So. 2d 296 (Fla. 5th Dist. Ct. App. 2003)   11-6:2
White Egret Condo. v. Franklin,
    379 So. 2d 346 (Fla. 1979)   2-2:1, 7-8:1
Wilshire Condo. Ass'n v. Kohlbrand,
    368 So. 2d 629 (Fla. 4th Dist. Ct. App. 1979)   7-2:2
Wilson v. Rex Quality,
    839 So. 2d 928 (Fla. 2d Dist. Ct. App. 2003)   2-2:1
Woodside Vill. Condo. Ass'n v. Jahren,
    806 So. 2d 452 (Fla. 2002)   1-1:2, 1-3:1, 1-3:2, 2-1, 2-8, 2-8:2, 7-1, 7-5
Zimmerman v. HBO,
    834 F.2d 1163 (3d Cir. 1987)   9-3

Index

A

AGE RESTRICTIONS, SELECTIVE ENFORCEMENT OF, 7–8:1

AGENCY REPORTS, DISCLOSURE OF, 10–2:4.2

ALTERNATIVE DISPUTE RESOLUTION
generally, 8–1
by condominium associations, 8–3
  procedures, 8–3:1
by homeowners' associations, 8–2
pre-suit nonbinding arbitration, 1–3:1

AMERICAN RULE, DETERMINING ATTORNEYS' FEES/COSTS, 11–2

ARBITRATION. *See also* ALTERNATIVE DISPUTE RESOLUTION; MEDIATION
for covenant enforcement disputes, 7–7:2
for election disputes, of board members, 4–2:5
procedures, 8–3:1
for recalling board members, 4–4:2

ARCHITECTURAL CONTROL, 7–3
condominium associations, 7–3:2
homeowners' associations, 7–3:1

ARTICLES OF INCORPORATION, 2–3

ASSESSMENT COLLECTION
generally, 9–1
delinquent assessments, interest on, 9–2:2
guarantees, 9–6
  condominium associations, 9–6:2
  homeowners' associations, 9–6:1
liability, 9–2
  condominium associations, 9–2:2
  following foreclosure sale, 9–1
  homeowners' associations, 9–2:1
  protection against unfair/abusive practices, 9–3
penalties, 9–5
slander of title, 9–8
validity of assessments, 9–1

ASSESSMENTS
by condominium associations, 5–3:3
by homeowners' associations, 5–2:3
  notice procedure requirement, 6–2:1

ATTORNEYS' FEES/COSTS
generally, 11–1, 11–7
the "American rule," 11–2
amount of, 11–5
  contingency risk multiplier, 11–5:1
arbitration procedures, condominium association disputes, 8–3:1
damages, discriminatory housing, 10–3:4
election disputes, of board members, 4–2:5
fees as sanctions, 11–4
losing entitlement to fees, 11–6
  failure to plead entitlement, 11–6:1
  before suit begins, 11–6:3
  time limit for motion service, 11–6:2
proposals for settlement, 11–3
slander of title, 9–8
written inquiries, board responding to, 5–8

B

BALCONIES, 5–5:3

BOARD MEETINGS
generally, 6–1
condominium associations, 6–2:2
homeowners' associations, 6–2:1
voting procedures, 6–4
condominium associations, 6–4:2
electronic voting, 6–4:3
homeowners' associations, 6–4:1

BOARDS OF DIRECTORS
generally, 4–1
developer-appointed boards, 4–3:3
developer obligations following
turnover, 3–4:2
discipline and removal, 4–4
civil penalty, 4–4:1
recalling, 4–4:2
duties of, 1–1:3, 4–3
business judgment rule, applied to
board members, 4–3:3, 4–3:5
compensation, 4–3:2
fiduciary duty, 4–3:1, 5–6:2
self-dealing and unjust enrichment,
4–3:4
election of, 4–2
election disputes, 4–2:5
filling vacancies, 4–2:4
procedures, 4–2:2, 4–2:3
qualifications, 4–2:1
hiring property managers, 5–9
competitive bids requirement,
5–9:1
liability insurance, 5–6:3
turnover of condominiums, developer
obligations, 3–5:1, 3–5:2
use restrictions as board-made rules, 7–2

BUDGETS, 5–2:1, 5–3:1

**BUSINESS JUDGMENT
RULE, 4–3:3, 4–3:5**

BYLAWS, 2–4
collecting assessment procedure
requirement, condominium
associations, 9–2:2
statutory procedures requirement,
board meetings notice, 6–2:2
statutory procedures requirement,
member meetings notice, 6–3:1, 6–3:2

C

CAMPGROUNDS, 1–4:2, 1–6:2

**"CATALYST THEORY," IN
FAIR HOUSING CASES, 10–3:4**

**CFR (CODE OF FEDERAL
REGULATIONS), 10–5**

**CHAPTER 607 (FLORIDA
BUSINESS CORPORATION
ACT OF 2012), 1–3:1, 4–3:3**

**CHAPTER 617 (FLORIDA NOT
FOR PROFIT CORPORATION
ACT OF 2012), 1–3:1**
articles of incorporation, defining, 2–3
board members, fiduciary duty of, 4–3:1

**CHAPTER 718
(CONDOMINIUM ACT
OF 2012)**
assessments
liability for, generally, 9–1
liability for, after foreclosure, 9–7
statutory definitions, 5–3:3
attorney's fees provision, 11–2
board elections
arbitration for disputes, 4–2:5
procedure exceptions, 4–2:2
procedures, 4–2:3
board meetings, 6–2:2
board members
compensation, 4–3:2
duties of, 4–3
emergency powers of, 5–1
fiduciary duty of, 4–3:1
recall of, 4–4:2
board vacancies, filling, 4–2:4
bylaws, 2–4
common elements, 5–5:1, 5–5:2
common elements, limited, 5–5:3
common expenses, 9–2:2
declarations, 2–2:1, 2–2:4, 7–2:2
developer disclosure obligations, 3–3:2,
3–5:2
developer-made contracts, 3–3:4
developer warranty, 3–3:3
disclosures prior to sale, 3–3:2, 3–3:5
disputes, mandatory procedures
resolving, 11–6:3

financial reporting, 5–4
flags, right to display, 2–7:2, 7:3–1
governing documents, amending, 2–8:2
hiring managers and professionals, 5–9
insurance, 5–6
mediation, mandatory, 7–7:2
non-binding arbitration requirement, 8–3
official records, requirements, 5–7:2
recreation facility leases, 3–3:1
reserves, 5–3:2
residential property insurance, 5–6:4
scope of, 1–2:3.2
transfers, approving, 7–6:1
turnovers, conditions triggering, 3–5:1
unit rentals, 7–6
voting procedures, 6–4:2

**CHAPTER 719
(COOPERATIVE ACT OF
2012), 1–2:3.1**
cooperative, statutory definition, 1–4:2
distinguishing features, 1–4:1
primary attorney's fees provision, 11–2
scope of, 1–2:3.2

**CHAPTER 720
(HOMEOWNERS'
ASSOCIATION ACT OF 2012)**
architectural controls, 7–3:1
assessments, 5–2:3, 9–1
assessments following foreclosure, 9–7
attorneys' fees, 11–2, 11–6:3
board meetings, 6–2:1
board members
    compensation, 4–3:2
    duties of, 4–3
    fiduciary duty, 4–3:1
    recall of, 4–4:2
    self-dealing and unjust enrichment,
    4–3:4
board membership, qualification for,
    4–2:1
board vacancies, filling, 4–2:4
bylaws, 2–4
common areas, 5–5:1
declarations, 2–2:1, 7–2:1
developer obligations, 3–2
election disputes, arbitration, 4–2:5
fees, of prevailing party, 11–5
fiduciary relationship, 1–2:2
financial reporting, 5–4
fines and suspensions, 7–7:1
flags, right to display, 2–7:1
governing documents, amending, 2–8–1
hiring managers and professionals, 5–9

legislative intent, 1–2:1
mediation, 7–7:2, 8–2
member meetings, 6–3:1
reserve funds, 5–2:2
scope, 1–2:3
    comprised of parcel owners, 1–2:3.3
    exclusion of condominiums and
    cooperatives, 1–2:3.2
    residential communities, 1–2:3.1
transfers, approving, 7–6:1
turnover, conditions triggering, 3–4:1
voting procedures, 6–4:1

**CHAPTER 721 (FLORIDA
VACATION PLAN AND
TIMESHARING ACT OF 2012),
1–6:1**

**CHAPTER 723 (MOBILE
HOME ACT OF 2012), 1–5**

**CHILDREN,
DISCRIMINATION AGAINST
FAMILIES WITH, 10–3, 10–5**

**CLAIM ANALYSIS, FAIR
HOUSING LITIGATION, 10–3**
discrimination in sale or rental, 10–3:2
    disparate impact, 10–3:2.2
    intentional discrimination, 10–3:2.1
reasonable accommodation, 10–3:3
    elements of claim, 10–3:3.1
    necessity and reasonableness,
    10–3:3.2
relief from discriminatory housing,
    10–3:4
standing, 10–3:1

**CLASS ACTION SUITS,
5–11:3**

**CODE OF FEDERAL
REGULATIONS (CFR), 10–5**

COLLECTION PRACTICES
generally, 9–1
guarantees, 9–6
    condominium associations, 9–6:2
    homeowners' associations, 9–6:1
liability, 9–2
    condominium associations, 9–2:2
    following foreclosure sale, 9–1

homeowners' associations, 9–2:1
statutory protection against unfair/
abusive practices, 9–3
lien rights, 9–4
condominium associations, 9–4:2
homeowners' associations, 9–4:1
penalties, 9–5
slander of title, 9–8

**COMMERCIAL
SELF-INSURANCE FUND
ACT OF 2012, 5–6:2**

COMMON AREAS, 5–5
common elements, limited, 5–5:3
common expenses, statutory definition,
9–2:2
condominium associations, 5–5:2
condominiums, features, 1–3:2
homeowners' associations, 1–2:4, 5–5:1
use restrictions on, 7–2:1
religious services in, 7–2:2
tenants, use restrictions on, 7–2:2

**COMMUNITY
ASSOCIATIONS. See
also CONDOMINIUM
ASSOCIATIONS;
HOMEOWNERS'
ASSOCIATIONS**
condominium associations, 1–3
condominium association tests,
1–3:3
condominiums, features, 1–3:2
governing statutes, 1–3:1
cooperatives, 1–4
features, 1–3:1
statutory definition, 1–4:2
duties and rights, generally, 1–1:3
governing documents, generally, 1–1:2
homeowners' associations, 1–2
common areas and individual
parcels, 1–2:4
fiduciary relationship, 1–2:2
Homeowners' Association Act,
1–2:1, 1–2:3
litigation, definition, 1–1:1
mobile home subdivision homeowners'
associations, 1–5
timeshare owners' associations, 1–6
Florida Vacation Plan and
Timesharing Act of 2012, 1–6:1
timeshare plan, statutory definition,
1–6:2

**COMMUNITY
ASSOCIATIONS,
OPERATION OF**
generally, 5–1
common areas, 5–5
common elements 5–5:2
common elements, limited, 5–5:3
condominium associations, 5–5:2
homeowners' associations, 5–5:1
condominium association finances, 5–3
assessments, 5–3:3
budgets, 5–3:1
reserves, 5–3:2
emergency powers, condominium
boards, 5–10
financial reporting, 5–4
hiring managers and professionals, 5–9
competitive bids requirement, 5–9:1
homeowners' association finances, 5–2
assessments, 5–2:3
budgets, 5–2:1
reserves, 5–2:2
insurance, Condominium Act and, 5–6
failure to maintain property
insurance, 5–6:2
multicondominium associations, 5–6:6
other types of insurance, 5–6:3
property insurance coverage, 5–6:1
reconstruction work after property
loss, 5–6:5
residential property insurance, 5–6:4
official records, 5–7
condominium association, 5–7:2
homeowners' association, 5–7:1
right to sue and be sued, 5–11
class action suits, 5–11:3
condominium associations, 5–11:2
homeowners' associations, 5–11:1
written inquiries, 5–8

COMPANION ANIMALS, 10–4
FHA and emotional support animals,
10–4:3
for mental/emotional disabilities, 10–4:1
service vs. emotional support animals,
10–4:2

**COMPENSATION (FOR
BOARDS OF DIRECTORS),
4–3:2**

**COMPETITIVE BIDS,
REQUIREMENT AND
EXCEPTIONS, 5–9:2**

CONCILIATION AGREEMENT (FCHR), 10–2:4

CONDOMINIUM ACT OF 2012 (CHAPTER 718)
arbitration (non-binding) requirement, 8–3
assessments
liability for, generally, 9–1
liability for, after foreclosure, 9–7
statutory definitions, 5–3:3
attorney's fees provision, 11–2
board elections
arbitration for disputes, 4–2:5
procedure exceptions, 4–2:2
procedures, 4–2:3
board meetings, 6–2:2
board members
compensation, 4–3:2
duties of, 4–3
emergency powers of, 5–1
fiduciary duty of, 4–3:1
recall of, 4–4:2
board vacancies, filling, 4–2:4
bylaws, 2–4
common elements, 5–5:1, 5–5:2
common elements, limited, 5–5:3
common expenses, 9–2:2
declarations, 2–2:1, 2–2:4, 7–2:2
developer disclosure obligations, 3–3:2, 3–5:2
developer-made contracts, 3–3:4
developer warranty, 3–3:3
disclosures prior to sale, 3–3:2, 3–3:5
disputes, mandatory procedures, 11–6:3
financial reporting, 5–4
flags, right to display, 2–7:2
governing documents, amending, 2–8:2
hiring managers and professionals, 5–9
insurance, 5–6
mediation, mandatory, 7–7:2
official records, requirements, 5–7:2
recreation facility leases, 3–3:1
reserves, 5–3:2
residential property insurance, 5–6:4
scope of, 1–2:3.2
transfers, approving, 7–6:1
turnovers, conditions triggering, 3–5:1
unit rentals, 7–6
voting procedures, 6–4:2

CONDOMINIUM ASSOCIATIONS, 1–3
aesthetic controls, 7–3:2
assessments

collection of, as "debts," 9–3
delinquent, penalties for, 9–5
guarantees, 9–6:2
liability, 9–2:2
board meetings, 6–2:2
civil penalty, board members, 4–4:1
common areas and individual parcels, 1–2:4
common elements, 5–5:2
common elements, limited, 5–5:2
use restrictions, by tenants, 7–2:2
condominium association tests, 1–3:3
condominiums, features, 1–3:2
developer obligations, 3–3
developer-made contracts, 3–3:4
developer warranty, 3–3:3
disclosures prior to sale, 3–3:5
recreation facility leases, 3–3:1
sale prior to completion, 3–3:2
disputes, 8–3, 8–3:1
elections of boards of directors, 4–2:3
flags, right to display, 2–7:1
governing documents
amending, 2–8:2
prohibited provisions, 2–7:2
required provisions in declaration, 2–2:4
governing statutes, 1–3:1
insurance, 5–6
failure to maintain, 5–6:2
multicondominium associations, 5–6:6
other types, 5–6:3
property insurance coverage, 5–6:1
reconstruction work after property loss, 5–6:5
residential property insurance, 5–6:4
meetings, 6–3:2
voting procedures, 6–4:2
official records, 5–7:2
operation of, emergency powers, 5–10
operation of, finances, 5–3
assessments, 5–3:3
budgets, 5–3:1
reserves, 5–3:2
religious services in common area, 7–2:2
right to sue and be sued, 5–11:2
rights of first refusal
prohibition against forced sales, 7–6:2.1
rule against perpetuities and, 7–6:2.2
tenants, use restrictions of common areas, 7–2:2
turnover, 3–5
conditions triggering, 3–5:1
developer obligations following turnover, 3–5:2
use restrictions, 7–2:2

CONDOMINIUMS
features, 1–3:2
Homeowners' Association Act of 2012, exclusion, 1–2:3.2
mixed residential-retail-commercial condominiums, 2–7:2
unit configuration, governing document amendments changing, 2–8:2
unit rentals, 2–8:2, 7–6

CONSTITUENCY TEST, DETERMINING CONDOMINIUM ASSOCIATION STATUS, 1–3:3

CONTINGENCY RISK MULTIPLIER, 11–5:1

CONTRACTS
competitive bids requirement to obtain, 5–9:1
Condominium Act on, hiring managers and professionals, 5–9
employment contracts, access to, 5–7:1, 5–7:2
statute of limitations for breach, 7–3:3

COOPERATIVE ACT OF 2012 (CHAPTER 719), 1–2:3.1
cooperative, statutory definition, 1–4:2
features, 1–4:1
primary attorney's fees provision, 11–2
scope of, 1–2:3.2

COOPERATIVES, 1–4
cooperative, statutory definition, 1–4:2
features, 1–3:1
Homeowners' Association Act of 2012, exclusion, 1–2:3.2

COUNTRY CLUB COMMUNITIES, MANDATORY MEMBERSHIPS IN, 7–4

COVENANT ENFORCEMENT
generally, 7–1
architectural control, 7–3
condominium associations, 7–3:2
homeowners' associations, 7–3:1
enforcement methods, 7–7
fines and suspensions, 7–7:1
mandatory mediation and arbitration, 7–7:2
statute of limitations, 7–7:3
estoppel, 7–8
selective enforcement, 7–8:1
governing documents, generally, 1–1:2
mandatory memberships, 7–4
scheme of development, 7–5
transfer restrictions, 7–6
association approval of transfers, 7–6:1
rights of first refusal, 7–6:2
use restrictions, 7–2
condominium associations, 7–2:2
homeowners' associations, 7–2:1

CRIMINAL BACKGROUND CHECKS, 7–6

D

DEBT COLLECTORS, PROTECTION AGAINST, 9–3

DECLARATIONS, 2–2
architectural controls, 7–3
characteristics, 2–2:1
condominium associations
aesthetic controls, 7–3:2
required provisions, 2–2:4
unit boundaries, 5–5:2
owner-adopted amendments to, 7–5
restrictions, 2–2:2, 7–1
invalid, 2–2:3
on transfers, 7–6
on transfers, association approval, 7–6:1
use restrictions, homeowners' associations, 7–2:1
rights of first refusal, 7–6:2
prohibition against forced sales, 7–6:2.1
rule against perpetuities and, 7–6:2.2
statutory rights *vs.*, in foreclosure, 9–7

DELINQUENT ASSESSMENTS, PENALTIES FOR, 9–5

DETERMINATIONS, ADMISSIBILITY OF, 10–2:4.1, 10–2:4.2

DEVELOPER GUARANTEES, ON ASSESSMENTS, 9–6:1, 9–6:2

DEVELOPER-MADE CONTRACTS
condominium associations and, 3–3:4
homeowners' associations and, 3–2:1
prohibited provisions for homeowners' associations, 2–7:1

DEVELOPER OBLIGATIONS AND TURNOVER
generally, 3–1
condominium associations and, 3–3
   developer-made contracts, 3–3:4
   developer warranty, 3–3:3
   disclosures prior to sale, 3–3:5
   recreation facility leases, 3–3:1
   sale prior to completion, 3–3:2
homeowners' associations and, 3–2
   developer-made contracts, 3–2:1
   disclosures prior to sale, 3–2:2
scheme-of-development test, 7–5
turnover of condominium associations, 3–5
   conditions triggering, 3–5:1
   developer obligations following, 3–5:2
turnover of homeowners' associations, 3–4
   conditions triggering, 3–4:1
   developer obligations following, 3–4:2

DISABILITY/MEDICAL ACCOMMODATIONS, 7–3:1

DISASTER PLANS (CONDOMINIUM ASSOCIATION EMERGENCY POWERS), 5–10

DISCIPLINE/REMOVAL OF DIRECTORS, 4–4
civil penalties, 4–4:1

DISCLOSURES. *See* **SALES, DISCLOSURES (BY DEVELOPERS) PRIOR TO**

DISCOVERY, IN ELECTION DISPUTES OF BOARD OF DIRECTORS, 4–2:5

DISCRIMINATION IN HOUSING. *See also* **FAIR HOUSING LITIGATION**
discriminatory practices, relief from, 10–3:4
familial status discrimination, 10–3, 10–5
intentional discrimination, 10–3:2.1
sale or rental, claim analysis, 10–3:2
   disparate impact, 10–3:2.2
   intentional discrimination, 10–3:2.1
sex offenders, 10–3:3.1
substance abuse, persons recovering from, 10–3:3.1

DISPUTES
attorneys' fees in prevailing litigation, 11–6:3
binding arbitration
   homeowners' associations, 8–2
   condominium association, 8–3
dispute, definition, 8–3
presuit mediation, 8–2

DIVISION OF FLORIDA CONDOMINIUMS, TIMESHARES, AND MOBILE HOMES
accessing records, 5–7:2
arbitration, 8–3
   procedures, 8–3:1
   of recall disputes, 4–4:2
civil penalties, board members, 4–4:1
limited proxy form, member meetings, 6–4:2
petition as precondition to suit, 7–7:1

DOCUMENT PRODUCTION IN ARBITRATION PROCEDURES, 8–3:1

DUTIES OF BOARD MEMBERS, 4–3
business judgment rule
   applied to board members, 4–3:3
   applied to community associations, 4–3:5
director compensation prohibited, 4–3:2
fiduciary duty, 4–3:1
self-dealing and unjust enrichment, 4–3:4

E

EASEMENTS, 5–5:2

ELECTIONS OF BOARDS OF DIRECTORS, 4–2
disputes, 4–2:5, 8–2
filling vacancies, 4–2:4
member voting rights, suspension of, 9–5
procedures, 4–2:2, 4–2:3
qualifications for board membership, 4–2:1

EMAIL ADDRESSES OF UNIT OWNERS, ACCESS TO, 5–7:2

EMOTIONAL SUPPORT ANIMALS, 10–4:1
FHA, HUD and VA on, 10–4:3
service animals *vs.*, ADA definitions, 10–4:2

EMPLOYMENT CONTRACTS, ACCESS TO, 5–7:1, 5–7:2

ENFORCEMENT FOR VIOLATIONS OF RULES AND REGULATIONS, 7–7
fines and suspensions, 7–7:1
mandatory mediation and arbitration, 7–7:2
statute of limitations, 7–7:3

ENGLISH RULE, DETERMINING ATTORNEYS' FEES/COSTS, 11–2

ENTITLEMENT TO FEES, LOSING, 11–6
failure to plead entitlement, 11–6:1
before suit begins, 11–6:3
time limit for motion service, 11–6:2

ESTOPPEL, 7–8

F

FAIR DEBT COLLECTION PRACTICES ACT (FDCPA), 9–3

FHA, EMOTIONAL SUPPORT ANIMALS AND, 10–4:3

FAIR HOUSING LITIGATION
generally, 10–1, 10–6
administrative process, 10–2
exhaustion of remedies, 10–2:1
FCHR, 10–2:3
HUD, 10–2:2
procedures, 10–2:4
claim analysis, 10–3
discrimination in sale or rental, 10–3:2
reasonable accommodation, 10–3:3
relief from discriminatory practices, 10–3:4
standing, 10–3:1
companion animals, 10–4
FHA and emotional support animals, 10–4:3
for mental/emotional disabilities, 10–4:1
service *vs.* emotional support animals, 10–4:2
housing for older persons, 10–5

FAMILIAL STATUS DISCRIMINATION, 10–5

FCCPA (FLORIDA CONSUMER COLLECTION PRACTICES ACT), 9–3

FCHR (FLORIDA COMMISSION ON HUMAN RELATIONS)
procedures, 10–2:4
admissibility of determinations, 10–2:4.1
post-determination proceedings, 10–2:4.2
process, 10–2:3

FDCPA (FAIR DEBT COLLECTION PRACTICES ACT), 9–3

FIDUCIARY RELATIONSHIP, 1–2:2, 1–3:1, 4–3:1

FINANCES
condominium association, 5–3
assessments, 5–3:3

budgets, 5–3:1
reserves, 5–3:2
financial reporting, 5–4
homeowners' association, 5–2
assessments, 5–2:3
budgets, 5–2:1
reserves, 5–2:2

FINANCIAL REPORTS, DEVELOPER OBLIGATIONS
before turnover, 3–3
following turnover, 3–5:2

FLAGS, RIGHT TO DISPLAY
condominium associations, 2–7:2, 7–3:2
homeowners' associations, 2–7:1, 7–3:1

FLOOD INSURANCE, 5–6:3

FLORIDA ADMINISTRATIVE CODE, 4–4:1, 8–3:1

FLORIDA BUSINESS CORPORATION ACT OF 2012 (CHAPTER 607), 1–3:1, 4–3:3

FLORIDA COMMISSION ON HUMAN RELATIONS (FCHR)
procedures, 10–2:4
admissibility of determinations, 10–2:4.1
post-determination proceedings, 10–2:4.2
process, 10–2:3

FLORIDA CONSUMER COLLECTION PRACTICES ACT (FCCPA), 9–3

FLORIDA FAIR HOUSING ACT (FFHA) OF 2012
Section 760.23, discrimination, 10–3
Section 760.23(2), protected classes, 10–3
Section 760.34, administrative remedies, 10–2:1

FLORIDA NOT FOR PROFIT CORPORATION ACT OF 2012 (CHAPTER 617), 1–3:1
articles of incorporation, defining, 2–3
board members, fiduciary duty of, 4–3:1

FLORIDA RULES OF CIVIL PROCEDURE
arbitration procedures, 8–3:1
class action suits, 5–11:3
Rule 1.442, proposals for settlement, 11–3
Rule 1.525, time limit for motion service, 11–6:2
Rule 1.720, dispute mediation, 8–2, 8–3

FLORIDA STATUTES.
See also **CHAPTER 718 (CONDOMINIUM ACT OF 2012); CHAPTER 720 (HOMEOWNERS' ASSOCIATION ACT OF 2012)**
Chapter 607, Florida Business Corporation Act of 2012, 1–3:1, 4–3:3
Chapter 617, Florida Not For Profit Corporation Act of 2012, 1–3:1
articles of incorporation, defining, 2–3
board members, fiduciary duty of, 4–3:1
Chapter 719, Cooperative Act of 2012, 1–2:3.1
cooperative, statutory definition, 1–4:2
distinguishing features, 1–4:1
primary attorney's fees provision, 11–2
scope of, 1–2:3.2
Chapter 721, Florida Vacation Plan and Timesharing Act of 2012, 1–6:1
Chapter 723, Mobile Home Act of 2012, 1–5
Section 57.105, fees as sanctions, 11–4
Section 768.79, proposals for settlement, 11–3

FLORIDA VACATION PLAN AND TIMESHARING ACT OF 2012 (CHAPTER 721), 1–6:1

FORECLOSURES
enforcement methods, 7–7:1
lien rights
by condominium associations, 9–4:2
by homeowners associations, 9–4:1
liability for assessments following, 9–7

FORM 903 ONLINE COMPLAINT (HUD), 10–2:2

FRAUD, BY BOARD MEMBERS, 4–3:3

FUNCTION TEST, DETERMINING CONDOMINIUM ASSOCIATION STATUS, 1–3:3

G

GOVERNING DOCUMENTS.
See also **COVENANT ENFORCEMENT**
generally, 1–1:2, 2–1
amending, 2–8
of condominium associations, 2–8:2
of homeowners' associations, 2–8:1
articles of incorporation, 2–3
assessment liability
condominium associations, 9–2:2
delinquent assessments, penalties for, 9–4
homeowners' associations, 9–2:1
bylaws, 2–4
conflicts between, 2–5
cooperative documents, 1–4:1
declaration, 2–2
characteristics, 2–2:1
invalid restrictions, 2–2:3
required provisions, condominium associations, 2–2:4
restrictions, 2–2:2
lacking, scheme-of-development test, 7–5
prohibited provisions, 2–7
for condominium associations, 2–7:2
for homeowners' associations, 2–7:1
restrictions
generally, 7–1
use restrictions, 7–2
rules and regulations, 2–6
suing to enforce, fines and suspensions, 7–7:1

H

HANDICAPPED, DEFINITION, 10–3:3.1. *See also* **REASONABLE ACCOMMODATION, CLAIM ANALYSIS**

HEARINGS
arbitration procedures, condominium association disputes, 8–3:1
election disputes, boards of directors, 4–2:5
FCHR- or HUD-instituted hearings, 10–3:4
housing discrimination, 10–2:4.2

***HOLLYWOOD TOWERS* TEST, 4–3:5, 7–5**

HOMEOWNERS' ASSOCIATION ACT OF 2012 (CHAPTER 720)
architectural controls, 7–3:1
assessments, 5–2:3, 9–1
following foreclosure, 9–7
attorneys' fees, 11–2, 11–6:3
board meetings, 6–2:1
board members
compensation, 4–3:2
duties of, 4–3
fiduciary duty, 4–3:1
recall of, 4–4:2
self-dealing and unjust enrichment, 4–3:4
board membership, qualification for, 4–2:1
board vacancies, filling, 4–2:4
bylaws, 2–4
common areas, 5–5:1
declarations, 2–2:1, 7–2:1
developer obligations, 3–2
election disputes, arbitration, 4–2:5
fees, of prevailing party, 11–5
fiduciary relationship, 1–2:2
financial reporting, 5–4
fines and suspensions, 7–7:1
flags, right to display, 2–7:1, 7–3:1
governing documents, amending, 2–8:1
hiring managers and professionals, 5–9
legislative intent, 1–2:1
mediation, 7–7:2, 8–2
member meetings, 6–3:1
reserve funds, 5–2:2
scope, 1–2:3
comprised of parcel owners, 1–2:3.3
exclusion of condominiums and cooperatives, 1–2:3.2
residential communities, 1–2:3.1
transfers, approving, 7–6:1
turnover, conditions triggering, 3–4:1
voting procedures, 6–4

**HOMEOWNERS'
ASSOCIATIONS, 1–2**
architectural control, 7–3:1
assessments
  delinquent, penalties for, 9–5
  guarantees, 9–6:1
  liability, 9–2:1
common areas and individual parcels,
  1–2:4
common property maintenance, 5–5:1
developer obligations, 3–2
  developer-made contracts, 3–2:1
  disclosures prior to sale, 3–2:2
fiduciary relationship, 1–2:2
finances, 5–2
  assessments, 5–2:3
  budgets, 5–2:1
  reserves, 5–2:2
flags, right to display, 2–7:1, 7–3:1
governing documents
  amending, 2–8:1
  official records, 5–7:1
  prohibited provisions, 2–7:1
lien rights, 9–4:1
meetings
  of board of directors, 6–2:1
  of members, 6–3:1
  voting procedures, 6–4
right to sue and be sued, 5–11:1
turnover, 3–4
  conditions triggering, 3–4:1
  developer obligations following, 3–4:2
use restrictions, 7–2:1

**HOUSING DISCRIMINATION.
See DISCRIMINATION IN
HOUSING**

**HUD (HOUSING AND URBAN
DEVELOPMENT), 10–2:2,
10–4:3**

**HURRICANE PROTECTION
MAINTENANCE, 5–5:2, 5–10**

I

**INSURANCE, CONDOMINIUM
ACT AND, 5–6**
coverage, 5–6:1
failure to maintain insurance, 5–6:2
multicondominium associations, 5–6:6
other types of insurance, 5–6:3
reconstruction work after property loss,
  5–6:5
residential property insurance, 5–6:4

**INTENTIONAL
DISCRIMINATION, IN
HOUSING, 10–3:2.1**

L

***LAMDEN* TEST
(CALIFORNIA), 4–3:5, 7–5**

**LANDSCAPING (FLORIDA-
FRIENDLY), 7–3:1**

LEASES, 3–3:1, 5–5:2

**LIEN RIGHTS, COLLECTION
PRACTICES, 9–4**

LITIGATION
attorneys' fees/costs
  contingency risk multiplier, 11–5:1
  in prevailing litigation, 11–6:3
defining, for community associations,
  1–1:1
fair housing litigation
  generally, 10–1, 10–6
  administrative process, 10–2
  claim analysis, 10–3
  companion animals, 10–4
  housing for older persons, 10–5

M

**MAINTENANCE
ASSESSMENTS,
COLLECTION OF, 9–3**

MANAGERS, HIRING OF, 5–9

**MARKETABILITY OF
PROPERTY, SLANDER OF
TITLE CLAIMS, 9–8**

***McDONNELL DOUGLAS V.
GREEN* BURDEN-SHIFTING
ANALYSIS, 10–3:2.1**

MEDIATION
choosing mediators, 8–3
homeowners' association disputes, 7–7:2, 8–2
losing entitlement before suit begins, 11–6:3

MEMBER MEETINGS
condominium associations, 6–3:2
homeowners' associations, 6–3:1
voting procedures, 6–4
condominium associations, 6–4:2
homeowners' associations, 6–4:1

MINUTES
access to
by condominium associations, 5–7:2
by homeowners' associations, 5–7:1
disclosing board member's interest in contracts, 5–9

MISREPRESENTATIONS IN DEBT COLLECTION PRACTICES, 9–3

MOBILE HOME ACT OF 2012 (CHAPTER 723), 1–5

MOBILE HOME SUBDIVISION HOMEOWNERS' ASSOCIATIONS, 1–5

MOTION PRACTICE, ELECTION DISPUTES OF BOARD OF DIRECTORS, 4–2:5

MULTICONDOMINIUM ASSOCIATIONS
budgets, 5–3:1
common elements maintenance, 5–5:2
insurance, 5–6:6

N

NECESSITY TO ENJOYMENT OF USE, FHA REQUIREMENT, 10–3:3.2

NEGLIGENCE, BY BOARD MEMBERS, 4–3:3

NONBINDING ARBITRATION REQUIREMENT, 8–3

NOTIFICATION. *See also* **ENFORCEMENT FOR VIOLATIONS OF RULES AND REGULATIONS**
for board meetings
condominium associations, 6–2:2
homeowners' associations, 6–2:1
of fines or suspensions, 7–7:1
of intent to lien/demand past due assessments
by condominium associations, 9–4:2
by homeowners' association, 9–4:1
for member meetings
condominium associations, 6–3:2
homeowners' associations, 6–3:1
Notice of Determination, 10–2:4.1, 10–2:4.2
of special meetings, 4–4:2

O

OFFICIAL RECORDS, 5–7. *See also* **GOVERNING DOCUMENTS**
condominium association, 5–7:2
homeowners' association, 5–7:1
privileged and confidential records, 5–7:1, 5–7:2

OLDER PERSONS, HOUSING FOR, 10–5

P

PARCEL OWNERS
architectural controls, 7–3:1
condominium, in declaration, 2–2:3
cooperative parcel, statutory definition, 1–4:1
Homeowners' Association Act of 2012, scope of, 1–2:3.3
homeowners' associations, 1–2:4, 6–3:1
use restrictions on, 7–2:1

PARKING SPACES, 5–5:3

PATIOS
estoppel, 7–8:1
insuring items on, 5–6:1n91
limited common elements, 5–5:3

PETITION FOR RELIEF
FROM A DISCRIMINATORY
HOUSING PRACTICE, 10–2:4.2

PETS. *See also* COMPANION
ANIMALS, 7–8:1

PRESUMPTION OF
UNCONSCIONABILITY IN
RECREATIONAL FACILITY
LEASES, 3–3:1

PREVAILING PARTY
ATTORNEY'S FEES. *See*
ATTORNEYS' FEES/COSTS

PRIVILEGED AND
CONFIDENTIAL
COMMUNICATIONS, 8–2

PRIVILEGED AND
CONFIDENTIAL RECORDS,
5–7:1, 5–7:2

PROPERTY INSURANCE.
See also INSURANCE
of condominium owners, 5–6:4
developer obligations to condominium
associations, 3–3
property loss, reconstruction work
after, 5–6:5

PROPERTY MANAGEMENT
COMPANIES
homeowners' associations, statutory
definition, 1–2:3.3
managers and professionals, hiring,
5–9

PROSPECTUS (OFFERING
CIRCULAR), PRIOR TO SALE
BY DEVELOPERS, 3–3:5

PROXY VOTING. *See* VOTING
PROCEDURES

R

REASONABLE
ACCOMMODATIONS
CLAIMS, 10–3:3
elements, 10–3:3.1
necessity and reasonableness, 10–3:3.2

REASONABLENESS TEST
application to governing documents,
7–4, 7–5
community associations' restraints on
alienation, 7–6
Lamden test (California), 4–3:5, 7–5

RECALLING BOARD
MEMBERS, 4–4:2, 4–2:5

RECEIVERSHIP, FILLING
VACANCIES ON BOARDS,
4–2:4

RECKLESSNESS, LIABILITY
OF BOARD MEMBERS FOR,
4–3:1

RECREATION
ASSOCIATIONS, 1–3:3

RECREATIONAL/COMMON
FACILITIES
developer-made contracts, 3–2:1, 3–3:4
leases of, developer obligations, 3–3:1
use restrictions on, homeowners'
associations, 7–2:1

RECREATIONAL VEHICLE
(RV) PARK. *See* MOBILE
HOME SUBDIVISION
HOMEOWNERS'
ASSOCIATIONS

RELIGIOUS GROUPS,
DISCRIMINATION AGAINST,
7–2:2, 10–3:1

RELIGIOUS OBJECTS, ATTACHING, 5–5:2, 7–3:2

RENTALS, 2–8:2, 7–6

RESERVE/OPERATING FUNDS, 3–2, 5–2:2, 5–3:2

RESTRICTIONS IN DECLARATION, 2–2:2, 2–2:3

RETIREMENT COMMUNITIES, QUALIFYING FOR, 10–5

RIGHT OF ACCESS, IMPOSING PENALTIES AND, 9–5

RIGHT TO SUE AND BE SUED, 5–11
class action suits, 5–11:3
condominium associations, 5–11:2
homeowners' associations, 5–11:1

RIGHTS OF FIRST REFUSAL, 7–6:2
prohibition against forced sales, 7–6:2.1
rule against perpetuities and, 7–6:2.2

RULES AND REGULATIONS
board-made rules, use restrictions, 7–2
enforcement for violations, methods, 7–7
fines and suspensions, 7–7:1
mandatory mediation and arbitration, 7–7:2
statute of limitations, 7–7:3
reasonableness test, 2–6, 2–8

S

SAFE HARBOR STATUTORY PROVISION, FORECLOSURE SALES, 9–7

SALES, DISCLOSURES (BY DEVELOPERS) PRIOR TO
condominium associations and, 3–3:5
homeowners' associations and, 3–2:2

SANCTIONS, ATTORNEYS' FEES AS, 11–4

SCHEME-OF-DEVELOPMENT TEST, PRIOR TO TURNOVER, 7–5

SEEING-EYE DOGS. See COMPANION ANIMALS

SELECTIVE ENFORCEMENT, 7–8:1. See also FAIR HOUSING LITIGATION

SELF-DEALING AND UNJUST ENRICHMENT PROHIBITION, 4–3:4

SETTLEMENT, PROPOSALS FOR, 11–3

SEX OFFENDERS, 10–3:3.1

SLANDER OF TITLE, 9–8

SOLAR COLLECTORS, ATTACHING, 5–5:2

SPECIAL ASSESSMENTS, CONDOMINIUM ASSOCIATIONS, 5–3:3, 5–10

SPECIAL (MEMBER) MEETINGS, 6–3:1

STATUTE OF LIMITATIONS, IN BREACH OF GOVERNING DOCUMENTS, 7–3:3

SUBSTANCE ABUSE, PERSONS RECOVERING FROM, 10–3:3.1

SUBSTANTIAL LIMITATION, DEFINITION, 10–3:3.1

T

TELEPHONE CONFERENCES, OF BOARD MEETINGS, 6–2:2

TENANTS
condominium associations, 7–2:2, 8–3
eviction of, 9–5

TESTS, CONDOMINIUM ASSOCIATION, 1–3:3

TIME LITIGATING FEE AMOUNTS, FEES FOR, 11–5

TIMESHARE CONDOMINIUMS
access to official records, distance requirement, 5–7:2
Florida Vacation Plan and Timesharing Act of 2012, 1–6:1
timeshare estates, 2–8:2
timeshare owners' associations, 1–6
timeshare plans, statutory definition, 1–6:2

TRANSFER RESTRICTIONS, 7–6
association approval of transfers, 7–6:1
rights of first refusal, 7–6:2
prohibition against forced sales, 7–6:2.1
rule against perpetuities and, 7–6:2.2

TURNOVER
after turnover, condominium associations' right to sue and be sued, 5–11:2
of condominium associations, developer obligations, 3–5
conditions triggering, 3–5:1
following turnover, 3–5:2
developer-controlled associations, reserve funds, 5–2:2, 5–3:2
of homeowners' associations, developer obligations, 3–4
conditions triggering, 3–4:1
following turnover, 3–4:2
pre-turnover contracts, disclosure rules, 5–9
prior to, scheme-of-development test, 7–5

U

UNFAIR/ABUSIVE ASSESSMENT COLLECTION PRACTICES, 9–3

UNITS, COMMON/LIMITED ELEMENTS, 5–5:2

USE RESTRICTIONS, 7–2
condominium associations, 7–2:2
homeowners' associations, 7–2:1

V

VETERANS AFFAIRS, DEPARTMENT OF, 10–4:3

VOTING PROCEDURES, 6–4
board meetings, 6–2
condominium associations, 6–4:2
homeowners' associations, 6–4:1
member meetings, 6–3
condominium associations, 6–3:2
homeowners' associations, 6–3:1

W

WARRANTIES, BY DEVELOPERS, 3–3:3. *See also* **DEVELOPER OBLIGATIONS AND TURNOVER**

WITNESS ATTENDANCE, AT ARBITRATION PROCEDURES, 8–3:1

WRITTEN INQUIRES, 5–8

Z

ZONING REGULATION WAIVERS, 10–3:3.2